THE SOCIAL MOVEMENT SOCIETY

Contentious Politics for a New Century

edited by
DAVID S. MEYER
and
SIDNEY TARROW

ROWMAN & LITTLEFIELD PUBLISHERS, INC.
Lanham • Boulder • New York • Oxford

ROWMAN & LITTLEFIELD PUBLISHERS, INC.

Published in the United States of America
by Rowman & Littlefield Publishers, Inc.
4720 Boston Way, Lanham, Maryland 20706

12 Hid's Copse Road
Cummor Hill, Oxford OX2 9JJ, England

British Library Cataloguing in Publication Information Available

Library of Congress Cataloging-in-Publication Data

The social movement society : contentious politics for a new century /
   [compiled by] David S. Meyer and Sidney Tarrow.
     p. cm.
   Product of a workshop held at Cornell University on March 1–3, 1996.
   Includes bibliographical references and index.
   ISBN 0-8476-8540-3 (cloth). — ISBN 0-8476-8541-1 (paper).
   1. Social movements—History.   2. Social action—History.
   3. Social change—History. I. Meyer, David S., 1958– . II. Tarrow,
  Sidney G.
  HM291.S58845   1998
  303.48'4'09—dc21
                                                97-30586
                                                  CIP

ISBN 0-8476-8540-3 (cloth : alk. paper)
ISBN 0-8476-8541-1 (pbk. : alk. paper)

Printed in the United States of America

♾ ™ The paper used in this publication meets the minimum requirements of
American National Standard for Information Sciences—Permanence of Paper
for Printed Library Materials, ANSI Z39.48–1984.

For Margaret
and
For Susan

THE SOCIAL MOVEMENT SOCIETY

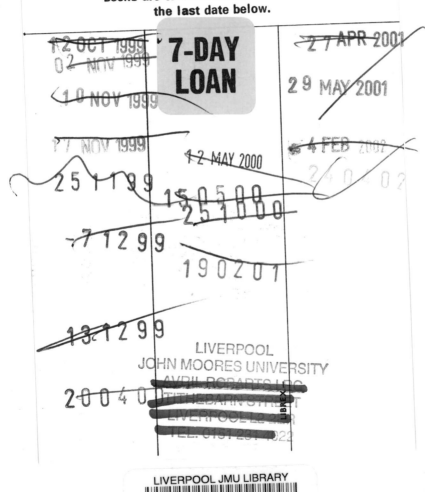

People, Passions, and Power
Social Movements, Interest Organizations,
and the Political Process
John C. Green, Series Editor

This new series explores the people, activities, and institutions that animate the political process. The series emphasizes recent changes in that process—new actors, new movements, new strategies, new successes (or failures) to enter the political mainstream or influence everyday politics—and places these changes in context with the past and the future. Books in the series combine high-quality scholarship with accessibility so that they may be used as core or supplementary texts in upper division political science, sociology, and communication studies courses. The series is consciously interdisciplinary and encourages cross-discipline collaboration and research.

Titles in the Series

The State of the Parties, Second Edition: The Changing Role of Contemporary American Parties (1996), edited by John C. Green and Daniel M. Shea
After the Boom: The Politics of Generation X (1997), edited by Stephen C. Craig and Stephen Earl Bennett
Multiparty Politics in America (1997), edited by Paul S. Herrnson and John C. Green

Forthcoming

Social Movements and American Political Institutions, edited by Anne N. Costain and Andrew S. McFarland
Cyberpolitics: Citizen Activism in the Age of the Internet, Kevin A. Hill and John E. Hughes
Social Movements Since the Sixties, edited by Jo Freeman and Victoria Johnson
The Changing Role of Labor Unions in American Politics, Herbert B. Asher, Randall B. Ripley, Karen Snyder, and Eric Heberlig

Contents

Acknowledgments

The essays in this volume are the product of a workshop, *Europe and the United States: Movement Societies or the Institutionalization of Protest?*, held at Cornell University on March 1–3, 1996. We thank Cornell's Institute of European Studies for support of that conference and Tammy Gardner and Jan McBride for coordinating the details of the meeting. We are also grateful to the other participants in the conference—David Blatt, Ulrike Liebert, David Ost, Jonas Pontusson, Roland Roth, and Elisabeth Sanders—for spirited discussions and generous comments that helped the chapter authors and us to do a better job in thinking and writing about these important issues.

A Movement Society: Contentious Politics for a New Century

David S. Meyer and Sidney Tarrow

From Berkeley to Berlusconi

It is October 1964 in Berkeley, California. On Sproul Plaza, outside the administration building of the University of California, a sprawling crowd of students surrounds and immobilizes a car full of police to prevent them from taking a student activist off to jail (Heirich 1971, chap. 6). Laughing gaily at their ability to immobilize the dreaded Berkeley police force, the students sing civil rights songs, a few pass out joints, and together they begin to form the collective identity that would eventuate in the Free Speech Movement. Without having the words to express it, they feel themselves to be in the presence of something new, at the center of a history they are making, and at the start of a new social movement. The sense of uncertainty and virtually unlimited possibility is pervasive.

The Berkeley students are not alone. In the months and years that follow, bolstered by their example, schooled by the experience of civil rights in the South, and exacerbated by the war in Vietnam, hundreds of similar demonstrations take place across America, adding new twists to the inherited repertoire of contention.[1] In Western Europe a new student rebellion, sparked by the Vietnam War, by dissatisfaction with overcrowded and badly equipped universities, and by the fading

We presented earlier versions of this chapter at graduate seminars at City University's Graduate Center and at Columbia University. We appreciate the helpful comments from participants at those sessions and also additional comments from Vince Boudreau, Russell Dalton, Margaret Groarke, Jack Hammond, Hanspeter Kriesi, Kelly Moore, Dieter Rucht, Ariel Salzman, and Charles Tilly.

appeal of the traditional parties of the left, spreads rapidly across West Germany, Italy, and France, paralyzing the French Fifth Republic, bringing universities to a standstill, and joining up, in some cases, with working-class insurgency and struggles over public housing, women's rights, and social services.

It is thirty-three years after the founding of the Free Speech Movement in Berkeley. On a windy Saturday morning in Rome, after a long and orderly march from the center of the city, a crowd of over five hundred thousand gathers in the Piazza of the Basilica of San Giovanni in Laterano—the scene of hundreds of previous demonstrations—to listen to its leaders oppose the government's *legge finanziaria*—a finance bill that proposes new taxes, does away with some old ones, revises income tax brackets, and would give the government a mandate to make new tax rules by delegation. The marchers wave banners, chant slogans, and shout their approval of their leaders' challenges. It is a demonstration like thousands of others that have wended their way through the main streets of Rome since the student movements of the 1960s. But there are some startling differences between this and the student protest in Berkeley in 1964.

First, in contrast to the Free Speech Movement in Berkeley, there is little spontaneity here. Under the watchful eyes of parade marshals, groups march under professionally lettered banners in orderly ranks, chanting rehearsed slogans calling for a reduction in taxes and the resignation of the government. Many have been brought to Rome by train or bus under the leadership of their political parties and professional organizations, which oppose the government's financial proposals and want to bring back the center-right government defeated in elections the previous spring (Sani 1996).

Second, these are no shaggy-haired students impassioned by general causes to benefit others or humanity, like the civil rights, peace, or environmental movements. These demonstrators are solid middle-class merchants and shopkeepers whose cause is the size of their own taxes and their fear that the recently elected center-left government will crack down on the lax tax collection practices of previous governments. Rather than putting forward utopian visions as demands, as their student predecessors did, they aim to put pressure on the government to modify its tax proposals over the next few days. Rather than calling for comprehensive reforms in the ways political decisions are made, bringing "participatory democracy," "power to the people," or "grassroots democracy," these marchers are interested less in changing the rules of institutional politics than in exercising greater influence within it.

But it is the leadership of this massive protest that causes the greatest clamor. In contrast to the bearded prophets of the New Left who traced this parade route in the sixties and seventies, its leaders are professional politicians: right-wing breakaway Christian Democrats; the reformed neofascists of the National Alliance; and the leader of the opposition—media magnate, soccer team owner, and department store mogul Silvio Berlusconi. With his designer suit and carefully slicked-back hair, the head of Italy's giant Finimnvest Corporation—himself under investigation for tax fraud—accuses the government of being in the hands of its Communist allies and shaping a dictatorship that will bankrupt him personally and throw the economy into a depression.

The left-wing daily and now-government organ *L'Unità* does not miss the ironies of a billionaire industrialist leading a mass demonstration in the traces of the revolutionary left of the 1960s:

> Who knows if the Honorable Berlusconi, buttoning up his double-breasted suit while he flies toward Piazza San Giovanni, felt the reassuring warmth of the middle class that surrounded him? We expect so, and we wish him well by it, because we know how incomplete life can be for a man who has had everything—but has never experienced the joy of marching in a protest demonstration. (*L'Unità*, 11 November 1996).

In summary, in Berkeley, we saw a new movement with new actors erupting on the scene of political struggle without a fully formed identity, whose actions would have an electrifying effect on their student community, on their opponents, and on their generation. These were people without substantial access to the institutions that made decisions about their lives, defining themselves and their claims in collective action outside mainstream institutions, chief among these claims was increased democratization of those institutions. In Rome, a well-known and "modular" form of protest (Tarrow 1994; Tilly 1995b) is employed by an established collective actor in the presence of the media and with a clear and limited political goal. Two days later, fueled by their success in the *piazza*, Berlusconi and his colleagues walk out of Parliament, leaving the government to pass its finance bill without opposition.

The reader may wonder why we have picked these cases out of a rich store of social protests and demonstrations over the last third of the twentieth century. Has something fundamental changed in the politics in contemporary industrial democracies? Are these two protests no more than variations around a theme, or do they exemplify a trend to a greater frequency, to broader diffusion, and perhaps to the institutionalization of collective action as the world approaches the new century? These are the questions that will animate this book. In this introductory chapter, we wish to lay them out in greater detail and introduce some suggestive findings from the work of our collaborators and other scholars, before raising some issues about the future of the movement society.

Toward a Movement Society?

Not long ago, one of us (Tarrow 1994, pp. 193–98) suggested that the social movement form of representing claims is becoming largely institutionalized in advanced industrial democracies—so much so that classical social movement modes of action may be becoming part of the conventional repertoire of participation.[2] The idea of a movement society advances three main hypotheses:

- First, social protest has moved from being a sporadic, if recurring feature of democratic politics, to become a perpetual element in modern life.
- Second, protest behavior is employed with greater frequency, by more diverse constituencies, and is used to represent a wider range of claims than ever before.
- Third, professionalization and institutionalization may be changing the major vehicle of contentious claims—the social movement—into an instrument within the realm of conventional politics.

To the extent that these three things are happening, the social movement may lose its power to inspire challengers and to impress antagonists and authorities; it may be moving from the edges of political legitimacy, where it has warranted special responses from the state and separate analytical treatment from social analysts, to become something more akin to interest groups and political parties. Before moving to any kind of grand generalization, however, we must examine the empirical facts of the frequency, diffusion, professionalization, and institutionalization of contentious politics and the social movement.

We begin from the assumption that the social movement is a *historical* and not a universal way of mounting collective claims. Movements, in our view, are best defined as *collective challenges to existing arrangements of power and distribution by people with common purposes and solidarity, in sustained interaction with elites, opponents, and authorities.* Movements became a viable way of making claims in national politics when the consolidated nation-state assured its citizens regular means of communication, created standard but fungible identities, and provided challengers with uniform targets and fulcra for acting collectively (Tarrow 1994; Tilly 1995b). But movements were never the only vehicles for contention; they acted in parallel and frequently intersected with other forms of collective action; with isolated incidents of collective violence; with strikes and campaigns mounted by unions or other institutional actors; and with the rebellions, insurgencies, and revolutions with which they have strong analogies (McAdam, Tarrow, and Tilly 1997). Not only that, they often acted *within* institutional politics and movement activists learned to combine institutional modes of action with noninstitutional contention (Tilly 1978; Tarrow, 1996a). Thus, if the definition of movements depends on a sustained, conflictual interaction with other actors, they have seldom been very far from institutional politics—especially in the pluralist democracies of the West.

If movements are historical phenomena and have always militated around the borders of the polity, it is surely a mistake to expect them to emerge and mobilize in characteristic forms as the world around them changes. Although few basic changes marked the national social movement's trajectory after its appearance in the eighteenth century up until the Second World War, the processes that first permitted movements to mobilize against powerful states have continued to evolve. New sets of claims and claimants have begun to emerge, even as the state's capacity to redress them has diminished (Ginsburg and Shefter 1990). Citizens with greater resources and increased skills have developed new capacities for action (McCarthy and Zald 1987a). With increased travel, communication, and education, the potential networks of activism have broadened beyond the state (Keck and Sikkink 1998). States have to some extent been losing control over national life as international news services, television broadcasting, and even electronic mail allow news of claims and events to spread within and across countries with astonishing speed.[3] These changes have increased the ease with which contention can be mounted and have created at least imagined commonalities among challengers across social groups and national states.

The rapid spread of contention across the globe and the increased capacity of citizens to mount it have been seen by some to portend a new and more chaotic era of global turbulence (Rosenau 1990) and, by others, to represent direct challenges to state sovereignty (Badie 1995; Cerny 1995). This view is supported by the spread of such militant movements as Islamic fundamentalism transnationally from Iran to Afghanistan and to North Africa and by the more recent appearance of extremist groups like American militias and European naziskins.

The dramatic rise of potentially violent movements belies the fact that over the longer run in the history of Western Europe and North America, there is evidence of declining violence in the repertoire of contention (Tilly 1995a) and of a greater ease of ordinary citizens in mounting contention, which suggests its acceptability and even legitimation by elites and authorities. By accepting and regulating contention, in this view, states may have learned to control it and, through this control, begun to domesticate the social movement within the political process. Even outside the democracies of the West, we see the largely institutional transnational activist networks described in this volume by Margaret Keck and Katherine Sikkink.

To examine the tenets of the movement society hypothesis and to understand the implications of the changes it suggests, we need to take it apart and examine its premises. In the next four sections, we will examine, first, whether contentious politics has increased in terms of the frequency of events and their commonality across industrial democracies—including some recently emerging democracies in East-Central Europe and the Third World. Second, we will look at the diffusion of contention to different social actors and at the equally important diffusion of particular forms of contention across different institutional sites. Third, we will turn to the professionalization of contentious politics, before examining, fourth, the entry of dissident claims and constituents into established institutions and the ongoing interaction of challengers and the state.

Has Contentious Politics Expanded?

In his fine textbook on citizen politics, American political scientist Russell Dalton (1996, p. 75) writes of survey results in the four liberal democracies he studied (the United States, Britain, Germany, and France), "In every nation unconventional political activities are more common at the end of the survey period [1974–1990] than at the first time point. . . . Protest is becoming a more common political activity in advanced industrial democracies."

In some ways, Dalton's results are unequivocal. For example, while only 22 percent of Britons surveyed in 1975 reported signing a petition, by 1990, the proportion had risen to 75 percent; and while 9 percent of Germans reported participating in demonstrations in 1974, by 1990, 25 percent said they had done so (p. 76). Dalton's findings are hardly peculiar or idiosyncratic; as Dieter Rucht shows in his chapter here, in Germany, the proportion of estimated protesters per year rose on the average from 1.45 percent of the total over his thirty-year period in the

1960s, from 0.94 percent in the 1970s, to 4.33 percent in the 1980s, before declining slightly to 3.30 percent in the early 1990s.

These changes were not linear or equal for all countries, but in countries as different as peaceful Switzerland and turbulent Italy, the end of the protest cycle that began in the late 1960s left a higher magnitude of contention than at its beginnings (Kriesi 1984; Tarrow 1989). For example, when Kriesi and his collaborators examined the trend of "new" social movements in four Western European countries, three of the four described protest cycles similar in shape to what Kriesi and Tarrow had found earlier for Switzerland and Italy; at the end of the 1980s, all three experienced a larger number of protests by such movements than in the mid-1970s (Kriesi et al. 1995, p. 74).[4]

In addition to being more frequent, protest appears to be employed by a wider variety of organizations than was the case thirty years ago. Particularly in the United States, there has been a dramatic increase in the number of interest organizations purporting to support either excluded constituencies or "the public interest"—that is, constituencies that were historically represented by social movements. Such organizations often combine institutional advocacy with extrainstitutional activity (Minkoff 1994; Walker 1991). Interestingly enough, as Verba and Nie (1972) noted in their pioneering study of participation in the United States, participation in protest activity has not come at the expense of other forms of participation but rather is cumulative with them: people who protest are more, not less, likely to vote and engage in the whole range of conventional citizen politics.[5]

What Does "More Protest" Mean?

But the story may be far more complicated than this; the proliferation of formal, bureaucratized, and relatively stable organizations like public interest groups mentioned earlier underscores two important issues regarding the meaning and implications of increased protest.

First, the increases in survey reports of nonelectoral participation between the 1970s and the 1980s were greatest for the *least* contentious forms of collective action—like petitions—while more contentious ones (e.g., building occupations and political violence) increased only slightly (Dalton 1996, p. 76) and in some cases—like Italy—actually declined after the protest excesses of the 1970s (della Porta 1990). In the United States, where the use of political violence decreased dramatically between the early 1970s and the late 1980s (Gurr 1989), the occasional dramatic incident, like the Oklahoma City bombing, was all the more shocking.

Second, "acceptance" of protests by the public is confined to a narrow range of protest activities, as Matthew Crozat shows in chapter 3, and has declined for most of the countries he analyzes. The one country we have examined in which the approval of more confrontational actions has increased since the 1960s is Germany (see Rucht's chap. 2). In Italy, it was dramatically reversed. In general, the evidence from both Europe and the United States suggests that the amount of highly contentious forms accepted and actually used by citizens seems to be more circumscribed than it was two decades ago.

Moreover, although survey results are good sources of systematic information about individuals over time, they do not easily translate into information about collective events or institutional trends in the histories of particular countries. For example, while contentious politics increased in Spain in the mid-1970s, this development was connected to the struggle over democratization and not part of a secular increase. Equally linked to specific conjunctures, Patricia Hipsher shows in chapter 7 on the demobilization of urban movements in Latin America that the trend to demobilization in recently democratized countries reflects responses to historical events and is not simply part of a larger trend independent of these events. The changes in protest propensity reported for African National Congress (ANC) supporters in South Africa by Bert Klandermans, Marlene Roefs, and Johan Olivier in chapter 8, though its transition is still under way, suggest a similar trajectory.

Nor do the survey data alone allow us to tap into protest traditions in particular countries. In a recent study, Patrice Mann (1990) shows how French winemakers repeatedly used and adapted the same basic protest tactics against a variety of opponents under changing circumstances over a thirty-year period. And in chapter 6 here, Jan Kubik shows that workers in Poland, enjoying one of the strongest economies in East-Central Europe, continue to strike far more than their counterparts in Hungary, Slovakia, and the once-Communist portion of Germany. Like collective events and institutional change, historical repertoires of collective action seem to affect the magnitude of contentious politics. National traditions influence both the form and frequency of collective action.

Even the national differences in the "new" social movements in the 1980s were as impressive as their commonalities. This can be seen in the four countries studied by Kriesi and his collaborators (1995). The new movements soared in conservative-ruled West Germany, whereas in neighboring Switzerland, both protest and the use of referenda and initiatives grew at the same time. But the same period saw new movement organizations coopted by the government in France, while the "old" politics of trade unions and material demands flourished. In the meantime, once-militant Italy witnessed apparent movement decline.

A similar picture of national differences emerges at the opposite end of the "old/new" spectrum; Peter Lange and Lyle Scuggs (1996) recently found that the strength of unions that many have seen declining all across the countries of the Organization for Economic Cooperation and Development (OECD) varied just as much as the "new" social movement events studied by Kriesi and his collaborators.[6]

One of the difficulties with using survey data to track the changes in contentious politics over time is that they seldom—if ever—allow us to compare a large number of countries with similar metrics and meanings. This is why some scholars are beginning to turn—if only as a rough guide—to the automated analysis of on-line newspaper or press agency reports of protest, which allows standard coverage over time for a large number of countries. Using this technique for a recent period (1983–1995), an automated time-series analysis of Reuter's European dispatches showed a relatively flat growth of contentious politics for the countries that were part of the European Union over these years (Imig and Tarrow 1996).

What inferences can we draw from these findings? According to some measures and some studies, the use of protest is progressively increasing, but it is also possible that the reported participation of more and more citizens in certain forms of contentious politics since the 1970s does not translate into increased contention generally. What we may be seeing is an increase in the more *institutionalized* forms of contention, like petitioning, and in the institutionalization of movement activity itself (Kriesi et al. 1995), as the most contentious forms fall into disuse. As we approach the beginning of a new century, what is the evidence that contentious politics is becoming more diffused, more professional, and more institutionalized? Let us turn to these aspects of contentious politics before asking how they affect the future of the movement society.

Contentious Diffusion

Thirty years separate the Berkeley student protests from the Berlusconi tax demonstration in Rome. We see many similarities in these two events, but we also perceive in Rome something new: people from a variety of walks of life, who probably would not have done so thirty years ago, used a contentious public performance to demonstrate a claim against political opponents and public authorities. The performance of contentious acts, albeit in less contentious forms and on behalf of narrower causes, has been diffused to broader sectors of the population. We will look at this process of diffusion across different social demographic groups and then across different geographic spaces. We will then turn to examine likely causes for diffusion.

Social and Demographic Diffusion

In one way the events in Berkeley in 1964 represented a popular image of the sixties: they overwhelmingly involved students and young people. It is still true today that young people are more likely to participate in protest activity than their seniors (Dalton 1996, p. 80).[7] But "the larger significance of protest politics," writes Dalton, "lies in its adoption by a wide variety of . . . citizen groups" (p. 81). In environmental protests, in tax revolts, in the peace movements of the 1980s and the activities of the religious right in the 1900s, age no longer seems to be a bar to participation in contentious politics.

In addition, social actors whose parents would not have dreamed of using contentious politics seem to do so increasingly today. The most striking shift is in gender. Although men still protest more often than women, this gap seems to be narrowing along with socially determined gender roles (Dalton 1996, p. 78; also see chap. 3). One outcome of feminist activism of the 1960s and 1970s is the increased visibility of women in leadership roles in both women's movements and all sorts of other movements (Meyer and Whittier 1994), from Phyllis Schlafly's anti-ERA campaign and Mothers against Drunk Driving in the 1980s to the antiabortion blockades and the Gay and Lesbian March on Washington, D.C., in 1994.

Women have also been playing an increasingly prominent role in contentious politics internationally. In Latin America, some of the most visible protests against military rule, torture, and disappearances were mounted by mothers' groups, while in Western Europe, mothers have been active in pushing governments to set up drug rehabilitation clinics. In Britain, the 1980s Greenham Common protests against nuclear armaments were organized exclusively by women, and the miners' strike of 1985 had substantial female participation (Beckwith 1996). On the right, women have emerged as major activists in the American antiabortion movement. Women's participation in the social protest movements has been mirrored in established political institutions as well. Although publicly mounted protests are particularly visible, less obtrusive activities may have more long-lasting effects. The growth of women's mobilization in politics and culture has expanded dramatically within established institutions, even those as unlikely as the military and the Catholic Church, as Mary Katzenstein shows in chapter 9 (also see Rochon, 1998).

Next, consider ideological positions. Although Dalton finds that those with a progressive political orientation are still more likely to protest than conservatives (1996, p. 80), antitax protests like those from Denmark to Italy were largely fueled by those of a conservative persuasion. The antiabortion movement in the United States and the anti-immigrant movement on the European continent involve people from the right in contentious and often violent activities (Koopmans 1995a). Even mildly progressive environmental protests like the anti–calf slaughter movement in Britain brought normally conservative middle-class professionals, matrons, and retirees into the streets to block trucks attempting to bring calves to continental slaughterhouses (Imig and Tarrow (1996). Indeed, many new political campaigns, such as for animal rights or against government property seizures, do not line up neatly as left or right on the old political spectrum, nor do they necessarily call for comprehensive social change. Note that successful protests on certain issues encourage other claimants to adapt protest tactics. Women's health care advocates, witnessing increased funding for AIDS research in response to political activism, for example, began to stage marches calling for funding of breast cancer research.

Nonetheless, Crozat's findings on the acceptance of protest still show an association between progressivism and protest that modifies the picture of protest repertoires spreading across the ideological spectrum. If we look at the French case, in which the extreme right has made the most dramatic leaps forward electorally, protest remains largely a tactic of the left and the unions; the National Front prefers to work beneath the surface in trying to organize police officers and public housing tenants. Moreover, progressive political orientations become more closely correlated with the use of protest the higher on the scale of contention we go—for example, in the approval of boycotts and wildcat strikes. In summary, however, the last thirty years have seen a generalization of the repertoire of contention across age groups, from men to women, from left to right, and from workers and students to other social groupings.

Spatial Diffusion

The tactics and symbols of social protest now appear to spread geographically more easily and more rapidly than they did in the past, both within nations and cross-nationally. When a new form of contention or a new campaign demonstrates its power to mobilize large numbers of citizens or shows up the state's vulnerability, its use is rapidly triggered elsewhere. We saw a vivid example of this kind of diffusion in the United States with the adoption of the"shantytown" protest tactic across college campuses in the 1980s to call for divestment of U.S.

investments in South Africa (Soule 1997). The shantytown identified an issue on which young people would mobilize and a tactic that would draw responses from both American universities and the mass media. Similarly, activists used the symbolic form of the AIDS quilt to mark the death of victims of AIDS in both Western Europe and the United States. And recently in Belgium, a *marche blanche* to protest the police mishandling of a grisly series of murders of young girls was transformed into a spontaneous national movement that forced the government to investigate its own police force.

The U.S. campus shantytowns reveal another trend in the diffusion of protest: indirect contacts between activists (Soule 1997). The protests of the 1960s were diffused mainly by "transitory teams" of activists, many of whom had met in the civil rights movement, maintaining and promoting personal contacts among activists across issues.[8] Today, protest is more often diffused through telephone and electronic communication, redefining the sorts of organization now required to mount protest. In part as the result of electronic communication, the transnational diffusion of protest is more rapid today than it was fifty or even twenty-five years ago. In the 1970s, American antinuclear power activists profited from studying West German activists' successful occupation of the proposed site of a nuclear reactor at Wyhl, modeling their campaign at Seabrook on it. Later, antinuclear campaigners in Germany looked to Seabrook for inspiration in their own blockades of missile bases. In both cases, information about events and tactics were disseminated on widely circulated films and videotapes. More recently, the use of the human chain across the Baltic states in 1989 to demonstrate citizens' desire for independence from the Soviet Union was modeled on the use of human chains in the Western European peace protests of the early part of the decade. These protests, in turn, were studied carefully by insurgents in Ukraine and the Caucasus (Karklins and Petersen 1995). Indeed, the rapid spread of strikingly successful independence and reform movements in Eastern Europe was promoted and accelerated by media reports of successful collective action in first one country then another, and particularly by no reports of violent Soviet responses. Marches that toppled communist governments reverberated around the world, encouraging democratic reformers in other contexts.

Social and Communicative Resources.

What factors explain such wide and rapid diffusion of contentious politics across social groups and between nation-states? We will address two, professionalization and institutionalization, in the next two sections. Here it is worth mentioning two sociological and cultural factors that make protest more readily available to more social groups than in the past. The first is the increase in education, and the second is the influence of universal access to the media.

Among the resources that have long been known to buttress collective action is education (Dalton 1996, p. 80). In the past thirty years, access to higher education has increased in every Western democracy and in many countries of the Third World. But with the end of the easy growth period in the West, access to higher education has not automatically brought about an increase in income or economic security. University graduates without access to professional jobs are probably no more likely to protest now than they were in the past, but there are many more of them than there were in the easy growth years following World War II. The content of education has also changed, with more students exposed to general, humanistically oriented subjects that broaden their perspectives to include "postmaterialist" concerns that often lead them to support—or at least tolerate—unconventional politics (Inglehart 1990). It seems evident that well-educated citizens who travel widely, read newspapers, and have increasing contacts with others outside their local areas will be more likely to join widespread protest movements than less educated citizens who do not read newspapers and spend most of their lives in their local areas.

The growth of the mass media, along with citizens' capacity to both consume and participate in it, has also increased the velocity of diffusion of contentious politics, for at least three reasons. First, when ordinary citizens see others like themselves demonstrating on television, they learn how protests can be mounted and occasionally how they can succeed—demonstrations have a demonstration effect. Second, television focuses attention not on discrete issues that can divide viewers from those they see protesting on the screen but on visual images that diffuse information about the routines of contentious politics, which can be used regardless of the content of demands. Third, because television broadcasters attract viewers through visual images, social actors with claims to make may learn to mount them through dramatic public performances that are more likely to attract the attention of the media then through less public forms of collective action.

Nor are activists and ordinary citizens any longer simply passive consumers of the media. Postmortem analyses of the student and antiwar movements of the 1960s recognized the importance of the media in defining the movement, not only to a broad public but to the activists themselves (see especially Gitlin 1980). Contemporary activists, recognizing the critical role of the media in projecting their activities and claims, have developed more sophisticated ways of influencing how their activities are covered, partly by being mindful of how the mass media work. Sociologist Charlotte Ryan (1991), surveying the scholarly literature on the mass media, provided a progammatic guide to help activists use it more effectively. And an organization like Greenpeace maintains a skilled staff that instantly diffuses images of its activists' dramatic activities to news sources around the world (Wapner 1995). Student and environmental activists have been particularly innovative in using the Internet to transmit information about issues and political activities.

In summary, although the evidence for the growing magnitude and the long-term maintenance of contentious politics is still an open question, the social movement's diffusion across both social and geographic boundaries has been both eased and accelerated by some of the central trends of social and cultural changes of our time. But ordinary citizens do not protest in a vacuum. We now turn to two other trends in contemporary societies that affect the social movements that attempt to mobilize them: professionalization and institutionalization. We will argue that both of these processes affect not only citizens' willingness to engage in collective action but the very nature of that action itself, which we think may be leading to a fundamental change in the nature of contentious politics.

Organized and Professional Amateurism

The conventional, albeit romantic, image of the social movement activist evokes Cincinnatus. The worker—or mother, or scientist, or student—leaves the routine of daily life to engage in collective action because she or he sees no alternative. Conditions in the plant, the home, the lab, or the university have become intolerable, and conventional means of changing them have proven ineffectual. Upon resolving this most pressing grievance, the activist returns to the plow—or home, or test tube, or textbook—to resume "normal"—that is, *not* activist, nonpolitical—activities.

However much truth this myth once held, we know that it is less true now. Although the mass movements that capture the imagination are invigorated by all sorts of people not normally engaged in contentious politics, they are organized through campaigns built by the ongoing efforts of organizers, for whom social activism is a vocation, to bring in others of a much less activist persuasion (Rucht 1991). Increasingly, core activists today support themselves through social change efforts, as organizing becomes a career option and social movement–related organizations differentiate. The mass movements of the past have given way to campaigns animated by small cores of permanent organizers surrounded by much larger numbers of people whose activism is episodic (Gerhards and Rucht 1992). Increasing professionalization and specialization in the nonactivist world also mean that activists who wish to return to the plow after campaign may find it increasingly hard to do so. They may instead move from movement to movement for both political action and employment.

A paradox is inherent in the professionalization of social movement organizations. Whereas the movements of the 1960s were animated by a democratic ethos that encouraged and legitimated participation at the grassroots of society, the following years demonstrated that the skills and resources for mounting the efforts that comprise a social movement could be, in fact, concentrated, reproduced, and professionalized. Those who developed those skills, taking them from one movement to another, may lose a connection with the groups they purported to represent. Professionalization is about drawing boundaries (Moore 1996) between accredited persons and others. Although the fuzzy boundaries between professional activists and their constituencies may support the ethos of democracy, they may also undermine the prospects of sustained and effective mobilization. Ironically, a movement organization concerned with effecting democratic reforms in the polity may be most effective by abandoning certain democratic and *amateurish* political practices. New technologies and forms of social organization have complicated this picture further.

From Mass Parties to Mobile Social Capital

Does this development mean we will see a return to the pattern of permanent, bureaucratic, and centralized mass parties of the European past? In 1973, American sociologists John McCarthy and Mayer Zald (1973, 1987a) first explained the rise of social activism in the 1960s by pointing to professionalization: to the increase in discretionary resources in an affluent society, to the intervention of foundation and government grants for social activism, and especially to the diffusion of professional social movement organizations (SMOs). These factors, in their view, support the permanent establishment of organizations concerned with challenging the establishment and are capable of expressing claims through a variety of means, including extrainstitutional action (see also Walker 1991).

Critics of this theory (e.g., Jenkins and Eckert 1986) noted that the period of greatest increase in mobilization in the 1960s was not when foundations or professional organizations were intensively active. After all, they reasoned, the height of the American civil rights movement was not driven by professional movement organizations but by loosely organized teams of activists converging on available local targets and attracting the temporary support of large numbers of citizens. Professional, bureaucratized, and better-financed organizations followed, rather than provoked, the heyday of movement activity (McAdam 1982).

A similar debate emerged after the high point of student mobilization in Western Europe in the late 1960s. In Italian universities, for example, small bands of activists had organized faculty occupations, drawing larger numbers of students into assemblies, teach-ins, and propaganda activities. Like their counterparts in the United States, the members of these small activist teams knew each other from earlier organized activities. Some had been members of traditional student organizations, while others had militated in the traditional parties of the left or in Catholic associations (Tarrow 1989, chap. 6). As in the Vietnam War protests in the United States in the same period, small cores of experienced activists organized protest campaigns around particular issues, drawing in much larger numbers of previously unmobilized or occasional activists.

But soon after the student movement collapsed as a mass movement, highly organized extraparliamentary groups, and then political parties, emerged from the ruins. Insurgency became tightly organized and organizations formalized, all under the banner of spontaneity. Formalization took three main forms: first, the increasingly routinized activities of the extraparliamentary groups, which organized territorially into sections, published their own newspapers, and elaborated formal ideological programs; second, the "hot autumn" of the labor movement, which created a new generation of professional activists within the unions (Pizzorno 1978; Reyneri, Regalia, and Regini 1978); and third, the creation by some former student activists and their successors of increasingly secret cells organized for armed struggle. These were the origins of the left-wing terrorists whose atrocities devastated the new left (della Porta 1990).

None of these variants was spontaneous in its organization (although the extraparliamentary groups encouraged tactical spontaneity in their supporters' actions), and all three were highly professional, in the sense that they turned part-time activists into full-time movement professionals, elaborated common methods of work, and directed their actions at agreed-on general goals and programs. However, none resembled the traditional mass organizations of the European left, with the permanent presences, bureaucratic structures, and centralized leaderships. This was a new kind of professionalization—often calling itself the opposite.

All of this is to say that professionalization raises more complicated issues than scholars initially thought. When we think of professional movement organizations, we too often think of the model of the European social democratic mass movements that flourished before and after World War I, and whose sterility and goal displacement were long ago foreseen by Robert Michels (1962). Following Michels, many analysts were quick to associate professionalization with the moderation of demands and tactics, drawing stark polemical lessons from organizations that "sold out" or "matured" into interest groups or parties. Critics on the left and right (e.g., Piven and Cloward 1979; Wilson 1973), who agreed on little else, concurred on this point, differing only in their normative evaluation of the process and compounding the misunderstanding.

Such claims, however, are based on too narrow a view of professionalization. As has been argued elsewhere (Tarrow 1994, chap. 8; also see Staggenborg 1988; Kleidman 1984), the permanent, bureaucratic, and centralized European mass movement, with its sorry heritage of goal displacement, is only one variant of the professionalization of movement organization. In the history of social movements, much more common have been looser, more decentralized networks of activists and leaders without strong central offices, organized around particular campaigns and claims. Like the movement organizations that emerged from the 1960s, the core participants of these movements are highly professional, even as they put forward ideologies of spontaneity and mobilize temporary coalitions of nonprofessional supporters around their campaigns.

The recent anti-immigration law campaign in France illustrates this new professionalism well. Frightened by a growth in far right, National Front votes, the center-right government of Alain Juppé passed a series of control laws aimed at illegal immigrants, laws with more than a passing resemblance to the anti-Semitic and antiforeigner legislation passed by the puppet Vichy regime during the Nazi occupation. This action led congeries of professional, civil rights, and union organizations to come together in a major series of protests and petitions calling for civil disobedience. The fact that the campaign first gained public notice when a group of moviemakers announced a civil disobedience campaign, and the fact that it was organized over only a few days in February 1997, made it seem spontaneous, but its organizational infrastructure was very much the same as that which had supported previous pro-immigrant protests and would survive the passage of the government bill to lead a massive protest against the National Front's national congress in Strasbourg in March.[9] No mass party or movement organization took place here but rather a campaign led by a small cadre of organizers and a much larger penumbra of usually inactive citizens.

Examples of lighter, more decentralized collectivities abound in the activism of the post-1960s decades: in the American peace movement studied by one of us (Meyer 1990); in the temporary coalitions of Berlin-based groups organized for brief campaigns studied by Gerhards and Rucht (1992); in the spectacular recent successes of the anti-Walmart protests in the United States, largely diffused through electronic communication by people who had never met (Yin 1996); and in transnational environmental organizations like Greenpeace, which combine small groups of high-risk activists with literally millions of inactive supporters around the world (Wapner 1995).

Such movements are not "new" in that they are "spontaneous," whereas their predecessors were "organized"; or in that they put forward "identity claims," in contrast to the supposedly more "instrumental" claims of "old" social movements; or even in that they routinely use unconventional forms of action (Rucht 1990).[10] What *is* new is that they have greater discretionary resources, enjoy easier access to the media, and have cheaper and faster geographic mobility and cultural interaction. Among them, these features have made permanent, centralized, and bureaucratic organizations less important than they once were in attempts to advance effective challenges to elites or authorities. In the movement society, it is possible for lighter, more decentralized, and temporary collectivities to gain the logistical and financial advantages that formerly inhered only in bureaucratic mass organizations. Professionalization then, needs to be conceptualized more broadly, as does the range of possible organizational forms dissidents may take.[11]

Unlike the stolid, bureaucratic organizations of the interwar period, contemporary activists possess what might be called "moveable social capital": the capacity of transitory teams to assemble coalitions of local and translocal groups and to mount collective action after relatively brief preparation in a variety of venues. Rather than declining in the age of the mass media as some have hypothesized (Putnam 1995), social capital may have simply become more mobile; though losing ground in the permanent associations of local life, it may be growing in the capacity of citizens to put together temporary coalitions for contentious politics. Hanspeter Kriesi's team's (1995) work on new social movement organizations takes us a step toward formalizing this insight.

The Growth and Differentiation of Movement-Related Organizations

Movements are generally composed of a number of organizations and affiliated organizations cooperating—to some degree—to advance political claims.[12] The form, organization, and relative prominence of movement organizations change over the course of a protest cycle. Key movement organizations are very seldom well structured during a movement's early phases. By using the term *well structured*, we follow Kriesi et al. (1995) in referring to their formalization, professionalization, centralized control, well-financed operations, and large number of supportive members. During their most protest-oriented phases, such organizations are usually in an emergent phase and depend more on protest as a resource with which to mobilize supporters than on more conventional internal or external resources (Lipsky 1968; Tarrow 1994). This finding has been confirmed in diverse contexts, including the American civil rights movement (Jenkins and Eckert 1986), the 1960s–1970s protest cycle in Italy (Tarrow 1989), and the new social movements in Western Europe in the 1980s (Kriesi et al. 1995). The major growth in movement organizations came *after* the height of both protest cycles.

Second, the strength of movement-related organizations cannot be measured simply by mass memberships. Social movements do not only produce organizations that aim at political mobilization toward authorities or others (SMOs); in fact, as we have just argued, such organizations are more likely to mature after the height of mobilization has passed. They can also turn into indirect forms of political representation, like parties or interest groups, or take on constituency/client-oriented activities that produce *non*political organizations, for either service or self-help purposes (Kriesi et al. 1995, p. 152 ff). This point suggests that movement organizations not only develop internally (e.g., greater formalization, bureaucratization, professionalization, and membership growth) but also put their energies into building other kinds of movement-related organizations—usually after their protest-related activities decline. As Kriesi et al. (1995, p. 156) note:

> An SMO can become more like a party or an interest group; it can take on characteristics of a supportive service organization; it can develop in the direction of a self-help group, a voluntary association or a club; or it can radicalize, that is, become an ever more exclusive organization for the mobilization for collective action.

More important here than the various trajectories, or their importance to different types of movements, is the recognition that the variety of organizational outcomes provides social movements with a wider range of possibilities for subsequent action than previous theories of social movements acknowledged. To the extent that a movement expands into other forms of movement-related organizations, it develops lateral constituencies and cadres of activists whose numbers or potential commitment will not be evident by looking at the figures for SMO membership. This is a crucial point that may help to interpret the fact that recent "new" SMOs tend to be more streamlined than older ones, in terms of both membership[13] and the number of their permanent organizational cadres. Roughly one-half of the groups Kriesi et al. examined had no paid staff at all; only in the German and Dutch SMOs was there more than an average of eighteen paid staff per organization; in France and Switzerland, the average was fewer than ten. But with affiliated self-help service, and party/political movement-related organizations, they may have a much larger activist cadre to draw on than appears evident from their number of members or permanent staff.

But there is another reason that the organizational diffusion described by Kriesi et al. is important for the movement society thesis: it suggests ways in which movement-originated identities, goals, and personnel may be blending into the structures of civil society without necessarily producing a higher visible level of protest, violence, or contention. Movement organizations need not be defined exclusively by the organization of protest campaigns, and more conventional political organizations may organize such campaigns (Burstein 1997). Indeed, much of the contention in contemporary societies does not come from movement organizations as such but from campaigns organized by parties, interest groups, professional associations, citizens' groups, and public servants. And this point takes us directly to the problem of institutionalization.

The Institutionalization of Movements

If social protest has become more common, more easily diffused and sponsored by increasing numbers and types of organizations, we must then ask, What sorts of protest? And what do they mean for the future of the social movement? Within the wide range of collective action forms in democratic states today, we find an apparent paradox: although disruption appears to be the most effective political tool of the disadvantaged (Lipsky 1968; Piven and Cloward 1979), the majority of episodes of movement activity we see today disrupt few routines, save perhaps those in the everyday lives of the protesters. As noted earlier, most contentious actions in Western industrial societies take the form of peaceful, orderly routines that break no laws and violate no spaces.

Why are conventional forms of collective action the ones most commonly employed, even in a tumultuous period of contention? Of course, part of the answer is tautological: what is conventional be-

comes so because it is commonly used, and the boundaries of acceptable conduct and claims are changed by social protest movements.
Demonstrations and petitions—once contentious, unpredictable, and
disruptive—are now less so. To understand what this means, we need
to look at the interests of both the state and dissidents in negotiating
means of claims making that are repeatable and routinized, regardless
of outcome.

For us, institutionalization is defined by the creation of a repeatable
process that is essentially self-sustaining (Jepperson 1991); it is one in
which all the relevant actors can resort to well-established and familiar
routines. For political movements, institutionalization denotes the end
of the sense of unlimited possibility of the kind we saw in Berkeley,
which paralyzed police and university administrators; for authorities,
it means the ending of the uncertainty and instability that can result
when unknown actors engage in uncontrollable forms of action. Institutionalization, in this view, is composed of three main components:

- First, the *routinization* of collective action, such that challengers
  and authorities can both adhere to a common script, recognizing
  familiar patterns as well as potentially dangerous deviations.[14]
- Second, *inclusion* and *marginalization*, whereby challengers who
  are willing to adhere to established routines will be granted access
  to political exchanges in mainstream institutions, while those who
  refuse to accept them can be shut out of conversations through
  either repression or neglect.
- Third, *cooptation*, which means that challengers alter their claims
  and tactics to ones that can be pursued without disrupting the
  normal practice of politics.[15]

These processes of routinization, inclusion/marginalization, and cooptation are distinct but complementary aspects of institutionalization
(Meyer 1993a), which allow dissidents to continue to lodge claims *and*
permit states to manage dissent without stifling it.

Authorities manage dissent by insisting clearly and acting consistently on a spectrum of behaviors, some of which will be tolerated
while others are either repressed or ignored. This has the effect of not
only enticing some actors to embrace institutional politics but also in-
ducing others to reject it, thus separating more radical activists from
their more moderate allies, fragmenting coalitions of challengers, and
weakening opposition overall. Institutionally oriented challengers are
rewarded for their choice by the prospect of meaningful political access, whereas those determined to make more comprehensive chal-

lenges avoid the compromises inherent in institutional politics but risk repression or simply irrelevance.

We can usefully think about this equation by starting from the activists' perspective. Challengers will adopt the form of claims making that they believe to be most effective and least costly. Most activists will abandon forms that seem unduly costly, eschewing actions that invite repression when meaningful alternatives seem available. For example, activists learn that they can march and offer even the most radical claims, provided they stay on negotiated parade routes. They learn to control extremist elements within their ranks and on their fringes, whose actions risk turning police cooperation into conflict. In the "American" model of police practice described by John McCarthy and Clark McPhail in chapter 4, they may even attend seminars organized by the police on proper demonstration behavior and marshaling techniques.

Just as pursuing strategies that invite repression can destroy movement organizations, adapting routinized forms of action is also costly. By reducing the uncertainty in their tactics and accepting compromises in their claims, challengers reduce their capacity to inspire supporters and to hold the attention of elites. At the same time, groups who choose the institutional path can gain compensations—which is why many often do. Ordinary people are more likely to want to participate in forms of collective action they know and understand than risk the uncertainty, particularly potential violence, of radical direct action. As a movement's chosen form of action crystallizes into convention, it becomes a known part of the repertoire and lowers the social transaction costs for organizers and their supporters (Tarrow 1994, chap. 2). Once learned, these practices can be redeployed, tinkered with, and combined with other forms, just as a jazz group improvises around a central theme (Tilly 1978). Perhaps most significantly, adopting routinized forms can lead to influence on public policy; challengers can win victories, even if often uncredited and more modest than activists might wish.

In the long run, the evolution of the repertoire results from the absorption of the innovations that work and the rejection of ones that fail. Over time, originally disruptive forms like the strike and the demonstration have become conventional because they presented effective challenges, maintained and built solidarity, and usually avoided repression by controlling uncertainty. In the early twentieth century, the invention of the institution of parade marshals in France and elsewhere showed how uncertainty could be controlled (Favre 1990). In the last thirty years of our century, once-disruptive forms like nonviolent collective action, sit-ins, and building occupations have begun to produce less disruptive equivalents.

How do ongoing changes in contemporary institutions affect the process of institutionalizing dissent? Three notable developments in contemporary protest politics seem to be particularly important.

First, social movement activists have learned how to move between conventional and unconventional collective actions, and even to employ both sorts of strategies in combination. As example, the civil rights movement in the United States began with legislative efforts and legal challenges and moved to mass marches and sit-ins in the next phase of its efforts. Similarly, European antinuclear groups deployed a panoply of tactics ranging from the high-risk blockades of nuclear energy facilities all the way to educational efforts and lobbying local politicians. While some organizations specialize in a particular set of tactics, they can work in combination with both other specialists and organizations that deploy diverse methods. Activists can thus adapt strategies to the targets, claims, opportunities, and constraints of the historical moment.

Entering mainstream politics or other well-established nonstate institutions does not mean eschewing challenging claims. In chapter 9, Mary Katzenstein examines two institutions that we would expect to be rather insulated from the effects of dissidents within them—the army and the Catholic Church—and finds that these institutions *sometimes* reformed and restructured themselves in response to new claims and constituents. To some extent, bringing new practices and even a new language to the heart of establishments like the armed forces or the Church may have had greater long-term effects than even the most dramatic mass protest does on the streets.

Second, police practices increasingly encourage the routinization of contention by cooperating with protesters in planning their events, avoiding provocations, and allowing them a public but circumscribed hearing. These practices vary among Western democracies, as the comparison of France and Italy in chapter 5 by della Porta, Fillieule, and Reiter shows. But they have consistently shifted in the direction of the apolitical management of protest, despite occasional outcroppings of politics or police-inspired violence. Police images of "good" and "bad" protesters are dependent not on dissident claims or ideology but on conduct. And police practices have diffused transnationally over time, just as activist strategies and claims have.

Police practice illustrates the process of institutionalization in microcosm. Demonstrators negotiate the date and physical boundaries of their challenges. Police, representing the state, agree not only to tolerate them but to protect them against countermovements. Demonstrators can even escalate the challenge by adding "civil disobedience" to their demonstration—as McCarthy and McPhail show in their discussion of the Justice for Janitors campaign. By informing police of planned challenges to the law—even asking lawbreakers to identify themselves with armbands—and agreeing to eschew violence, activists can make the experience of breaking the law safe and predictable. Police know what to expect, lay on stretchers and buses, and inform demonstrators how to avoid being hurt while they are carried off to be booked. Everyone can get home by the end of the day to observe the event on the evening news.

Do movements that routinize their practices in cooperation with the police eventually have to accept the other two aspects of institutionalization—inclusion and cooptation? Although this progress seems to have an inexorable logic, this is not necessarily the case. If we accept that movements can pursue system-challenging claims even *within* the institutions of the state, we have no reason to believe that routinized forms of contention are necessarily less challenging than their unruly cousins or that they determine other aspects of movement/state relations. In fact, putting half a million people in the streets for an orderly demonstration may push policies in activists' preferred direction more than the more dramatic and disruptive efforts of a few militants who firebomb opponents' offices or turn over cars.[16]

Third, the tactics used by movement organizations and those used by more institutionalized groups increasingly overlap. Just as movement leaders have become skilled at using the law, legislation, and the media, interest groups and parties frequently resort to the kinds of public performances that used to be identified exclusively with social movements. When Democratic members of Congress hold mock hearings on the steps of the Capitol to demonstrate their being shut out by the Republican majority or get arrested outside the South African consulate to protest apartheid, when members of a representational artists' association demonstrate outside the Museum of Modern Art in New York to protest their exclusion from the museum's exhibits, and when members of the Royal Association for the Prevention of Cruelty to Animals block calf-carrying trucks in British ferry ports, the instruments of social protests have indeed become modular. We now reach our final concern: a reflection on how social movements are conceived, operationalized, and how they relate to conventional politics.

Politics, Contentious Politics, and the Movement Society

In the preceding discussion, we have tried to move from current debates on social movements to frame important unresolved issues in understanding the changing relations between contemporary politics and contention. A number of important dilemmas remain—some methodological, some theoretical, and some historical. The following chapters should answer some of them, but we wish to mention three here to alert the reader to the fact that all the issues raised by the movement society thesis are by no means settled. The methodological issue is the relation between social movements and the forms of contention they use; the theoretical and historical ones are the future of the social movement and the impact of selective institutionalization on violence.

We have observed that one of the characteristics of the movement society is that social movements can combine disruptive and conventional activities and forms of organization, while institutional actors like interest groups and parties increasingly engage in contentious behavior. The methodological issue that this raises is obvious: if we are correct, it will be increasingly difficult to expect that by tracing protest activities in a given society we will have an accurate record of social movement activities—and *only* of them; we will also find that we have included some of the activities of *non*social movements in our record of contention.

As in all serious methodological issues, the solution to this dilemma will only come through a combination of conceptual and methodological work. A first step is to recognize that social movements are by no means the only participants in contentious politics. A second would be the classification of both movements and other actors in terms of the centrality of contentious forms of action in their repertoires, and the collection of data about other kinds of actors in contentious politics that will permit us to see who uses it and under what conditions. To go back to one of the cases sketched at the beginning of this essay: the occasional recourse to public demonstrations on the part of politicians like Silvio Berlusconi should not be enough to lead us to classify such individuals as the leaders of social movements.

But, second, and more fundamentally, precisely because of the increasing incentives to engage in socially controlled collective action in our societies today, can we still regard the social movement in its classical form as a major player in the political struggle? Movements historically gained their power to build constituencies and occasionally influence authorities with their power to disrupt, to surprise, and to create uncertainty. We have seen that the movement society provides incentives for the professionalization of movement organizations, for their ability to shift into other organizational forms, for their institutionalization, as well as making it profitable for ordinary interest groups to adopt the methods traditionally associated with the social movement. To what extent have these changes done away with the special role of the social movement as a challenger to the polity? Further, if protest is no longer the exclusive province of those on the margins of the polity, do those groups still have some way to make claims effectively?

Finally, if states have become adept at institutionalizing movements and activists are becoming both more professional and more interchangeable with interest groups in their activities, what will happen to those actors who refuse the blandishments of recognition and legitimation? Will they profit as free riders from the institutionalization of protest? Will they simply fade away, returning to private life or becoming isolated sects of devotees? Or will they react to the institutionalization of other movements by radicalizing their appeals and their own modes of action? As we can recall from earlier periods of protest, the institutionalization of most mainstream movements at the end of a protest cycle can lead to radicalization and violence on the part of their competitors (Tarrow 1989, chap. 11). The recent outbreaks of militia violence in the United States may be related to the simultaneous "mainstreaming" of the Christian Right and other conservative groups into the ranks of the Republican party.

These are questions for future research. For the moment, we think it enough to ask our authors whether they see a more or less linear increase in protest and in the acceptability of protest; whether unconventional politics is diffusing more rapidly and finding activists in once-quiescent sectors of the population; and whether this expansion of protest is producing an institutionalization so great that the social movement as we have known it in the history of the West is losing its power to surprise, to disrupt and to mobilize, and to provide a meaningful and effective alternative form of politics for those without access to more conventional means of influence.

Notes

1. On the repertoire of contention, see Tilly (1978, 1995), Tarrow (1994), and Traugott (1995). On the connections between civil rights and the student movement of the late 1960s, see McAdam (1988).

2. Although the first statements of the "movement society" idea were proffered as possibilities rather than as explicit hypotheses, in this fragmentary treatment, Tarrow tried to distill a few key issues that recur in the literature. For other attempts to do the same, see Neidhardt and Rucht (1993), where the term first appears; Fish (1995), where it is used somewhat differently; Minkoff (1994); and Meyer and Staggenborg (1996).

3. For a sampling of the rapidly growing literature on transnationalization

of movements, see Keck and Sikkink (1998), Rucht (1996c), Sikkink (1993), Smith, Pagnucco, and Chatfield (1997), and Wapner (1995).

4. The exception was France, both because the "cycle" of new social movement activity came earlier in the fifteen-year period and because the cooptation of a number of movement organizations by the Socialist-led government resulted in an overall reduction of protest activity during the 1980s. Note that France's level of protest activity appears to have reversed course in the 1990s, especially on issues of immigrant rights and in the "old" sector of industrial conflict.

5. Also see Barnes et al. (1979), Conway (1991), and Rosenstone and Hansen (1993).

6. When we break down the generic term *protest* into its main components, the incidence of particular forms of contentious politics is by no means uniform. For example, the World Values Study of 1990–91 shows that the signing of petitions—the least contentious form of unconventional politics covered by that survey—was reported by 77 percent of respondents in Canada but by only 18 percent in Spain; while the use of more contentious acts (e.g., lawful demonstrations, boycotts, unofficial strikes, or building occupations) varied on the average between 52 percent in East Germany (in 1990) and 12 percent in Japan. Not only that: with the exception of the peculiar case of East Germany, the countries in which higher proportions of citizens reported using these more contentious forms are by no means the same ones as those in which high proportions signed petitions.

For example, the United States, which ranked fourth in the proportion of citizens who reported signing petitions, ranked twelfth in the proportion reporting participation in more contentious forms of protest; and Italy, which ranked fifteenth in signing petitions, ranked second in participation in the more contentious forms of protest (figures reported by Dalton [1996, p. 74]). The use of contentious politics has risen throughout the West, but it has done so unevenly over time and to different degrees for different forms of protest across national and cultural boundaries.

7. In the United States, Germany, and France, Dalton (1996, p. 80) shows that age is correlated with protest activity at about −0.25, rivaled only by left/ right position in Germany (0.25) and France (0.29). Note that controlling for other factors, the correlation between left/right position and acceptance of protest is still significant but shows a lower coefficient of correlation in Crozat's chapter in this volume.

8. McAdam (1988) demonstrates the continued activism of Freedom Summer volunteers, long after the Mississippi project had ended. Activists trained in one movement become resources for subsequent social protests on other issues (Meyer and Whittier 1994).

9. This summary of events is based on the personal experience of one of the authors and will be reported in a later publication.

10. For the archetypical "new" social movement claim, see Cohen (1985) and Cohen and Arato (1992). For a more historically based view that finds both instrumental and identity claims in previous waves of movement, see D'Anieri, Ernst, and Kier (1990) and Calhoun (1995b).

11. Scholars have lately examined the "organizational repertoire" from which dissidents can choose; see Clemens (1993) and Minkoff (1994).

12. For a more developed statement of the coalitional aspects of social protest movements, see Meyer and Rochon (1997).

13. For example, Kriesi et al.'s (1995, p. 172) data on the most important SMOs in the four European countries he examined show clearly that, with the exception of Greenpeace, average membership is much lower for those organizations created after 1965 than those already on the scene in that year.

14. For example, so routinized has the *manifestation* become in France that political scientist Pierre Favre (1990) is able to chart a schema of its constituent elements graphically.

15. We follow Selznick (1949) here, rejecting the narrower definition of co-optation of some analysts that implies the abandonment of political goals.

16. The trade-off between numbers and intensity of participation required presents an intriguing puzzle that activists confront regularly but in scholarly research has been addressed only at a formal theoretical level (De Nardo 1985). Although we might assume an inverse relationship between numbers participating and the risk and cost of participation, we need empirical research to confirm this assumption and to examine the relative influence of different tactics on public policy.

2

The Structure and Culture of Collective Protest in Germany since 1950

Dieter Rucht

Collective protest was—and still is—an endemic feature of politics in Western societies. Many different types of protests complement, and sometimes challenge, the well-established means of participation in social and political life. In spite of the ubiquity and relevance of collective protest, we have had only a sketchy knowledge of changing patterns over the last decades. For the most part, we have had to rely on impressions rather than systematic empirical investigation. This was also true for West Germany, which, according to some observers, has a particularly vigorous protest sector. This chapter focuses on the changing patterns of collective protest in West Germany. It aims to offer at least preliminary answers to two questions: What are the main *structural* changes that West German protests have undergone since 1950? Have changes also taken place in the *culture* of protest as expressed in the use of language, symbols, and very specific tactics?

Thanks to recent research, we no longer have to rely on vague impressions or risky generalizations from a few case studies to provide a picture of the structure and culture of collective protests in West Germany. First, we can draw on protest event data from a cross-national project that includes France, the Netherlands, and Switzerland from 1975 through 1989 (Kriesi et al. 1992, 1995) and more extensive work on West Germany (also see Koopmans 1993, 1995b). Second, we now have protest event data from an ongoing project with the short title

An earlier version of this chapter was presented at the Tenth International Conference of Europeanists, Chicago, March 14–16, 1996. I am grateful to Peter Hall, David Meyer, and Sidney Tarrow for their comments on the earlier version. I would also like to thank Gabi Rosenstreich for her editorial assistance.

"Prodat" (discussed later). It currently provides comprehensive and detailed data on West Germany from 1950 to the early 1990s. These data enable us to place the number and structure of protests in West Germany in a comparative perspective and to draw a more detailed picture of West German protest over a considerable period of time.

Before presenting the database and empirical results, I will first clarify some of the key concepts used here. In contrast to other scholars who have attributed all collective protests to social movements (e.g., Kriesi et al. 1995), I argue for the analytical separation of the two categories. By *collective protest* I mean any kind of group activities carried out by nonstate actors designed to express and enact dissent publicly with societal and/or political conditions, institutions, norms, and/or forces. This definition of *collective protest* comes close to Tilly's "contentious gathering,"[1] but it does not necessarily imply the physical presence of the protesters at the same place at the same time (as evoked by the term *gathering*). Thus, a mail-based collection of signatures against whaling and their subsequent publication in a newspaper advertisement would qualify as a collective protest, and so would a citizen group that litigates against the construction of a nuclear power plant regardless of whether the group's members are present in the courtroom.

This definition of a collective protest is fairly inclusive, but my understanding of a *social movement*[2] is more restrictive. This latter concept contains two additional criteria that many protests do not meet. First, a social movement ultimately struggles for or against a new societal order.[3] This is certainly not the case in the numerous protests that are limited and very specific in their thematic concern (e.g., protests against a corrupt politician, a tax increase, or the establishment of a supermarket). Second, a social movement is based on a broad network of groups and organizations. Only when an individual group shares the movement's beliefs and is connected to its network can we consider this group and its activities as part of the movement. Collective protest is the key resource of most social movements because they usually lack other resources, such as money, formal power, or expert knowledge. Protest can, however, be used by various kinds of actors who are not necessarily part of a social movement. Consider, for example, a new political party that organizes a demonstration to demand changes in a voting system that disadvantages newcomers. Or consider a group of homeowners opposing the construction of a nearby street. Although the homeowners may tactically promote environmental arguments, their underlying motive may be to prevent a decline in their property values. Having neither a genuine belief in environmentalism nor any links to the respective networks, this group's protest can hardly be attributed to the environmental movement.

In many cases, particularly when collecting newspaper-based data on large numbers of protests in large geographic areas, we lack the information necessary to decide whether the two additional criteria of a social movement—orientation toward societal change and embeddedness in a larger movement network—are fulfilled. Therefore, in the context of this chapter and its underlying research strategy, it seems more appropriate to stick with protests rather than movements as a unit of analysis.

Finally, the notions of structure and culture need some clarification when applied to the context of protest analysis. By *structure of protest* I refer, speaking metaphorically, to the "hardware" of protest—for example, occurrence in time, location, size, duration, organizing groups, types of action, level of mobilization, and targets. These kinds of features are relatively easy to identify and aggregate because they involve characteristics for which common indicators or categories are available. It is thus no surprise that these aspects are usually part and parcel of the standard coding schemes used for documenting protest events. Although each individual protest has its own structure, in the context of this chapter the term *structure* refers to patterns in the aggregate level of protest in the same way as we characterize, say, class structure or the structure of criminal behavior in a given society.

By *culture of protest* I refer to its "software," notably the framing of action in terms of content, meaning, and reasoning by the use of language, symbols, and very concrete behaviors (Swidler 1986). These are, of course, guided and shaped by underlying values, interests, and experiences. Hence, unlike scholars who have conceptualized political culture mainly as a set of values[4] that cannot be directly observed, I stress its dual character. On the one hand, culture has a manifest side as represented in behavior, acting, and talking. On the other hand, it comprises a latent basis formed by particular interests, values, and experiences, which, shaped by situational factors, translate into manifest behaviors, words, and tangible cultural symbols. From these observable "collective representations" (Durkheim, 1995, p. 46), we may indirectly deduce the underlying intrapersonal basis—a strategy that phenomenologists and behaviorists prefer. But we may also ask individuals directly about their intrapersonal world, as many survey researchers do, or combine both approaches.

Protest culture is part of the broader political culture.[5] The latter can be defined as the set of elementary values, interests, and experiences that, as expressed in manifest forms of behavior, help to legitimize or delegitimize political institutions and decisions. Parts of the political culture are contested terrain, in which different claims are made about what is right or wrong, whom to blame, and what to do. This is what protest is all about. Typically, in Western democracies protest is not so much geared to physical dominance but to hegemonic cultural interpretations (Touraine 1985; Melucci 1985, 1997). Because of the democratic nature of core processes of legitimation, political protest is directed not only at the opponents but toward the wider audience (Gamson 1995). The aim is to achieve "power in numbers" (De Nardo 1985) and thereby have an impact on political decision making.

The Scope and Profile of Protest in West Germany from a Comparative Perspective

Before describing the changes in West German protest in some detail, it may be instructive to know whether the amount and composition differ significantly from that of other Western European countries. In this regard, we can draw on the four-country study mentioned earlier. The main sources used for data on protest events were the Monday issues of one major national newspaper in each country.[6] Although this study has a particular emphasis on "new social movements," it also includes other protest domains such as labor, regionalism, and right-wing protests.

In relative terms, when taking into account the different population sizes and referring only to unconventional events, we see that from 1975 through 1989 protest groups in France mobilized the most people (403,000 participants per million inhabitants), followed by West Germany (248,000), the Netherlands (221,000), and Switzerland (158,000).[7] France's leading position is mainly the result of the high level of strike activity, which accounts for 56 percent of the total mobilization in the country. Strike activity varies enormously, with 225,000 participants per million inhabitants in France, 37,000 in Germany, 23,000 in the Netherlands, and only 2,000 in Switzerland.[8] Once strikes are excluded, mobilization in unconventional events in all four countries lies roughly in the same range, with West Germany in the lead (211,000 participants) and Switzerland at the end (156,000) (Kriesi et al. 1995, p. 22).

In all four countries, mobilization by radical right-wing groups was very low, with slightly higher levels in France compared to West Germany. Moderate right-wing groups mobilized more participants in West Germany than in the three other countries but even here represented only 2.8 percent of the total mobilization. For the "new social movements," which Kriesi et al. (1995) defined as the aggregate of ten individual movements,[9] West Germany's lead is much more pronounced (168,000 participants), and the gap between West Germany and France, the country with the lowest new social movement mobilization (with 43,000 participants), is considerable. Because peace protests—as well as labor protests—will be examined in more detail later, it is interesting to single out their mobilization capacity. According to the events data, peace protests were very prominent in West Germany and the Netherlands (with 111,000 and 92,000 participants, respectively) but modest in Switzerland (25,000) and France (14,000). Considering the figures referred to earlier on the aggregate of new social movements, the German political scientist Roland Roth (1985, p. 20) may well be correct in assuming that "these new concerns are promoted more clearly and strongly in West Germany than anywhere else" (my translation). Overall, however, we have no indications that West Germany exhibits extraordinarily high levels of protest mobilization. But are West German protests special in qualitative terms? Is it correct to attribute a "fundamentalist" attitude (Sontheimer 1983) and a leaning toward "total critique" (Pulzer 1989) to them? Although no cross-national content analysis of the protesters' ideologies is available, we could look for other indicators. For instance, we may assume that the predominance of fundamentalist attitudes will translate into a relatively large share of radical activities. Again, Kriesi et al. provide an answer; the authors condensed a larger list of protest forms into three broad categories: demonstrative, confrontational, and violent actions.[10] Compared with the other three countries, West Germany displays the highest proportion of demonstrative and a medium proportion of confrontational and violent protests (Koopmans 1995b, p. 82). A telling indicator of the actual degree of violence is the average number of casualties in those protest events that resulted in personal injuries. According to this measure, the new social movements are much more violent in West Germany (17.2 casualties) than in the Netherlands (3.5), Switzerland (2.0), and France (1.2) (Koopmans 1995b, p. 83). By contrast, protests that do not occur in the context of the new social movements are certainly much more violent in France than in West Germany. The relevant figures are not displayed by Kriesi et al., but data from the *World Handbook of Political and Social Indicators* indicate a relatively high level of unruliness in France compared with that in West Germany (Taylor and Jodice 1983).

In conclusion, it seems safe to assume that in the aggregate West German protests are not exceptional in terms of either frequency or radicalness in comparison with those in neighbor states. This does not, however, preclude that subsets of the protest sector (e.g., antinuclear protests or squatter protests) may exhibit very distinct features.

The Changing Structure of Protest in West Germany

The Prodat data allow us to look more closely at changes in the structure of protest in West Germany from the 1950s onward. In the following section, I will first describe the database and then present selected findings regarding the frequency, size, forms, and carriers of protest.

Database and Methods

Prodat covers all types of collective protest in West Germany (since 1950) and East Germany (since 1989) based on reports in two national newspapers using a sampling strategy (see appendix). Currently, the complete sample has been collected from 1950 through 1960 and from 1979 through 1992. A complete time series of all weekend protests from 1950 through 1992 is also available (West Germany, $N = 5{,}264$).

Depending on the research question, I will use the weekend protests and, for selected periods, the complete sample. I will focus mainly on long-term changes by comparing the 1950s with the 1980s. Moreover, because the whole data set involves a broad range of protest areas that cannot all be presented and discussed in this chapter, I will pay particular attention to two major protest domains: labor and peace. These domains have been chosen because of both their prominence and their relative continuity during West German history since the 1950s. Together, they represent nearly 30 percent of all events and involve nearly 40 percent of all participants in protests in the period under investigation.

In interpreting the data, it is important to stress that these events represent only what has been reported in the general sections (excluding the state and local sections) of two national newspapers. According to findings from various countries that have used police data to control for the selection bias of mass media in specific localities, these reported events represent only a small proportion of all events that actually occurred (McCarthy et al. 1996; Fillieule 1995). In testing the selectivity of the Prodat data set, Hocke (1996) has found that it contains only 12 percent of the events reported by a local newspaper in the city of Freiburg and 4.6 percent of the events reported by local police. Whereas from a purely technical perspective this high selectivity may appear disturbing, it is not so from another viewpoint. The vast majority of protests remain unnoticed because they reach neither the wider populace nor the political decision makers. By contrast, protests that are reported by major mass media are the ones that may be relevant in terms of public awareness and, eventually, policy impact. Hence, essentially, we do cover the politically relevant protests.

The other aspect that makes the selectivity bias less problematic is the underlying pattern of media attention. Though national newspapers cover only a small proportion of all protest events, this proportion probably represents 70 to 80 percent of the actual mobilization as measured in terms of participants. Also, the fact that in 45.7 percent of all reported events journalists do not provide figures on the numbers of protesters should not cast serious doubts on the participation figures. These missing data refer mostly to small protests, including those in which protesters tend to hide their identity (e.g., arson).

The Volume of Protest

The first and foremost feature of the structure of collective protest is its volume as measured in the occurrence of and participation in protest events. Consider first the distribution of all registered weekend protests from 1950 through 1992 as indicated by the upper line in Figure 2.1. The significant peak in the late 1960s and the second crest in the first half of the 1980s are probably in line with what most informed observers would have expected. The late 1960s were the heyday of the student rebellion, and the early 1980s were marked by an extraordinary wave of peace protests. However, other features might come as a surprise. Most striking is the finding that 1991 and 1992 equaled the peak year of 1981 in terms of numbers of protests.[11] Another point is less salient, and contrary to conventional wisdom: a considerable level of protest was found in the 1950s, though still markedly lower than in the whole period from 1966 onward.

Regarding the distribution of mobilized people in these events over time, we see a completely different pattern when looking at the upper line of Figure 2.2. The absolute peak of mobilization occurred in 1980 (mainly because of a single but huge event involving the collection of 4.7 million signatures), followed by peaks in 1955, 1983, and 1992. The late 1960s and in particular most parts of the 1970s represent periods of modest protest participation, while considerable mobilization took place in the first half of the 1950s.

When comparing Figures 2.1 and 2.2, it is striking that the peaks and valleys of protest event numbers are not parallel to those of mobilized participants. The fact that both curves hardly co-vary points to the remarkable changes in the average sizes of protests across time. Obviously, relatively many protests of a smaller size occurred in some periods, (e.g., the late 1960s), whereas the opposite holds true for other periods (e.g., the mid-1950s). This finding suggests an important methodological conclusion. It could be misleading to make strong statements about changing levels of protest by looking at only the

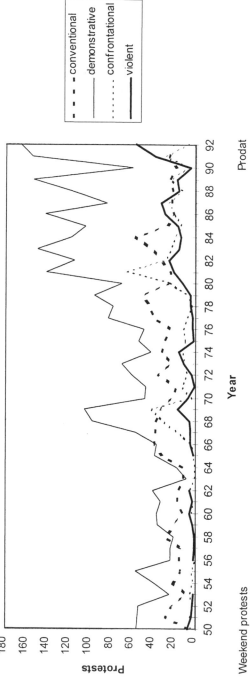

FIGURE 2.1. Protests in West Germany 1950–1992

FIGURE 2.2. Participants in Protests, West Germany 1950–1992

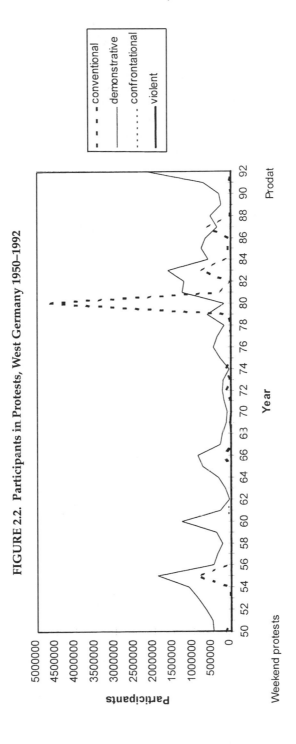

frequency of events or number of mobilized protesters. Both measures have to be taken into account to control whether the respective trends run parallel or diverge.

These variations in the frequency and size of protests also become obvious once we compare across decades. Table 2.1 displays the average yearly values per period. As the average values per year for each of the five periods show, the frequency of protest increased from decade to decade. It still remains to be seen whether the 1990s will turn out to be the decade with the most protests in (West) German history, as the first three years in this decade indicate. In contrast to the frequency of events, the yearly number of participants per decade decreased over the first three periods but then, in the 1980s, reached an unprecedented high. In the first three years of the 1990s, average mobilization was lower than in the 1980s but still significantly higher than in the 1950s. The average sizes of protests in the five periods under consideration vary considerably, with extremely large events in the 1950s and very small events in the 1970s. Thus, in the 1950s protests were relatively rare, but when they occurred, they attracted generally far more people than in later periods. This suggests that the underlying mobilization structure has changed over time (see later discussion).

The Forms of Protest

Figures 2.1 and 2.2 also include information on the respective weight of various forms of protest. To obtain an overview, the list of twenty-one specific forms (plus one open category) has been condensed into four broader categories: conventional, demonstrative, confrontational, and violent protests.[12] When considering the relative importance of

TABLE 2.1
Protests and Participants per Period, West Germany 1950–1992*

| Period | Proportion of protests per | | Proportion of participants per | | Participants per protest |
	Period	Year	Period	Year	
1950–1959	11.9	1.19	22.9	2.29	12.241
1960–1969	17.0	1.70	14.5	1.45	5.436
1970–1979	21.1	2.11	9.4	0.94	2.828
1980–1989	38.4	3.84	43.3	4.33	7.185
1990–1992	11.6	3.87	9.9	3.30	5.439
Sum or mean	100%	2.32	100%	2.32	6.372
N		5,264		33,540,996	

*Weekend protests.

these four categories, again it is crucial to distinguish between the numbers of events and participants. In terms of events, Figure 2.1 shows that demonstrative protests clearly prevail, whereas confrontational and violent events are only significant in some periods. In the aggregate of the whole period, demonstrative protests comprise 59.7 percent, conventional protests 21.5 percent, confrontational protests 10.3 percent, and violent protests 8.4 percent of all weekend events (when weekday protests are included, the respective percentages are 55.2, 22.8, 11.7, and 10.3 percent). Figure 2.5 shows that participation in confrontational and violent protests is virtually negligible. Over the whole period of investigation, confrontational events mobilize only 2.0 percent and violent events the tiny proportion of 0.2 percent of all participants in weekend protests, whereas the proportion of conventional protests is 25.4 percent and that of demonstrative protests is 73.6 percent. It follows that an assessment of the role of confrontational and violent events would be completely one-sided and therefore misleading if only the number of events or participants is taken into account.

Behind these aggregate data on protest forms lie considerable shifts over time, as shown in more detail elsewhere (Rucht 1996a, b). Overall, both illegal and violent protests increased remarkably from the 1950s through the 1990s, though participation in these events still remains very low even in later periods. Whereas the proportion of violent events compared with all weekend events in the 1950s was 3.9 percent, the respective numbers rose to more than 5 percent in the 1960s and 1970s, 10.3 percent in the 1980s, and a stunning 17 percent in the early 1990s. This most recent increase is mainly due to the extraordinary wave of right-wing radicalism that culminated in 1991 and 1992 (Rucht 1997). When regarding other indicators for changes in the degree of radicalness of protests, the pattern of a rising intensity of conflicts is also confirmed. The amount of damage to property rose enormously from the 1950s to the 1980s and early 1990s. The number of casualties increased from 137 in the 1950s to 2,791 in the 1980s, and that of arrested people from 1,130 to 7,949. Thus, we have clear evidence that collective protests in West Germany have become more radical from the 1950s through the 1980s. However, we should keep in mind that a very small proportion of protesters participated in confrontational events, and an insignificant proportion in violent events.

Domains and Carriers of Protest

Themes of protest have been coded in a rather detailed manner. We can group them together in twelve broader categories. These "protest

domains" have been chosen for purely pragmatic reasons, and in practice they sometimes overlap. For instance, when a women's group
stages a peace protest, this could be attributed to the domain of either
women or peace.[13] Table 2.2 displays the distribution of weekend protests across these domains.[14] A relatively large number of protests
focus on civil rights, followed by peace and, to a much lesser degree,
labor and environmental issues. In terms of participants, this rank
order changes significantly. With nearly one-third of all participants,
the peace protests are most prolific, closely followed by issues of German unification/European integration (which ranks eighth in numbers
of protests), labor, and democratic rights. Note that labor protests will
be underrepresented because these calculations are based on weekend
protests only.

These aggregate data spanning forty-three years hide potential
changes in the composition of protest domains over time. A detailed
analysis of these changes is beyond the scope of this chapter. As for
the domains of labor and peace, some information on their changing
relevance is provided later. In addition, three other trends are worth
mentioning. First, environmental concerns achieved a remarkable position from the 1970s onward. As for weekend protests, their share rose
from about 1.1 percent in the 1950s to 16.6 percent in the 1980s. By
contrast, the relative weight of protests in the domains of social welfare, ideology (e.g., protest for or against communism), and—most

a
self
organised

TABLE 2.2
Relevance of Protest Domains, West Germany 1950–1992

Domain	Protests (%)	Participants (%)
Democratic rights	25.4	7.2
Peace	18.5	31.5
Labor	9.3	8.3
Environment (including nuclear power)	9.3	5.8
Ethnic issues/asylum	6.9	5.9
Infrastructure	6.7	4.8
Ideology	6.6	1.5
(Divided) Germany/Europe	6.4	27.5
Social welfare	4.5	5.3
Education	2.4	1.0
Women	2.2	0.8
Farmers	1.0	0.4
Other	0.8	0.0
Total	100	100

*Weekend protests.

pronounced—divided Germany/Europe declined over the last four decades. While the latter issue accounted for 20.3 percent of all weekend protests in 1950s, the respective proportion was only 1.6 percent in the 1980s. Third, we find an unsteady proportion of protests focusing on democratization over time. Their share of all protests per decade rose from 17.7 percent in the 1950s to 36.1 percent in the 1970s and then declined to 21.6 percent in the 1980s.

For the most part, protests do not occur spontaneously but are planned and carried out by distinct groups or organizations. Those serving as sponsors of protests almost always also participate, so that these two roles can only rarely be separated when information is derived from newspaper reports only. Detailed analysis of the groups that organized and/or participated in protest events (in the following referred to as protest groups) will be reserved for a separate analysis. However, to get a general sense of the changing weight of different types of protest groups, it may suffice to consider three broad categories consisting of (1) informal groups and networks (predominantly citizen initiatives), (2) more formal and institutionalized pressure groups (e.g., business associations and trade unions), and (3) political parties. To determine roughly their differential weight, we can see how often these groups are listed as the key actors in protests, ignoring at this point instances of combined participation. Table 2.3 shows a significant decrease in formal pressure groups acting as carriers of protest from the 1950s onward, though these kinds of actors still remain dominant. In the overall trend, informal groups and networks have roughly tripled their proportion as key organizers in the period investigated, whereas the political parties experienced a smaller increase in their relative weight.

In 48.9 percent of all weekend protests, we have information about

TABLE 2.3
Types of Groups as Key Organizers*

Type of Group	1950–1959 (%)	1960–1969 (%)	1970–1979 (%)	1980–1989 (%)	1990–1992 (%)
Informal groups/ networks	9.7	26.6	36.9	36.9	37.2
Formal pressure groups	78.7	62.8	39.6	43.3	46.0
Political parties	11.6	10.6	23.5	20.1	16.8
Total	100	100	100	100	100
N	423	444	742	1,309	250

*Weekend protests.

the number of groups that took part. In the case of one major peace protest, as many as two thousand groups were involved, but relatively few protests include more than five different groups. The overall trend toward alliances and closer cooperation among protest groups is clearly indicated by the average number of groups involved per event. This figure was 1.4 groups in the 1950s, 1.6 in the 1960s, 4.3 in the 1970s, and 9.6 in the 1980s.

Taken together, the data on the distribution of types of groups and joint activities indicate a notable trend in the underlying mobilization structure. In the 1950s protests were typically staged by large individual organizations (e.g., a major trade union, a federation of war victims, or an alliance of German refugees). In the 1970s and 1980s the mostly informal groups and networks of the new social movements became relevant protest actors. In many cases, dozens of such groups coordinated joint protest campaigns.[15] Interestingly, the role of political parties as protest actors has also grown over time. This trend cannot be attributed to "movement parties" such as, most notably, the Greens. As Table 2.3 shows, the proportion of political parties as key organizers was highest in the 1970s before the Greens were founded. This finding, confirmed by examining the spectrum of parties involved in protests, supports the idea of separating protest analysis from social movement analysis.

A Closer Look at Labor and Peace Protests

As we have seen, aggregate data are hard to interpret unless they are broken down into more specific subsets. Only then can we evaluate, for example, to what extent particular kinds of protests influence the overall trends and whether stable aggregates mask significant changes that, because of their divergent trends, neutralize each other when lumped together.

In the following section, I examine two protest domains that represent substantial parts of the total mobilization (see Table 2.2). We can expect these two domains to vary in a number of aspects. For instance, labor conflicts tend to be carried out by well-structured actors in a widely institutionalized setting, which is hardly the case in the domain of peace protests. We can also assume that the role of the state will differ substantially in these two domains. Only a few traits of these two areas of protests can be analyzed here. For the most part, the 1950s will be contrasted with the 1980s onward rather than providing an analysis over a continuous period of time. Beside weekend protests, this data set also includes protests occurring from Monday through Friday every fourth week.

Volume of Mobilization

There were roughly the same number of labor and peace protests during the 1950s and 1980s, respectively. However, in both domains there were three times as many protests in the 1980s as in the 1950s. Labor protests mobilized about the same number of people across the two decades; in contrast, participation in peace protests reached extraordinarily high levels in the 1980s. Accordingly, the average participation per event varied considerably across the two decades. The average size of labor protests decreased from the 1950s to the 1980s, whereas the opposite holds for peace protests (see Table 2.4).

The data presented on participation suggest that labor protests follow a more continuous course than peace protests. This is confirmed by looking at the occurrences of participation in labor and peace protests annually (data not provided here). Peace protests exhibit several outstanding peaks of participation (e.g., in the mid-1950s, the late 1960s, and the early 1980s).

Types of Action

Table 2.5 displays the distribution of six different forms[16] of labor and peace protests in the 1950s and 1980s. Demonstrative protests are by far the most common in the case of the labor movement. Within this category, strikes clearly prevail. Surprisingly, violent labor protests are virtually absent in both decades. Demonstrative activities also play an important role in peace protests, though to a lesser extent than in labor protests. Appeals were the most important category of peace protests in the 1950s (with 49 percent), but in the 1980s their proportion declined to 21.8 percent. Both the decrease in appeals in the 1950s and the strong increase in confrontational and violent activities in the 1980s show that peace protests have become more unruly over time. When we also control for a separate variable noting the legal status of the action (legal, illegal, unclear) it becomes obvious that while peace pro-

TABLE 2.4
Labor and Peace Mobilization in Selected Periods, West Germany*

	Labor		Peace	
	1950–1959	*1980–1989*	*1950–1959*	*1980–1989*
Protest events	234	634	200	662
Participants	2,242,360	2,345,474	1,710,133	8,733,477
Participants per event	9,583	3,699	8,551	13,193

*Full sample.

TABLE 2.5
Types of Action in Labor and Peace Protests, West Germany*

	Labor		Peace	
Type of Action	*1959–1959 (%)*	*1980–1989 (%)*	*1950–1959 (%)*	*1980–1989 (%)*
Appeal	9.4	5.7	49.0	21.8
Procedural	6.8	2.1	3.0	0.8
Demonstrative	78.6	87.8	45.0	55.6
Confrontational	4.7	3.6	1.5	15.4
Light violence	0.0	0.0	0.0	0.6
Heavy violence	0.4	0.8	1.5	5.9
Total	100	100	100	100
N	234	632	200	648

*Full sample

tests have become more unruly over time, the proportion of confrontational and violent labor protests was stable. The proportions of illegal protests in both areas were roughly the same in the 1950s (5.8 and 7.7 percent, respectively). However, while the proportion of illegal labor protests then decreased to 3.3 in the 1980s, the corresponding figure for peace protests was 23.1 percent in the 1980s. Again, when interpreting the growing number of unruly peace protests, we should also consider participation in these events. For instance, the 6.1 percent violent peace protests (of all peace protests in the 1980s) have attracted only 0.016 percent in terms of participants.

Targets

Labor and peace protests differ in their main targets. Whereas labor conflicts in Germany are mainly considered to be a matter of self-regulation between labor and capital, peace protests are primarily addressed to the state. Our data show that this overall pattern holds for peace protests, but not necessarily for labor protests. Of all peace protests, 94.5 percent targeted the state in the 1950s and 92.8 percent in the 1980s. As for labor protests in the 1950s, 45.7 percent targeted private enterprises and 41.8 percent the state (remaining targets were parties, trade unions, etc.). For the 1980s, the respective proportions were 41.2 percent (against private enterprises) and 56.9 percent (against the state). These figures demonstrate the important—and increasing—role of the state, which, beyond its role in public employment, is an important factor in various types of labor policies.

Territorial Scope of Mobilization

Given the modern communication media and the trend toward political centralization and even globalization, we would expect the protest groups would increasingly shift from smaller to larger territories when mobilizing for collective action. Following Charles Tilly (1978), who observed a historical shift of the "repertoire of contention" from local to national concerns around the turn of the nineteenth century, other researchers have assumed that today's protest politics are shifting from the national to the transnational level (Imig and Tarrow 1996; Smith et al., 1997). However, as the figures in Table 2.6 demonstrate, the latter shift is hardly observable for either labor or peace protests in West Germany. The proportion of nationwide mobilization decreased slightly for labor and more clearly for peace protests. International mobilization is negligible, or irrelevant, in the labor domain and modest in the peace domain. Most remarkable, however, is the growing relevance of local mobilization in the case of labor. This trend also holds for the aggregate of protests in all protest domains: the national level loses and the local level gains relevance (these data are not displayed here).

Some Observations on the Changing Culture of Labor and Peace Protests

As mentioned earlier, the cultural side of protest events is not represented by these statistics. The following section will shed some light on the changing culture of protests by providing a few illustrations of

TABLE 2.6
Territorial Scope of Mobilization for Labor and Peace Protests*

Territory of Mobilization	Labor		Peace	
	1959–1959 (%)	1980–1989 (%)	1950–1959 (%)	1980–1989 (%)
Local	15.8	35.0	18.5	16.5
District/regional	50.4	39.0	19.0	23.9
State	20.9	14.7	19.0	18.1
National	10.3	8.7	32.0	25.1
International	0.9	0.9	6.5	9.8
Unknown	1.7	1.7	5.0	6.6
Total	100	100	100	100
N	234	634	200	662

*Full sample

both mass mobilization and disruptive labor and peace protests in the 1950s and 1980s. Particular attention will be given to the novelty of particular forms of protests and their expressive and symbolic elements. My information is mainly derived from the same sources as the quantitative data, articles in two national newspapers, the *Frankfurter Rundschau* (FR) and the *Süddeutsche Zeitung* (SZ). The protest domains of labor and peace have been chosen because they represent a significant proportion of all protests and are spread over the entire time span of more than four decades.

Mass Protests in the 1950s and 1980s

The 1950s

In February 1957 some 1,800 winegrowers went to the nation's capital to claim state subsidies to compensate for cheap wine imports and crop failures. Prior to this event, the organizers urged all participants to sign a "list of solidarity," which included a promise not to disturb or violate public order during the protest (FR, February 7, 1957). Although such a preventive act was by no means the rule, it was conceivable at that time but not after the mid-1960s. Until then, disruptive protest behaviors were mainly associated with communist groups or youth gangs, while most other groups, such as the winegrowers, were eager to be perceived as "serious" and "lawful."

Overall, in the 1950s and early 1960s, orderly, well-prepared, and peaceful events dominated the protest picture.[17] This is particularly true for mass protests, which were mostly labeled in neutral terms, such as *Kundgebungen* or *Versammlungen* (gatherings, meetings). Usually these mass gatherings focused on an appeal or a resolution. In the case of the peace movements, such appeals were addressed to "those who govern" or, as in the case of a gathering of the "World Association of the Mothers of all Nations," to "all powerholders in the world" (FR, July 1, 1958). Only on a few occasions do we find other forms of mass protest, such as a march carrying torches (*Fackelzug*) or a silent march (*Schweigemarsch*) with no speeches or chanted slogans. Most of these events were sponsored by formal associations or, occasionally, by political parties. Typically, representatives of these groups or even state officials served as speakers. In peace protests in particular, references to moral obligations, to the individual's consciousness, to responsibility for humankind, and so forth, were prevalent. Police accompanying these protests hardly ever became the subject of critique or aggression. This even held when, in a few cases, the police—on highly dubious legal grounds—required the protesters to show their banners in advance to check whether these were tolerable. Highly restrictive measures to channel protest continued to be used in the early 1960s. In the case of the annual Easter marches staged by peace groups, administrators and police prevented foreign delegations who wanted to participate from entering the country, forbade marches through city centers, and suppressed the use of certain slogans and songs (Otto 1977, p. 128).

In the case of labor protests, mass meetings in public places were relatively rare. If they occurred, they were related to either (1) larger strike activities, (2) fundamental political decisions (e.g., the Corporate Constitution Bill in 1952 [*Betriebsverfassungsgesetz*], the introduction of the forty-hour week in 1953, and the downsizing of coal mining since 1958), or (3) ritual occasions such as Labor Day. From today's viewpoint, these mass gatherings were very conventional. Officials stood on a podium in front of an attentive and silent crowd, speckled with some banners, and delivered their speeches. Then the crowd disassembled. Deviation from this pattern of mass protest, such as silent marches or traffic blockades staged by the peace movement, occurred only rarely.

The annual Labor Day gatherings in the first half of the 1950s were large and impressive. In West Berlin, they were attended by 600,000 people in 1950, 1951, and 1953. Across the country, Labor Day events consisted of up to 1,800 individual gatherings (as in 1958). In the early 1950s, these gatherings were also marked by more general political themes, and not only labor issues. The 1950 Labor Day slogan in West Berlin, for instance, was "Peace in Liberty." It seems that the participants in these events took a strong ideological stance and were "true believers," as exemplified by a report on the Munich event in 1950: "Deeply impressed [by the speech], the densely packed crowd, predominantly the older generation, took off their hats and sang: 'Brothers, toward the sun, toward liberty' " (SZ, May 2, 1950, p. 1; author's translation).

Occasionally Labor Day events were marked by internal conflicts among the participants. When communist groups displayed their own banners and placards, the large majority of leftist but noncommunist protesters reacted with hostility and even outspoken aggressiveness toward their codemonstrators. The rivalry between communist and noncommunist groups was particularly strong in the divided but still not totally split city of Berlin. Consider the example of the Labor Day events of the 1950s. In the western part of the city, a huge but somewhat amorphous crowd gathered close to the border with the eastern part. Essentially, it was composed of individuals and families. Many participants wore a button with the letter *F*, for *Freiheit* (liberty), to distinguish their event from the one occurring simultaneously in East Berlin. The Eastern event took a very different shape. Recruited en bloc by factories, schools, and party-controlled mass organizations, the participants first met at twenty-five predesignated places in a bloc by bloc formation. Then they moved to a central location to form one huge parade. Led by the *Volkspolizei* ("People's Police") marching band, they eventually marched in accurate rows of twenty-four people through a huge "May Gate." This was decorated with large placards and slogans and had been erected specifically for this day (SZ, May 2, 1950).

Competition between the "free" and the "communist" Labor Day events continued and even intensified in the following years, as indicated by a report headlined "War of the Flyers in Divided Berlin." During the parallel and virtually adjacent gatherings on both sides of the border, each party shot rockets with flyers over to the other gathering, which the recipients on the other side then burned demonstratively (SZ, May 5, 1954). These incidents highlight the fact that, despite the prevailing language of antagonism between capital and labor, the majority of the West German labor force eagerly tried to keep clear of communist groups. Probably also because the communists in the West were more prepared to ignore the restrictive rules regarding legal and orderly protest, the majority of the Western labor force shied away from any kind of disruptive action that could be interpreted as inspired or guided by the communists.

The 1980s

In the 1980s and early 1990s, the face of mass protests is very different from the 1950s. The large peace protests, be they conventional demonstrations, marches, or other kinds of activities, have become more colorful and lively. As a rule, the organizers are no longer single associations but broad alliances, which, in many cases, encompass dozens of national, regional, and local groups with a variety of ideological positions. Sometimes, these protests resemble fairs or festivals, dominated by young people, and families and children of all ages participating. Large rows of tables and booths are erected on the fringes to offer flyers and brochures and to sell books, buttons, balloons, food, and other goods. Numerous speakers from different backgrounds gather on the stage, selected in long and cumbersome negotiations among the organizing groups,[18] and they often do not represent a particular organization but speak as "a woman," "a foreigner," or "somebody from a grassroots group." Many people do not listen to the speeches but chat or stroll around. Between the speeches, a folk or rock band plays; somebody reads a telegram from a foreign peace group expressing solidarity, or a speaker announces that a child is looking for his or her parents. The police also seem to be contaminated by this friendly and fairlike atmosphere, chatting with the protesters, accepting flyers and flowers—all this in stark contrast to protests during the 1950s.

Though this pattern may be typical for peace protests in the 1980s, it represents only one side of the coin. Other mass protests in the 1980s were marked by tensions between police and protesters, and occasionally they erupted into violent clashes, particularly in the case of the antinuclear and some kinds of urban protests. As we saw in the quantitative data presented earlier, the proportion of illegal and/or violent protests was considerably higher in the 1980s than the 1950s.

Mass labor protests have also changed since the 1950s, perhaps best indicated by Labor Day events. Above all, they have become smaller. Instead of hundreds of thousands, they have attracted at best tens of thousands since the early 1980s.[19] Moreover, the former spirit and language of class struggle have waned. Demands for fundamental social and political change are largely absent. Despite their rhetorical efforts, the speakers seem to be toothless. The demands are moderate, specific, and defensive: reduction of mass unemployment, reconciliation of economic and environmental needs, an end to cuts in welfare provisions. Critique of "the system" has been replaced by criticisms of particular political leaders or measures. The mass of demonstrators have become, quite literally, an audience. Most participants passively endure the speeches made by politicians and union representatives, no longer exhibiting the emotion and strong ideological commitment that prevailed in the early 1950s. The formerly broader audience has now been reduced to the hard core of union members and Social Democrats who remain faithful to their organizations but do so more out of a sense of obligation than intrinsic emotional drive. It is no wonder that, from an outsider's perspective, Labor Day events are perceived as an empty ritual.[20]

Occasionally, there are still small skirmishes within the ranks of the demonstrators. However, the unwanted minorities on the fringes are no longer the traditional old guard of communists but rather the so-called *Autonome*, members of a militant political youth culture. Apart from romantic reminiscences of struggles between labor and capital, the average worker in the crowd and the young radicals in their black attire have nothing in common.

Innovative and Disruptive Protests in the 1950s and 1980s

Beyond the mostly conventional mass gatherings,[21] provocative and disruptive protests are a constituent part of the modern protest repertoire. Usually these protests are carried out by relatively small numbers of highly motivated people who are prepared to take risks. Some examples of disruptive protests may illustrate the differences across protest domains and time.

In the 1950s, as we have seen, disruptive, illegal, and/or violent protests were rare in the domains of both labor and peace. Still fewer protests can be deemed innovative. Scanning many articles on labor protest, I could not find a single example. Among the small proportion of confrontational labor protests, the wildcat strike is probably the most frequent. Disruptive labor protests in the 1950s addressed almost exclusively concerns such as higher wages and other kinds of remuneration, reduction of working hours and weekend labor, worker participation, resistance to privatization, and shutdowns. Only occasionally were demands made on other issues, such as protests against West German rearmament. Striking for political purposes was illegal and therefore occurred rarely. Equally rare were other forms of protest, such as "flags of mourning," blaring sirens to oppose the shutdowns of a plant, or threatening to destroy machinery that was to be dismantled and transferred somewhere else. Overall the labor force in early West Germany was far from quiet, but nearly all protests were orderly and disciplined, exhibiting a collective effort to be seen as serious and responsible.

By contrast, peace activities in the 1950s exhibited much greater variation in tactics. Although the usual spectrum of petitions, demonstrations, and marches prevailed, the protesters were more creative and often more prepared to be disruptive. A few examples serve to illustrate this: the occupation of tiny Helgoland to protest against the bombing of the island by British warplanes in a military exercise (FR, December 22, 1950); the walling up of niches in bridges designed to hold explosives in the case of a war; a school strike in a village to protest against the negative effects of military exercises, a vigil held by Berlin youth groups "against atomic death"; setting fire to an old barn to protest the creation of the European Defense Union; staging a jazz concert as a protest against the equipping of the West German army with atomic weapons; sit-ins; nightly placarding of walls; the distribution of faked letters to individuals calling them up for the draft or equally faked orders that city administrations vacate public buildings so that military troops could be hosted there.

In the 1980s, the more disruptive labor protests still resembled those of the 1950s. A few new elements were introduced, however, most prominently in the case of announced plant shutdowns. Once the more conventional spectrum of protest activities has been applied without success, workers sometimes move toward more disruptive and innovative forms. For instance, in the Rheinhausen case, where a large plant was to be closed, activists staged a variety of innovative protest actions in 1987 and 1988, but all without success (Jäger 1993). Among other activities, religious services were held inside and outside the plant, twenty-five thousand people blocked streets and a bridge crossing the Rhine, and trees were planted near the factory.[22] Another highly provocative protest was waged by angry workers who felt threatened by job loss. They invaded the mansion of the Krupp industrialist dynasty, where everything was set up for a superb meal. Without hesitation, the workers wolfed down the cold buffet reserved for their bosses and their invited guests.

Compared with the general picture of very traditional labor protests, the peace domain from the early 1980s onward appears to be a true laboratory for the adoption, forging, and probing of new forms of protest activities. A few examples illustrate the wide variety of creative and innovative protests. Among these are a women's group's impersonation of a military maneuver; symbolic die-ins adopted from the Vietnam War protests;[23] the disruption of military exhibitions and weapons fairs; the noisy disturbance of public ceremonies for new recruits; the erection of a monument to war deserters; blockades at the entrances of military bases and arms depots; the destruction of an imitation wooden tank; the use of large balloons to prevent low-flying air force exercises; the symbolic siege of the national parliament and party offices; hunger strikes and hunger marches; concerts and exhibits; human chains that, in one case, spanned over 110 kilometers. Sometimes these protests also exhibit a sense of irony and fun[24] that would have been unthinkable in the 1950s.

Beside these mostly symbolic actions, more aggressive forms of peace protest were also staged in the 1980s. Some were carried out strictly in the spirit of civil disobedience. For example, a small group of activists from the plowshare network secretly entered a military base, destroyed some weapons, and then turned themselves in to the military officials and the police (Sternstein, n.d.). Other activities include the destruction of SS officers' graves and arson against military facilities. However, as we have seen from the statistical figures presented earlier, such acts were extremely rare.

Conclusion

The data and material presented here are too copious and, for the most part, too selective and insufficiently analyzed to allow for strong, all-embracing conclusions. Nevertheless, some sound results can be summarized and interpreted.

First, over more than four decades, protest in West Germany has undergone major changes, in terms of both its structure and culture. The 1950s were marked by fewer protests than the 1980s, although they were more frequent than common perception suggests. In terms of protest participation, the 1950s exceeded the mobilization of the 1960s and 1970s, contrary to most observers' assumptions. The 1950s were dominated by relatively few but large protests, whereas the opposite holds for the later periods under study. Another surprise is the high level of mobilization in the early 1990s with regard to both the frequency of protest events and the number of participants. More than ever, protest has become a part of everyday politics, a process that has been called the "normalization of the unconventional" (Fuchs 1991). Thus, as far as West Germany is concerned, we find the trend toward a "protest society" (Pross 1992) or "movement society" (Neidhardt and Rucht 1993; Tarrow 1994).

Second, beyond changes in the sheer frequency of protests and numbers of mobilized people, other long-term trends can be observed. One is the change in forms of protest. Most notably, the proportion of illegal and violent protests is increasing, although these protests still mobilize only a tiny number of participants. A second remarkable trend is the growing relevance of informal and mostly small protest groups as primary organizational carriers that, over time, tend toward closer cooperation—as indicated by the strongly growing average number of groups involved in individual protests. This shift toward a more informal and cooperative mobilization structure is accompanied by the growing importance of local mobilization—again a finding that few would have predicted.

Returning to the notion of a "movement society," we can state that two of the three traits that Meyer and Tarrow (see the introduction) attribute to this notion could be found: first, protest has become a perpetual element in modern life, and, second, it has been employed with greater frequency by more diverse constituencies. Whether protest also covers a wider range of claims than in earlier periods still needs to be investigated. However, no evidence was found regarding the third trait. Professionalization and institutionalization, which certainly characterize many protest groups, have not resulted in a "deradicalization" of protest. At the same time, it may well be that both power holders and bystanders have become more accustomed to even radical challenges and thus tend to react in a more relaxed fashion. Probably it is precisely this effect that drives protesters to use more disruptive tactics to impress their audiences.

Third, a closer look at the structure of labor and peace protests has revealed that these two domains differ in several respects. Mobilization of labor protests is relatively continuous in terms of events and—to a lesser extent—participants, whereas peace mobilization is more discontinuous. A more comprehensive view across the whole period on a yearly basis would reveal that peace mobilization is highly dependent on specific external constellations and decisions, such as West German rearmament, plans to equip West Germany with atomic weapons, the Vietnam War, the NATO double-track decision to deploy nuclear missiles, and the Gulf War (see Cooper 1996). Very few violent protests were found in the domain of labor, whereas peace protests tended to be more unruly, particularly in the 1980s. While it is trivial to find that the main target of the peace movement is the state, it comes as a surprise that the state has increasingly become the primary target for labor protests.

Fourth, a more detailed analysis of West German protests in the past few years and especially a comparison with East German protests are beyond the scope of this chapter, though some general tendencies can be mentioned here. In the early 1990s we find a reversal of several long-term trends in West Germany and some striking differences between East and West. For instance, the "postmaterialist" issues promoted mainly by the new social movements (such as civil rights, peace, women, environment, and the Third World) become less salient in West Germany but still remain more relevant than in East Germany, where bread-and-butter issues prevail. To an extraordinarily large extent, the state is (still) the major target of protest in East Germany. In the case of labor, the state attracted 92.5 percent of all protests from 1990 to 1992 (compared with 36.2 percent in West Germany). Also striking is the rise of radical right-wing and xenophobic protest, more common in East than in West Germany, though mobilizing only a tiny proportion of all participants in both parts of the country.

Fifth, beyond statistical figures, information was given on the culture of the labor and peace movements in West Germany across time, by means of a few illustrations. Overall, protests in these domains tended to be orderly and disciplined in the 1950s, particularly in the case of labor. In that era, labor protest was still shaped by a strong ideological commitment, as can be seen in the Labor Day demonstrations. Beyond these types of gatherings and, of course, strike activities, other forms of labor protests were very rare. The repertoire of the early peace movement was more heterogeneous but also tended to be orderly.

By the 1980s, however, the overall picture had changed considerably. For labor protests, Labor Day demonstrations may be indicative. Participation is low, claims are pragmatic and defensive, and the protesters

no longer exhibit the former symptoms of strong ideological commitment. Labor Day has become an empty routine that has lost its attrac-
tion and former class spirit. The traditional labor protest in the plants
and shops continues and, in rare cases, is complemented by more disruptive and creative forms that seem to have been adopted from the
new social movements. Most significantly, the protest repertoire of the
peace movement has become broader, more creative, and more disruptive in the 1980s. I assume that many of these changes have to do with
the watershed years of the late 1960s, in which new forms of protest
were invented that then spread out to other movements.

Finally, as indicated by several social scientists, the political culture
of (West) Germany has undergone considerable changes since the immediate postwar years (Conradt 1980). It has often been asserted that
the early postwar period was still marked by an authoritarian tradition
and strong reservations toward outspoken and nonparliamentary political conflict (Greiffenhagen 1984). By contrast, today's Germany is
perceived as an active and lively democracy, in which many citizens
feel free to take strong stances, to criticize authorities, and to make use
of a broad variety of protest forms, including more disruptive activities. Some observers have even stated that a "participatory revolution"
has taken place (Kaase 1982). As far as protest is concerned, this overall
picture is supported by empirical evidence, although the vitality and
breadth of protest evident in the 1950s tends to be notoriously underes-
timated.

The most profound change probably cannot be grasped by statistical
figures. It lies in an attitudinal shift regarding the status of protest.
Not only the protesters but also a significant proportion of the wider
population as well as scholarly observers consider protest to be a legitimate and elementary part of a democratic political culture—an expression of "democracy from below" (Roth 1994; Koopmans 1995b). They
interpret collective protests as a sign of vitality rather than a threat,
although—and because—it constantly questions what is politically
right and wrong.

Notes

1. "A contentious gathering is an occasion on which a number of people
(here, a minimum of ten) outside the government gathered in a publicly accessible place and made claims on at least one person outside their own number,
claims which if realized would affect the interests of their object" (Tilly 1995a,
pp. 32–33).

2. I define a social movement as an action system composed of mobilized

networks of groups and organizations that, based on a collective identity, attempt to achieve or prevent social change by means of protest.

3. In a classic formula: "Social movements can be viewed as collective enterprises to establish a new order of life" (Blumer 1939, p. 225).

4. This is a dominant tradition of research in political culture, ranging from Almond and Verba (1963) to Inglehart (1990). The latter defines political culture as "a system of attitudes, values and knowledge that is widely shared within a society and transmitted from generation to generation" (p. 18). Beyond its restriction to the intrapersonal world, one might question this definition because it excludes minority and/or deviant cultures.

5. For a more recent overview of this concept, see Lane (1992).

6. For methodological details, see the appendix in Kriesi et al. (1995).

7. These figures result from the sum of participants in all conventional events in a country in the period from 1975 to 1989, divided by the number of inhabitants (in millions).

8. Data on strikes are not based on newspaper reports but on figures from the International Labor Organization.

9. The foci of these movements are nuclear weapons, other peace issues, nuclear energy, ecology, antiracism, other solidarity issues, squatting, other countercultural issues, homosexuality, and women's issues.

10. Examples of a demonstrative event are a public rally or a protest march; for a confrontational event, a hunger strike or a disruption of institutional procedures; for a violent event, property damage and physical violence against persons. For a detailed categorization, see Kriesi et al. (1995, p. 267–68).

11. There were 252 protests in 1981, 248 in 1991, and 253 in 1992.

12. This categorization follows that of Kriesi et al. (1995). *Conventional* protests consist of signature/petition/resolution/public letter, press conference, leaflet, procedural complaint, litigation, and inside assembly/teach-in. *Demonstrative* protests, if legal, include nonverbal protest, demonstration march, public protest assembly/rally, and strike. *Confrontational* protests are composed of defamation, disturbance/hindrance, blockade/sit-in, occupation, theft/burglary, and all (other) illegal demonstrative activities. *Violent protests* consist of minor damage to property, aggressive bodily contact, severe damage to property/arson/bombing, personal injuries, and homicide/murder.

13. The coding scheme allowed for multiple answers when categorizing the theme or demand of a protest event, though arranged in a hierarchical order based on specific rules. In this chapter, only figures based on the primary theme or demand are displayed.

14. Note that the aggregate is still composed of different samples over time. From 1961 through 1978, it includes only weekend protests and thus will undercount, for instance, strikes that predominantly occur on weekdays.

15. For an analysis of two major protest campaigns, in each of which more than 130 groups participated, see Gerhards and Rucht (1992).

16. Building from the categories presented earlier, conventional protests are broken down into appeals (signatures, leaflets) and procedural protests (formal complaints, litigation). Violent protests are classified according to whether light or heavy violence is involved.

17. Notable exceptions were the activities of aggressive youth gangs, the *"Halbstarken."* On one occasion, after having watched the cult movie *Rebel without a Cause*, about a thousand of these "rowdies" vandalized the inner city of Dortmund, breaking windows and demolishing cars, without articulating specific demands (SZ, December 12, 1956). For an extremely comprehensive and detailed documentation of protests in Germany from 1949 through 1959, see Kraushaar (1996).

18. An organizer of the Easter March for Peace in Bremen describes the underlying criteria for the selection of speakers: "They ought to represent, if possible, all 'colors,' i.e. all political strands of the peace movement. Criteria of prominence and appeal also came into play. Moreover, we sought to include foreign guest speakers, representatives of the US peace movement, and delegates from Bremen's official partner cities" (Butterwege et al. 1990, p. 44; author's translation.)

19. Even the central demonstrations, held in a different city each year, remained relatively small, with ten thousand in 1980 (Stuttgart), twenty thousand in 1981 (Duisburg), ten thousand in 1982 (Frankfurt) eight thousand in 1983 (Bremen), and—probably the highest number in the 1980s and 1990s—forty thousand in 1984 (Hamburg). The German Federation of Unions (*Deutscher Gewerkschaftsbund*) claimed a total of about one million participants in the Labor Day events in 1986. However, the central demonstration in Hannover was attended by only eighteen thousand people in that year.

20. Fritz Teufel, a well-known exponent of the student revolt of the late 1960s, has probably best characterized the meaninglessness of the ritual. In response to the traditional rallying cry "Rise up on the first of May!" (*Heraus zum 1. Mai!*), he sarcastically stated: "To me, any other day would be just as good."

21. For a more detailed analysis of mass protests in Germany from 1950 to 1992, see Rucht (1996a).

22. These kinds of activities, adopted from other movements, may illustrate to what extent modern forms of protest have become "modular" (for this concept, see Tarrow 1993).

23. For preconditions and processes of diffusion and adoption of protest repertoires, see McAdam and Rucht (1993) and McAdam (1995).

24. The ironic undertone of some protests was a legacy of the idea of the *Spaßguerilla* (fun guerilla) that emerged in the late 1960s rather than an invention of the 1980s peace movement.

Appendix: Basic Information on the Prodat Project

Prodat's official title is "Documentation and Analysis of Protest Events in the Federal Republic of Germany." Located in the research unit "The Public and Social Movements" at the Wissenschaftszentrum Berlin für Sozialforschung, the project was funded mainly by the German

Research Council (*Deutsche Forschungsgemeinschaft*). Principal investigators are Friedhelm Neidhardt and Dieter Rucht.

The basic unit of analysis is the *protest event*, defined as a "collective, public action of non-state actors who articulate some sort of critique or dissent together with societal or political demands" (Rucht, Hocke, and Ohlemacher 1992, p. 4). The key variables are time, location, duration, form, legal status, theme, claim, policy area, territorial range of the concern, organizing groups, territorial range of mobilization (local, regional, international), number of participants, embeddedness of the event in a campaign, and immediate (e.g., arrests, injuries) and long-term consequences of action (e.g., trials).

The data are drawn from two national "quality" newspapers, *Die Süddeutsche Zeitung* and *Frankfurter Rundschau* (excluding reports in the state and local sections). The full sample covers protest events on all weekends plus all weekdays of every fourth week (46.6 percent of all days). Protest events are coded when occurring in West Germany (including West Berlin) from 1950 onward and, since 1989, also in East Germany.

As of April 1997, 8,914 protest events have been coded from 1950 through 1992. These events include all weekend protests for these forty-three years ($N = 5,264$). Data from the full sample, however, are so far only available from 1950 to 1960 and 1979 to 1992. Coding of the subsequent years (1993–94) and of the missing part of the full sample, from 1961 to 1978, is under way. For the 1950s and 1980s, 11,503 additional protest events with unknown location have been registered and roughly categorized, but they are not part of the core data set. Among these additional events, 52 percent are strikes.

Beyond the core project, Prodat comprises the collection and analysis of additional data sets that, in part, serve to assess the selection bias of the core data set. Among these, there is (1) a local study on protests in the city of Freiburg from 1983 to 1987, based on data from local police archives and the local newspaper (see Hocke 1996); (2) a collection of protests based on the national leftist-liberal newspaper *Die Tageszeitung* in selected years during the 1990s; and (3) a collection of antinuclear power protests from 1968 to 1992.

The overall research design is presented in Rucht and Ohlemacher (1992). Both a German version of the codebook (Rucht et al. 1992) and a detailed report on coder reliability (also in German) are available on request. An updated version of the codebook is in preparation. Methodological issues in the project are discussed in Rucht, Hocke, and Oremus (1995) and Rucht and Neidhardt (1995). For the first data analyses, see Rucht (1996, a,b,c; 1997).

3

Are the Times A-Changin'?
Assessing the Acceptance of Protest
in Western Democracies

Matthew Crozat

Democracies are built around the act of voting. It is the manner the state provides for citizens to express their displeasure or satisfaction with government policies collectively. To rely only on this form of conventional participation, however, means that citizens must wait until the next election before they can offer opinions. Even then, voting is a blunt instrument: it is easy to pass judgment on a candidate but very difficult to register unhappiness with a specific policy, let alone recommend alternatives with this form of participation. Protest, on the other hand, can be used by groups of people to convey more specific and timely messages. Protest may be a way to speak without elections (Tilly 1983), but what will be heard by the rest of society depends greatly on how the message is conveyed. A petition, for example, might not offend anyone, but it is also not likely to be noticed, whereas violent uprisings will surely be noticed and generate widespread attention and animosity. The differences between the forms of protest that could be employed matter because of how the public receives them. Socially unacceptable forms of protest will gain attention precisely because they are socially unacceptable. If protesters know the effect they want to create, they need to have some idea of how the protest form they employ will be received.

The effectiveness and impact of protest forms changes over time along with societal perceptions of them. In this chapter, I will consider *modular* forms of protest—that is, those actions such as petitions or demonstrations that can be used by just about anyone to make any kind of point the protestor wants (Tarrow 1994, p. 33; Tilly 1995b). Although the forms themselves do not change, public responses to them might. I will examine whether the consistent protests of the recent past have desensitized society to various forms of protest. If so, then forms that once might have shocked a nation now are used commonly, meaning that more threatening means would be necessary to capture a country's attention. I will examine five prominent forms of protest that comprise the modular repertoire of contentious collective action that has spanned the last few decades. I will show that popular attitudes toward this repertoire have changed only minimally over the last two decades. Furthermore, the only apparent evidence of attitudinal change indicates that the public has become less accepting of protest, not more.

 Sidney Tarrow (1994, pp. 187–98) argues that the late twentieth century could be described as an era of a movement society. In an increasingly global economy, national borders do not have the constraining effect they once did. As commerce and capital move more freely across nations, movements are also transnational forces not necessarily aiming at any one state. Moreover, modern communications allow the diffusion of movements—both issues and methods—in a matter of minutes. "In Western Europe, as in the United States, the relatively stable social and political life of the 1950s and 1960s was replaced by social unrest, political protest, and social movements during the late 1960s and 1970s" (Gundelach 1995, p. 412).

"The general acceptance of protest politics," Russell Dalton (1996, p. 82) writes, advancing the argument, "is what has transformed the style of citizen politics." The argument that society has become more protest oriented has two sides to it. First, it implies that protest is becoming more common in current society: there are more protests and more protesters. The second side, however, focuses on the society as a whole. If we do live in a protest society, we would expect that protest itself has become more acceptable. This view considers protest as merely an extension of a citizen's political repertoire. What I am interested in presently is how, if at all, attitudes toward protest have changed in advanced western societies over the last couple of decades and who holds what attitudes, the second part of the social movement society argument.

This premise suggests many implications worthy of examination. For example, if it is true that protest has become more acceptable, to what extent should we think of it in the same way that we thought of protest in the past? Even more clearly, if protest draws its strength from its contentious nature, then the degree of contentiousness matters. We want to have some understanding of contentiousness to understand how protest should be placed in the context of a larger society. One profitable route would be to examine public attitudes about protest. How we think of protest will depend on how we define it. Protest takes a variety of empirically observable forms; these forms will be the focus of my discussion. Taking this approach allows me to distinguish among types of contentious behavior. There is a difference, for example, between signing a petition and occupying a building, although each is a form of protest. The difference is in the degree of contentiousness of the acts. I will argue that this degree of contentiousness is important to understanding the relationship between protest and society over the last twenty years.

I will present two variants to this claim that we now live in more protest-oriented, movement society. The first variant says that Western societies have become increasingly contentious. This line of argument leads to the assumption that people have begun to accept all forms of protest no matter how contentious they are. They have turned away from traditional outlets for expressing dissatisfaction and have instead begun to use more direct methods (Rosenau 1990, pp. 368–73). The second variant—we can refer to it as the conventionalization of protest—claims not only that less contentious forms of protest become more acceptable but also that they have actually become part of the conventional political action repertoire. However, on the other side, highly contentious acts have, if anything, become less tolerable. "It is now safe to conclude that legal forms of direct action, such as boycotts, citizen initiatives, and demonstrations, have become a standard part of the citizen repertory of political behaviour in modern pluralist democracies" (Kaase and Newton 1995, p. 50). This has been a reoccuring theme in work done on political participation in the last twenty years (Barnes et al. 1979; Dalton 1996; van den Broek and Heuncks 1994; Jennings et al. 1990; Gundelach 1995). Working from this observation, scholars have debated whether this trend has come at the expense of conventional forms of participation (Kaase 1990; Koopmans 1996). To test these arguments, I will use the Guttman scaling technique to analyze how protest attitudes have evolved.

Data

In this chapter I look at the "acceptance" of protest. I will use "acceptance" in two stages: first, how the concept is defined will be laid out, then the concept will be defended against other possible approaches. The path-breaking *Political Action* (Barnes et al. 1979) study of the mid-1970s asked respondents a series of questions about whether they would use a particular form of political protest. The individuals from the cross-national sample could say that they had used the form of protest, they would use it, they might use it, or that they would never use it. Of the eight protest forms the survey examined, I explore five: petitions, lawful demonstrations, boycotts, unofficial (wildcat) strikes, and occupying buildings (sit-ins). By my approach, respondents "accept" a protest form if they indicate that they have already used it, would use it, or might do so. Equivalently, acceptance can be thought of as everyone except those who would never use that form of protest and those who did not answer the question.

I use acceptance, rather than self-reported participation, for two reasons. First, although the *Political Action* study did ask the acceptance question directly, the question of intent is more appealing. A glib (though not inaccurate) answer would be to quote Ralph Emerson's famous line "What you do speaks so loudly I cannot hear what you say." If a respondent were to say that he or she finds demonstrations acceptable in the abstract but would never actually participate in one, how credible is this acceptance? The concept of interest here is an individual's personal attitude about a form of protest, not whether it is alright for others. Put somewhat differently, a direct question of whether a person finds demonstrations acceptable could be interpreted as to divorce the respondent from the answer—"It's alright for those kids, but I'd never do it"—but what I care about is whether the form of protest is *personally* acceptable to the respondent. Second, the question of acceptability was not directly asked again. Even if it had been followed up years later, I do not believe that I would use it because it misses the mark for which I am really aiming: the personal attitudes of the respondents.

This focus on attitudes also needs to be defended. Barnes et al. (1979) combined this set of questions with another of the perceived effectiveness of protest forms to create their "protest potential" scale. This approach has since been reconsidered and discarded on the grounds that it conflates evaluations, behavior, and attitudes (Inglehart 1990; Kaase 1990; Gundelach 1995). Kaase (1990) avoided this problem of how to define the variable of interest entirely by constructing five separate scales from which the reader could choose one to his or her liking. Inglehart (1990) and Gundelach (1995) were less ambiguous and chose to focus solely on the self-reporting of whether or not a respondent had already used a certain form of protest. Apparently preferring the "concreteness" of what has happened to the vagueness of what might in the future, the authors proceed with little justification for their decision. My focus is on the popular acceptance of each of these forms of participation—an attitude. I define respondent acceptance of an action as agreement with any of the first three responses—have/would/ might—use the form of protest. Wilson (1990) uses this method in his treatment of the same question, and it is equivalent to one of the five scales presented by Kaase (1990) in his reevaluation of the *Political Action* project.

Attitudes are a more reliable indicator of the issues I want to examine. Consider Kaase (1990), who compares the attitudes of young and old toward protest and then self-reporting of these groups of having actually participated in protests. He finds that, on the one hand, younger people indicate that they are willing to participate in protest much more than their elders; however, when it comes to self-reported protest participation, the differences between young and old diminish. The implication here is that the youth might talk a big game when it comes to protest, but when push comes to shove, they stay on the sidelines. But given the way the question is asked, this makes perfect sense. An eighty-year-old person asked whether she has ever participated in a protest activity has had many more opportunities to do so than has someone who is twenty-five. If this eighty-year-old woman did not participate in her protest activity until she was forty-five, how fair is the comparison to the twenty-five-year-old? Any question that asks whether a person has ever had a life experience will almost invariably be biased toward older respondents simply because they have had more experiences from which to draw. This is especially important if we take seriously Tarrow's notion of protest cycles: the full repertoire of protest forms is not available at all times. If we could normalize the variable by determining how many protest actions in which the person has participated per year, this effect would go away. However, the surveys were not structured in this manner, which means that the examination of a very important variable—age—will be inherently suspect.

A hypothetical example helps to clarify this point. Let us take the equivalent wording of the question, but rather than ask whether the respondent has ever participated in a protest activity, ask whether the person has ever been involved in an automobile accident. I would venture to guess that we would find older respondents much more likely to respond affirmatively to the question. Would we then want to conclude that older drivers are more accident prone? Should older drivers be paying more for automobile insurance than younger ones? Of course not, and the reason for this sort of result is obvious: the older person has been driving for many more years than the younger one and has therefore had many more opportunities to be in an automobile accident than has the youth. Yet if we were to look at the average number of accidents per year, we would undoubtedly find that the rate for younger drivers is much higher than for older ones, thereby justifying the near-extortionary insurance rates for drivers under twenty-five.

Given my approach to the concept of "acceptance," my defense of the other methodological decisions makes more sense. The have/would/might/never series of questions has been asked in five major cross-national surveys: Political Action (1974), World Values Survey I (1981), Political Action II (1983), Eurobarometer 31 (1989), and World Values Survey II (1990). We know that attitudes can take a long time to change, especially when generational replacement is a likely cause. To give as much time as possible to pick up these changes, I wanted to use the time points with the largest temporal spread. Five nations were surveyed in both the 1974 *Political Action* study and the 1990 World Values II study: Great Britain, West Germany, the Netherlands, Italy, and the United States, all of which are included in this project.

A Cross-National Sketch of the Terrain

Now that we know what we are looking at, we can begin to make a thumbnail sketch of how these five nations compare with one another. Figure 3.1 presents the data for 1974. In general, we see that the lines slope downward, as we would expect: as protest forms become more contentious, popular acceptance of them dwindles. This same pattern is even more clearly seen in Figure 3.2 showing the same data for 1990. Is it possible to say that some countries are more protest oriented than others? Yes, it is, but we have to pay close attention to where we look to get a good answer. For example, if we just looked at petitions in 1990, we would get the idea that Great Britain was more accepting of protest in our study. However, if we moved over one notch to demonstrations, we would see that Great Britain was the least supportive of this form of protest, which would lead us to conclude that Great Britain was the least accepting of protest. Which conclusion is more valid? Neither; protest is a broad concept not adequately defined by any one form. One of the most important themes of this chapter is to remember that as we are trying to characterize individual attitudes about protest, *the degree of contentiousness matters*. Let us now examine each nation in our study using the information contained in Figures 3.1 and 3.2.

We can safely say that relative to the other nations in this study, Great Britain was less accepting of the less contentious forms of protest in the mid-1970s. With only three-quarters of the respondents accepting petitions and just a bit over half accepting demonstrations, Great Britain was noticeably behind the other countries. In the same year only 46 percent found boycotts acceptable—a figure greater only than

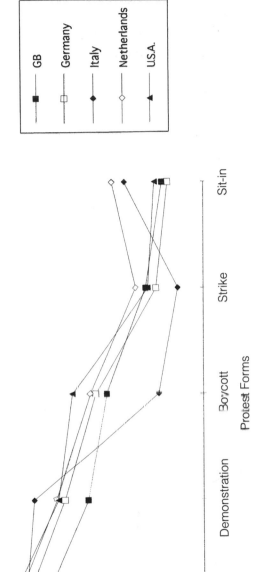

FIGURE 3.1. 1974 Protest Acceptance

Matthew Crozat

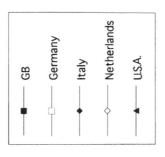

FIGURE 3.2. 1990 Protest Acceptance

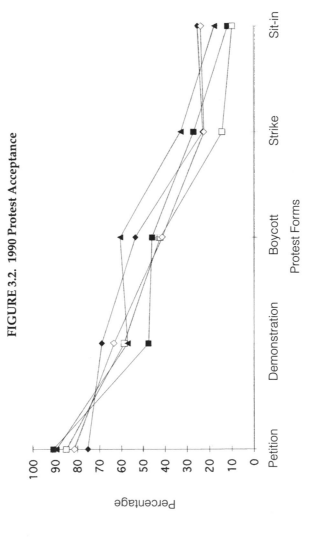

the startlingly low number from Italy. Given the popular attitudes toward these forms, it is somewhat surprising that wildcat strikes are more accepted in Great Britain than anywhere else except the Netherlands. This may be an artifact of the long British history of labor protest in response to early industrialization rather than a more general embrace of contentious political actions since we can see that building occupations are relatively unpopular. Moving forward to 1990, we see a remarkable jump in the popularity of petitions in Great Britain. After petitions, not much had changed with Great Britain from 1974 to 1990. Compared with results sixteen years before, demonstrations and sit-ins were a bit *less* popular, whereas boycotts and strikes were accepted at about the same level as before.

The first three protest forms for West Germany in 1974 suggest that the country is fairly typical: about 84 percent accepted petitions, 65 percent were amenable to demonstrations, and a shade over 50 percent found boycotts acceptable. Yet as we move toward the most contentious forms, German support drops off. Only 22 percent of West Germans accepted wildcat strikes (only Italy was lower), and just 17 percent accepted sit-ins—the lowest in the group. This data from 1974 present an image of a nation that tolerates the less contentious forms of protest but will not tolerate the more contentious ones. This conception is supported by the 1990 data. The relative position of West Germany only changes with regard to boycotts, which West Germans accept only marginally more than the Dutch, who have the lowest rate. Acceptance of petitions in West Germany did not change much from the mid-1970s, and acceptance of demonstrations actually increased a bit. West Germany was not becoming more protest oriented across the board; acceptance rates for boycotts, wildcat strikes, and peaceful building occupations all fell between 7 and 9 percent. The 1974 image of a nation that will not tolerate contentious forms of political action is even more valid in 1990.

The 1974 data for Italy present a very different profile. Demonstrations are almost as popular as petitions, with acceptance of the former at 83 percent and the latter at 79 percent. Yet, only 21 percent accepted boycotts and 12 percent wildcats strikes. By way of comparison, the next lowest rate of acceptance for boycotts is 46 percent in Great Britain, and only 22 percent condone strikes in West Germany. Does this mean we can characterize Italy in 1974 in the German mold as a nation that accepts less contentious forms of protest but not more contentious ones? Not really, for 37 percent accept sit-ins, second only to the Netherlands. Is there something unique about Italy in 1974 that might make its figures look so different from those for the other nations? By 1974, Italy was at the end of what Tarrow has called "a long wave of collective action" (1989, p. 5) in which the other nations had seen their protest waves subside. If being beset by protest alters public acceptance of protest, then we would expect that data from the calmer 1990 would be more in line with those from other nations. This is what we see, but that result does not imply that there is anything typical about Italy. Petitions are less accepted in Italy in 1990 than anywhere else (75 percent), but demonstrations are still the most accepted here (69 percent). More typical are Italy's attitudes toward boycotts (54 percent) and strikes (24 percent). Building occupations are more accepted in Italy than anywhere else in 1990 (26 percent). Though the picture is not clear, Italians appear to have relatively little use for as relatively passive a tool as a petition and would rather take to the streets, or maybe even the buildings, to express their demands.

The Netherlands in 1974 can be classified as a protest-oriented society: for every protest form, it is one of the two most accepting nations. Fully 88 percent of Dutch respondents were amenable to petitions, 68 percent to demonstrations, and 53 percent to boycotts; all ranked second compared with the other countries in the study. The Netherlands had the largest percentage of respondents who accepted wildcat strikes (32 percent) and building occupations (43 percent) of the five nations. This description is not really accurate as we move to 1990. Acceptance of every form of protest dropped in the Netherlands from 1974 to 1990. In the end, the Netherlands looks something like a toned-down Italy in the sense that, comparatively, demonstrations and building occupations are reasonably well tolerated.

If the Dutch in 1974 are an example of a protest society that would generally embrace contentious forms, the Americans in 1974 are an example of a protest society less willing to do so. Over 90 percent of Americans found petitions acceptable in 1974, the most of any nation in our sample. Just a fraction of a percentage less than the Dutch, almost 68 percent of those in the United States said demonstrations were acceptable. Considerably more than anyone else, 61 percent of Americans were amenable to boycotts. Acceptance of protest in the United States is more typical with regard to wildcat strikes and building occupations, supported by 26 percent and 23 percent, respectively. This trend holds up a little better over time in the American case than in the Dutch. In 1990 almost 98 percent still accepted petitions. Those approving of demonstrations dropped by ten points to 57 percent (greater than only Great Britain), whereas support of boycotts stayed up around 61 percent. The rate of acceptance for wildcat strikes rose only to one-third, yet sit-ins fell to 19 percent. Though by no means definitive, the conception of the United States in 1990 is one that is relatively tolerant of unconventional forms of political participation—even the rather contentious ones.

Scaling a Wall to Evaluate the Arguments

The view we get from looking at nations as a whole is interesting, but the claims I am trying to evaluate make arguments about the attitudes of individuals. To carry out analysis at the individual level, we need to organize the information provided by the respondents. By creating a scale, we can condense the information contained in the respondent's answers to the questions of whether they accept each of the five protest forms described here into a single number that can be compared across individuals. One method is to create a simple scale by counting the number of unconventional actions accepted by the respondent. This simple scale, however, is problematic. When we see a value—say, 1—affixed to a respondent, all we can say is that of the five protest forms, one was acceptable; we want to know which one that might be. In this context, we would be grouping together someone who only finds petitions acceptable with someone who only finds building occupations acceptable.

Gundelach (1995) and Inglehart (1990) offer an alternative method. They define a respondent as a protester if he or she claims to have participated in more than one protest action. This dichotomizing throws away a lot of useful information and makes it difficult to understand gradations of contentiousness. For example, using this method, a person who has signed one petition and attended one rally is placed in the same category as an extremely protest-oriented individual who has repeatedly employed even the most contentious forms. Another difficulty is that, using their approach, we have no way of being sure that the one protest form used by an individual is an uncontentious one, such a signing a petition, thereby warranting inclusion in the "nonprotester" category. Intuitively, we can see that the uncontentious forms are more likely to be used by most people, but it would be nice to rely on something stronger than intuition. The main problem is that this dichotomizing paints with too broad a brush, especially when more nuanced measures can be created.

As an alternative, I will employ a Guttman scale, a method that makes a strong statement about the data. The score for a respondent allows us to know not only how many forms of protest are accepted by the respondent but also which ones. Guttman scaling works when the potential answers can be ranked based on the rationale "If form Z is acceptable to the respondent, then so too must forms X and Y." In other words, Guttman scaling works from a cumulative ranking: if a person responds affirmatively to the third item on a Guttman scale, then we know that he or she also responds affirmatively to the first two items as well. The score on a Guttman scale is the point at which the respondent says, "I will go this far, but no farther." It is precisely this hierarchical aspect of the data that I want to analyze. Figure 3.3 illustrates an ideal Guttman scale. These data are said to scale perfectly because no respondent answers affirmatively to an item without doing the same for all previous items.

Measures can be used to determine whether the data come close enough to this idealized form. Should the data conform to a Guttman scale, we will be able to count the number of protest forms each person finds acceptable and make reasonable assumptions about their attitudes. The first assumption would be that if a respondent only finds one form of protest acceptable, then we can surmise that it would be petitions. Furthermore, if a person finds three protest forms acceptable, we could assume with confidence that they would be petitions, demonstrations, and boycotts. Thus, we would have a means to compare respondents quantitatively by scoring them from 0 to 5 and know exactly what that score represents.

Three criteria must be satisfied to say that the data conform to a Guttman scale. First, we would like to know just how often the responses fit the ideal pattern shown in Figure 3.3; the coefficient of reproducibility tests this fit. For the data to conform to a Guttman scale, the coefficient of reproducibility should be at least 0.90; this means that at least 90 percent of the responses were in line with the ideal pattern. As Table 3.1 shows, the 1990 data satisfy this criteria safely, whereas the 1974 data do so only marginally. The second criterion for accepting the Guttman scale is that the value of the minimal marginal reproducibility, which is the average of the overall frequency of each response, not be too close to the coefficient of reproducibility. This step is to

FIGURE 3.3
An Ideal Guttman Scale

Respondent	Petitions	Demonstrations	Boycotts	Strike	Sit-in
A	N	N	N	N	N
B	Y	N	N	N	N
C	Y	Y	N	N	N
D	Y	Y	Y	N	N
E	Y	Y	Y	Y	N
F	Y	Y	Y	Y	Y

TABLE 3.1
Protest Scale Results

Test	1974	1990
Coeff. of Reproducibility	0.898	0.921
Minimal marginal reproducibility	0.706	0.657
Coeff. of scalability	0.654	0.771

ensure that the coefficient is not spuriously high. Both years appear to satisfy this vague requirement. The minimum marginal reproducibility value of 0.706 in 1974 may seem close to the coefficient of reproducibility of 0.898, but from the way the former is constructed, its minimum possible value is 0.500. The final, and perhaps most important criterion, is the coefficient of scalability, which is a measurement of the proportional reduction in error. The rule of thumb for this statistic is that we want the coefficient of scalability greater than or equal to 0.60, which we have. As we can see, both the 1974 and 1990 data satisfy all three criteria to be classified as a Guttman scale (McIver and Carmines 1981; Barnes 1979).

Now that we know the data correspond to a Guttman scale, we can move to the substantive issues. The first variant of increasing societal contentiousness would predict an increase in the mean value of the Guttman scale: that would imply that contentious protest has become more acceptable. Table 3.2 shows this is not the case; evidence actually indicates that there is less, not more, support for contentious actions in 1990. This finding does not necessarily refute the second variant of protest conventionalization; after all, this argument claimed that while more contentious forms were being repudiated, less contentious ones were becoming so accepted that they could be considered conventional. However, no evidence exists for this contention either, as Table 3.3 shows. The percentage who accepted petitions in 1990 is about the same as in 1974—nearly 86 percent—but there was a drop from 68 percent to 60 percent among respondents who approved of peaceful demonstrations, the second least contentious form of protest. The per-

TABLE 3.2
Protest Scale (min. = 0; max. = 5)

Year	Mean	Standard Deviation
1974	2.597	1.514
1990	2.446	1.521

TABLE 3.3
Percentage Accepting Protest Forms

Year	Petitions	Demonstrations	Boycotts	Strikes	Sit-ins
1974	86	68	52	27	27
1990	87	60	52	26	19

centage supporting boycotts stayed constant at about 52 percent, as did the percentage accepting unofficial strikes at 27 percent. Support for sit-ins fell from 27 percent to 19 percent.

The Guttman scale allows us to say with confidence that these percentages are actually representative of the data. If we were to rely solely on the aggregate percentages, we would be unable to reject the possibility that there are two classes of citizens divided over protest. The first group would be relatively law-abiding and supportive of only the most conventional forms of political action. The second group, on the other hand, might reject these mainstream political channels on the grounds that they are an ineffectual waste of time and opt instead for the most direct and radical forms. Using the Guttman scale, we know that, to the extent the second type of citizen exists, they are few and far between.

Who Accepts Protest?

Using the two data sets previously discussed, we can see which citizens' attitudes toward protest have changed since the mid-1970s. From the previous phase, we know that there is not support for the notion that society has become dramatically more protest oriented; within this context, we can examine how various groups in the society have changed their attitudes toward unconventional political participation. To do this, I will use a series of probits—that is, discrete choice, nonlinear models, with a host of explanatory variables that should be instructive: age, gender, education, union and party membership, ideology, religiosity, income, and country-specific dummy variables.

Three independent variables form the backbone of all studies in this area: age, gender, and years of schooling. All previous studies have shown age as one of the best indicators of an individual's attitude toward protest: younger people are more willing to protest than older ones (Barnes et al., 1979; Dalton 1996; Inglehart 1990; Kaase 1990; van den Broek and Heunks 1994; Kaase and Newton 1995; Gundelach 1995). The arguments that society is becoming more protest oriented suggest that age effects should be less important in 1990 than they were in 1974, on the grounds that even older people are more accepting of protest than they used to be. On the other hand, such a finding could imply that younger respondents are less approving of protest than were their counterparts in the earlier survey.

Conventional wisdom holds that because women tend to be less aggressive, they are less likely to approve of contentious political actions than men, if we assume protest is a form of aggressive behavior (Barnes et al. 1979, p. 106). We would therefore expect negative coefficients in our results (because gender is coded 1 for female, 0 for male). The question is whether this variable has changed significantly over time. Dalton (1996) claims the "gender gap" in attitudes toward protest has narrowed over the course of the 1980s. This view would make sense if we accept the *Political Action* analysis that the primary explanation for the gender gap was the differences in education levels between men and women (Barnes et al. 1979, p. 148). In this analysis both education and gender will be included as independent variables, which will allow us to see whether gender has any independent explanatory power.

Years of education has also been shown to be positively associated with acceptance of protest (Dalton 1996, p. 79; Kaase 1990, p. 42; Gundelach 1995, p. 425; Barnes et al. 1979). This relationship can be taken as evidence that protest is a function of personal resources, or "human capital." Mirroring the accepted relationship between conventional participation and schooling, the connection between protest and education was a major piece in the argument advanced in *Political Action* that unconventional participation was an extension of the political repertoire of citizens rather than an alternative to it. With this in mind, the belief that society has become more protest-oriented over the last couple of decades makes a great deal of sense because we know that the level of education has increased over that time.

I include dummy variables to pick up membership in either a union or a political party, because these organizations are at once a means of political socialization and part of the conventional political system. As Barnes et al. (1979) argue that protest is merely an extension of the conventional forms of political participation, it is reasonable to examine the manner in which these bonds have evolved over the last two decades. It is difficult to hazard a guess as to how this variable might react. On the one hand, social movements and unconventional forms of political action have been seen as an alternative means of interest articulation to political parties and conventional participation—a dealignment hypothesis (Dalton 1996, p. 71; Wallace and Jenkins 1995). On the other side, we might expect a counterbalancing effect as movements "evolve" into parties, as we have seen most starkly with the Greens in Germany and the Netherlands (Kaase 1990, pp. 61–62). One other notable feature of unions and parties is that membership in each has been reported to be on the decline for most of the last twenty years.

Respondents in both sets of surveys were asked to place themselves ideologically on a ten-point scale from left (1) to right (10). In the 1960s protest was most clearly associated with the political left, but the 1980s saw a rise of militant abortion protests in the United States as well as a resurgence of the German far right; we have reason to expect that some change toward the right would occur. Such a finding would lend some credence to the idea that we are witnessing the emergence of a social movement society: if ideological differences are shrinking, it is a sign that these unconventional forms of political action are indeed becoming more and more accepted by the society as a whole.

Wallace and Jenkins (1995) contend that more religious respondents are less disposed to support protest. They see religiousness as an indicator of postindustrialism, which, in itself, is a potential explanation for an increase in protest. Because the survey question asked respondents whether they are somewhat, very, or not at all religious, the measure for religiosity is broken out into two dummy variables: the first is coded 1 if the respondent indicated that he or she is very religious and 0 otherwise, while the second is defined in the same manner with respect to whether the respondent is somewhat religious.

Income has been shown to correlate positively with protest in past studies—partially confirming a resource mobilization thesis. This variable is measured on a ten-point scale in local currencies. Because of the local currencies and the inability to control for inflation, this variable should be viewed more as a control than an explanatory variable.

Finally, dummy variables for whether the respondent lived in the United States or Italy were included in the analysis. The inclusion of these variables implies that something about the political culture of these nations might help to explain attitudes toward protest. All of the nations in the study could not be included because that would violate the requirement for full rank. The United States and Italy were chosen not only for their familiarity, but also because of their histories regarding protest in the last thirty years. The polarizing protest campaigns for civil rights and against the Vietnam War in the United States during the 1960s and 1970s reaffirmed a national propensity to protest. Italy was witness to violent protests in the 1970s creating a backlash effect against what is essentially a national pastime in the country.

Model and Results

To determine the impact that these variables will have on a person's willingness to accept protest, we need to fit a model to the data that will allow us to sort out the relative effects of a host of demographic variables. I will examine each of the forms of protest separately to allow for more nuanced results. Because the probit model is different than an ordinary regression, we must take care in how we interpret the results. First, we will look at the significance of the independent variables and their sign as reported in Table 3.4. In this manner, interpretation of the results is straightforward, but the explanatory power is limited because we cannot accurately comment on the magnitude of the effects. We can use this method of interpretation to understand whether an increase in the explanatory variable will increase or decrease the probability that a person would accept the protest form.

TABLE 3.4
Significance of the Independent Variables

Variable	Petition	Demonstration	Boycott	Strike	Sit-in
1974:					
Intercept	1.033*	1.137*	0.477*	0.743*	0.755*
Union	0.008	0.131*	0.066	0.238*	0.066*
Party	0.130*	0.116*	0.160*	0.124*	0.191*
Very religious	−0.085	−0.172*	−0.367*	−0.411*	−0.422*
Somewhat religious	0.055	0.002	−0.263*	−0.241*	−0.202*
Ideology	−0.034*	−0.073*	−0.087*	−0.112*	−0.143*
Female	−0.024*	−0.319*	−0.173*	−0.258*	−0.185*
Age	−0.013*	−0.020*	−0.012*	−0.024*	−0.022*
Education	0.067*	0.048*	0.069*	0.037*	0.037*
Income	0.052*	0.047*	0.030*	0.021*	0.010
United States	0.613*	0.291*	0.409*	0.188*	0.048
Italy	−0.157*	0.493*	−1.042*	−0.730*	0.276*
−2 Log (L0/L1)	401.239	818.371	957.372	900.493	933.696
1990:					
Intercept	1.220*	0.696*	0.213	0.488*	0.076
Union	0.157	0.287*	0.235*	0.271*	0.257*
Party	0.273*	0.496*	0.274*	0.347*	0.387*
Very religious	−0.058	−0.058	−0.158*	−0.273*	−0.306*
Somewhat religious	−0.032	−0.072	−0.030	−0.125	−0.148
Ideology	−0.055*	−0.089*	−0.106*	−0.141*	−0.153*
Female	−0.080	−0.026*	−0.129*	−0.149*	−0.060
Age	−0.012*	−0.018*	−0.013*	−0.016*	−0.018*
Education	0.059*	0.083*	0.071*	0.033*	0.063*
Income	0.071*	0.021*	0.047*	0.003	−0.015
United States	0.388*	−0.023*	0.568*	0.523*	0.233*
Italy	−0.036	0.727*	0.662*	0.249*	0.726*
−2 Log (L0/L1)	362.339	900.063	870.030	704.904	767.057

*Statistically significant at the .05 level using a Wald test.

Later, we will take a more detailed look at some of the more important explanatory variables. Let us first examine 1974.

We can see that with the exception of the Italy variable, we do not have a significant independent variable that changes sign as the forms of protest become more contentious. This reassures that the explanatory variables are working in the way we think they are. We see that for three of the protest forms, being a member of a union is significant and increases the probability that the individual will accept that form of protest. Similarly, membership in a political party has a positive effect on the probability of condoning the unconventional political action, but it is significant in all cases. With the less contentious forms of protest in 1974, being somewhat religious is not a statistically significant factor in the probability of accepting a form of protest, but with the three most contentious forms, it is significant and the effect is negative. The very religious variable shows a similar pattern: though not significant for petitions, it is relevant in the other models and has the effect of decreasing the chances that the protest form will be accepted. Keeping in mind that higher values represent a move rightward on the ideological spectrum, we see that in all cases ideological self-placement is significant and negatively associated with the political right. Our models show that being a woman matters for all forms of protest, and the effect is always negative. As we would expect, age matters: older people are more reluctant to accept any given form of protest. Education and income are positively associated with acceptance of protest and are significant in all cases, although income is not relevant to explain sit-ins. As for the countries, Italy shows an interesting pattern that we saw in Figure 3.1: in 1974 Italians accepted demonstrations and building occupations, but rejected petitions, boycotts, and wildcat strikes.

The models for 1990 show some subtle differences from 1974, but, in general, the directions of the variables do not change much. Union membership is only irrelevant for petitions in 1990, and the effect is still positive. Belonging to a party is significant in all cases and does improve the probability that the protest form will be accepted. Probably most interesting in this set of models is that being somewhat religious is not significant in any case, whereas being very religious has a negative impact but is only relevant for the three most contentious forms of protest. Ideology is still significant and negatively associated with political conservatives. In 1990 gender is no longer relevant for explaining the acceptance of the least contentious act (signing petitions) or the most contentious act (occupying a building), though it is significant and negative for the other forms. Age still matters in 1990, and getting older continues to have a negative effect on the probability of accepting protest. Education remains relevant and positive, while income also has a positive effect but is only significant for the three least contentious forms of protest. Being American is relevant in every case and only negative with regard to demonstrations, which basically confirms what we saw in Figure 3.2. Being Italian has a positive impact on the likelihood of accepting a form of protest with the exception of petitions, where it is not relevant.

We can compare the relative importance of an independent variable in 1974 and 1990, but we can only look at one at a time. I have picked interesting values for the other independent variables and held them constant to examine the effect of changes in the variable of interest. To aid in comparison, I present three hypothetical "archetypical individuals" to use for our examinations in each case: one is "normal," one predisposed to protest, and one protest averse. Let me begin by describing the "normal" individual, a fifty-year-old man who does not live in the United States or Italy. He does not belong to a union, but he is a member of a political party. He is not religious at all and places himself in the middle of the ideological spectrum. He has ten years of formal schooling and an average income. With this information I can use the results in Table 3.4 to compute the probability that our normal person would have accepted petitions in 1974 would have been 0.89. Now, to see how relevant belonging to a party is to this person's probability of accepting petitions in 1974, we can recalculate it by keeping all of the other factors constant but setting the party membership variable to 0. Doing this, we can compute that the probability of a normal person who does not belong to a party accepting petitions in 1974 is 0.86. Using this technique of creating a general profile of a type of person, then altering one variable while holding everything else constant, we can get an idea of how important that altered variable is.

Next is the person who is predisposed to protest. This individual is a twenty-year-old American man who belongs to both a union and a political party. He places himself to the left of the ideological spectrum and is not religious. He has twelve years of formal education, and his income is a bit above average. In contrast to this pro-protest individual, we also have a person who is averse to protest. This person is an eighty-year-old woman who does not belong to a political party or a union. Though not religious, she is conservative. Her income is below average, and she has eight years of formal education. She lives in neither the United States nor Italy. I want to reiterate that these personality profiles are the same for all of the models with just one variable being allowed to move in each case.

Party Membership

Table 3.5 presents the probability of an individual accepting a protest form in either 1974 or 1990. First I will focus on the normal person.

TABLE 3.5
Party Identification

	Normal		Pro-Protest		Averse	
	0	1	0	1	0	1
1974 petition	0.86	0.89	0.99	0.99	0.63	0.68
1990 petition	0.89	0.93	0.99	1.00	0.65	0.75
1974 demonstration	0.68	0.72	0.97	0.98	0.20	0.23
1990 demonstration	0.60	0.77	0.94	0.98	0.21	0.38
1974 boycott	0.61	0.67	0.94	0.96	0.24	0.29
1990 boycott	0.46	0.57	0.95	0.97	0.12	0.18
1974 strike	0.28	0.33	0.85	0.88	0.02	0.03
1990 strike	0.25	0.37	0.86	0.93	0.04	0.07
1974 sit-in	0.26	0.32	0.74	0.80	0.02	0.03
1990 sit-in	0.15	0.25	0.71	0.83	0.01	0.03

We see that the probability of the individual accepting petitions in 1974 increases by only 0.03 if he belongs to a party. In 1990 party membership increases probability by just 0.04. If he belonged to a party in 1974, the probability of our normal person accepting demonstrations was a mere 0.04 greater than if he did not belong; however, in 1990 the difference was over four times that—an increase in probability of 0.17. Though demonstrations show it most dramatically, as we look at the other forms of protest we see a trend that party membership had a stronger effect on our normal person in 1990 than it did in 1974. For our pro-protest individual, the effects of party membership are generally less than for the normal person. Some evidence indicates that belonging to a party was more significant in 1990 than it was in 1974—this is most evident with sit-ins—but the differences are not quite as striking as in the previous profile. For the protest-averse person, the effects of belonging to a political party are minimal as the protest forms are more contentious, as are the differences across time. We can see that party membership is rather significant for a person averse to protest in 1990 as to whether he or she will accept demonstrations and petitions. The main theme from this set of calculations is that party membership is more important in 1990 than it was in 1974.

Ideology

Table 3.6 presents the probability of accepting a protest form with the variable for the ideological self-placement of the respondent being allowed to take three values. If we look at our first profile, we can

TABLE 3.6
Ideology

	Normal			Pro-Protest			Averse		
	2	5	8	2	5	8	2	5	8
1974 petition	0.91	0.89	0.87	0.99	0.99	0.99	0.71	0.67	0.63
1990 petition	0.95	0.93	0.91	1.00	1.00	0.99	0.76	0.71	0.65
1974 demonstration	0.79	0.72	0.64	0.98	0.96	0.94	0.34	0.26	0.20
1990 demonstration	0.84	0.77	0.68	0.98	0.96	0.93	0.40	0.30	0.21
1974 boycott	0.75	0.67	0.57	0.96	0.93	0.88	0.42	0.33	0.24
1990 boycott	0.69	0.57	0.45	0.97	0.95	0.90	0.30	0.20	0.12
1974 strike	0.46	0.33	0.22	0.88	0.80	0.69	0.09	0.05	0.02
1990 strike	0.54	0.37	0.23	0.93	0.85	0.73	0.17	0.08	0.04
1974 sit-in	0.49	0.32	0.19	0.80	0.66	0.49	0.12	0.06	0.02
1990 sit-in	0.42	0.25	0.13	0.83	0.68	0.51	0.10	0.04	0.01

clearly see that as the form of protest becomes more contentious, the importance of ideology increases. With petitions, being on the left as opposed to the right only increased the probability of acceptance by 0.04 in both 1974 and 1990; but with building occupations, the increase is about 0.30 for both years. For both boycotts and wildcat strikes there is a noticeable difference between 1974 and 1990, with the more recent year showing a stronger effect of being on the left, but this is not pervasive across all protest forms and not noticeable at all with our protest-friendly person. Our individual predisposed to protest shows a pattern similar to our normal person in that the effect of being on the left is much higher for the most contentious political actions. The protest-averse profile does not show the same force for being on the left with sit-ins and boycotts on first glance, but considering the probabilities were low even for those who placed themselves on the left, the value could not drop that far and still stay a non–negative number.

Age

We would expect that age would be an important consideration in whether a person accepts protest, and Table 3.7 shows this. The first thing we notice from our normal profile is that the effects are larger across the board than for any of the other variables. The effects of age are not as clearly linked to the contentiousness of the protest as was the case with ideology. With the exception of boycotts, the magnitudes of the difference between being twenty and eighty are more muted in 1990 than they were in 1974. With our protest-favorable individual, a person's age becomes really important as we get to strikes and sit-ins, where the effect of being younger can increase the probability of accepting protest by as much as half. The protest-averse profile shows

TABLE 3.7
Age

	Normal			Pro-Protest			Averse		
	20	50	80	20	50	80	20	50	80
1974 petition	0.95	0.89	0.80	0.99	0.99	0.96	0.87	0.77	0.63
1990 petition	0.97	0.93	0.88	1.00	0.99	0.98	0.86	0.77	0.65
1974 demonstration	0.88	0.72	0.50	0.98	0.92	0.80	0.63	0.40	0.20
1990 demonstration	0.90	0.77	0.58	0.98	0.93	0.83	0.61	0.40	0.21
1974 boycott	0.78	0.67	0.53	0.96	0.91	0.84	0.49	0.36	0.24
1990 boycott	0.72	0.57	0.42	0.97	0.94	0.87	0.36	0.22	0.12
1974 strike	0.61	0.33	0.12	0.88	0.67	0.38	0.29	0.10	0.02
1990 strike	0.56	0.37	0.21	0.93	0.83	0.68	0.20	0.09	0.04
1974 sit-in	0.58	0.32	0.11	0.80	0.57	0.31	0.24	0.09	0.02
1990 sit-in	0.46	0.25	0.11	0.83	0.65	0.43	0.14	0.05	0.01

that the effect of age is not as pronounced in 1990 as it was in 1974. Again it seems that age becomes less relevant as the protest form becomes more contentious, but especially with wildcat strikes and building occupations, the probability of acceptance really cannot drop any lower. There is one striking trend that holds up across profiles: *age is not as significant in 1990 as it was in 1974.*

Gender

From Table 3.4, we noted that the female dummy variable was not statistically significant for petitions and sit-ins; therefore, only the remaining forms of protest will be analyzed. The most striking feature of Table 3.8 is that gender is consistently less important in 1990 than in 1974. This fits nicely with the earlier result that being female was not even a statistically relevant factor in explaining the probability of ac-

TABLE 3.8
Gender

	Normal		Pro-Protest		Averse	
	0	1	0	1	0	1
1974 demonstration	0.72	0.61	0.98	0.95	0.30	0.20
1990 demonstration	0.77	0.76	0.98	0.98	0.20	0.19
1974 boycott	0.67	0.60	0.96	0.94	0.21	0.16
1990 boycott	0.57	0.52	0.97	0.96	0.14	0.12
1974 strike	0.33	0.24	0.88	0.82	0.02	0.01
1990 strike	0.37	0.32	0.93	0.90	0.04	0.03

0 = male; 1 = female.

cepting petitions or sit-ins. Across all profiles, being a male at most increases the probability of acceptance by 0.05, but usually not even that high in 1990. There is no discernable pattern as far as the contentiousness of the protest form and the magnitude of the impact from the profiles.

Conclusion

I began this chapter by discussing the notion that society has become more accepting of protest. In the first part of this analysis, I show that with respect to the actual forms that protest may take, the story is not well supported; society has not become more accepting of these forms of protest. This finding does not imply that protest has become any less prominent in Western society. Protest methods may well have been employed more often and by a wider panoply of groups than twenty years ago, in spite of the fact that popular acceptance of the forms has not changed considerably. What this would mean is that the increase in the frequency of protest has not desensitized the observing public to the actions themselves. The evidence presented here would also lead us to believe that the pool from which protesters are being drawn is not a rapidly expanding one.

If it were true that the public were becoming more accepting of unconventional political action, then the weight associated with these forms of protest would have been altered. But this has not happened: popular attitudes about the forms of protest have not changed markedly. I believe that these results give us reason to believe that the protest forms I have examined have been *institutionalized* as part of the modern political repertoire. An institution, in the sense used here, can be thought of as a set of mutual expectations based on past experiences. I argue here that part of the expectation involved is the type of public reaction that will be generated by use of a protest form. Though these forms have become institutionalized, they have not necessarily become accepted. Does this make sense? Absolutely. If part of what makes protest effective is this ability to disrupt, the lack of acceptance is precisely what makes the more contentious forms of protest appealing to the protester. Although society may not have become more contentious, that might mean that we have seen the institutionalization of these forms.

4

The Institutionalization of Protest in the United States

John D. McCarthy and Clark McPhail

Media coverage of protest at the 1996 Democratic National Convention in Chicago repeatedly contrasted the actions and interactions of police and protesters at the 1968 Democratic National Convention in Chicago with their 1996 counterparts. The Chicago Study Team of the President's National Commission on the Causes and Prevention of Violence (Walker 1968) called the 1968 interactions "a police riot," a characterization subsequently substantiated by independent social science inquiry (Stark 1972). The Study Team further documented that the 1968 demonstrators were also confrontational, provocative, and aggressive in their contacts with police.

In 1996 the police were repeatedly portrayed in the media as protectors of protesters' First Amendment rights, almost imperturbable in the face of occasional provocations and restrained on the few occasions when arrests were made. Whereas protesters found it almost impossible to obtain demonstration permits in 1968, an elaborate lottery system was established in 1996 under the guidance of U.S. District Courts and the supervision of the prestigious accounting firm of Ernst and Young. The system allocated time slots to protest groups at three designated sites that provoked controversy and some legal action. At issue were which streets demonstrators could use for marches (near, but not past the convention center), the designated rally sites (two blocks and twelve blocks from the convention center), and the "metal cage" on the

We thank Michael Foley, David Meyer, and David Schweingruber, who provided helpful comments on an earlier draft of this chapter. An earlier version of the essay appears in *les Cahiers de la Securité Interieure*.

sidewalk near the convention center from which protesters could speak to and leaflet any passing delegates. But the vast majority of the protesters were portrayed by the media as cooperative and for the most part willing to accept the tight restrictions imposed on the "time, place, and manner" in which they could demonstrate.

Police in 1968 often attacked protesters, sometimes with a great deal but more often with very little provocation, and they arrested hundreds. The 1996 demonstrators found it very difficult to get arrested, even after deliberate provocation. One protest veteran of the 1968 Chicago convention who returned in 1996 was David Dellinger (one of the infamous Chicago Seven tried for conspiracy after the 1968 demonstrations). In 1996 he tried to get arrested for five days before he finally succeeded. Federal Protective Service officers arrested Dellinger along with ten other people from the Not on the Guest List Coalition when they tried to stage a sit-in outside the Kluczynski Federal Building office of U.S. Sen. Carol Moseley-Braun. According to one source, "Dellinger could not get arrested by Chicago police. The feds obliged him. In fact, Chicago police obliged few others, in part because so few challenged them" (Black and Hill 1996, p. 5). A 1996 leader of the Chicago People's Convention Coalition asked the twenty-odd people in his group whether they would risk arrest by leaving the sidewalk and marching down Michigan Avenue. A loud "no" came from the ranks. The leader's collaborator shouted, "Into the street," but no one followed. The leader then responded, " 'Well, guys, we've got the permit for the sidewalks. Shall we just do that? Sidewalks OK with everybody?' It was. Nobody ventured into the streets" (Warren and Warren 1996, p. 2). In short, there was little sustained civil disobedience throughout the 1996 convention and virtually no resistance if and when police did intervene and make arrests; and, of the total of eighteen demonstrator arrests made in Chicago during the 1996 convention, only seven were by Chicago police compared with hundreds of arrests in 1968.

These contrasting images of protest and police behaviors in 1968 and 1996 accurately reflect, in our judgment, the continuing institutionalization of protest that has occurred in the United States over the last three decades. Citizen protest has now become a normal part of the political process, its messages seen as a legitimate supplement to voting, petitioning, and lobbying efforts to influence government policy and practice. At the same time, the recurring behavioral repertoires of both protesters and police, and their interactions with one another, have become institutionalized and therefore routinized, predictable, and, perhaps as a result, of diminishing impact.

Institutions are cultural rules. In the simplest possible terms, social institutions are routinized solutions—a pattern of activities by various interacting groups—to recurring problems. Consistent with Scott and Meyer (1994, p. 10), we conceive of "[*I*]*nstitutionalization* . . . [a]s the process by which a given set of units and a pattern of activities come to be normatively and cognitively held in place, and practically taken for granted as lawful (whether as a matter of formal law, custom, or knowledge)." Our conception of the process of institutionalization of protest reflects the major themes of recent institutional analysis: that particular organizational structures and routines reflect wider institutional environments; that their constituent elements are created, therefore, only partly based on internal technical and functional logics; and that environmental templates are adopted through a variety of processes, only one of which reflects patterns of interorganizational authority (Scott and Meyer 1994, pp. 2-3).

In the following pages, we describe the most important changes in the protester and police repertoires, their connections with one another, and the several interacting processes we believe are responsible for these changes: (1) the transformation of the legal context within which public protest and its social control takes place; (2) the emergence and stabilization of a public order management system; (3) the transformation of standard protest policing procedures; (4) the transformation of social movement organizations (SMOs), which are the principle sources of contemporary protest; and (5) the diffusion of police structures and practices throughout the United States. We conclude with an assessment of the consequence of these shifts for the role of public protest in democratic societies.

The Transformation of the Legal Context of Protest

The First Amendment to the U.S. Constitution, as interpreted and reinterpreted by the U.S. Supreme Court, has defined the evolving rights of protest by U.S. citizens. And, while states and local jurisdictions make and enforce laws governing protest, Federal Constitutional doctrine defines the limits and boundaries of that authority. The cycle of labor protest that occurred in the United States during the 1930s initiated a major legal reinterpretation of citizen protest rights. The 1960s cycle of civil rights and antiwar protests took place within a changed legal context of substantially broadened rights of protest. The extensive litigation that resulted from widespread confrontations between authorities and protesters during that cycle led to further articulation of those rights. This in turn formed the basis for the design of routinized public order management systems (POMS) across the country and the development of a new standard repertoire of police practices for dealing with public protest.

The 1930s protest cycle was central to the subsequent transformation of legal guarantees for U.S. citizens' right to protest. Although demonstrators had few well-established rights during that cycle, their protests were important in shaping political processes that led to a series of crucial Supreme Court appointments. That Court's response to subsequent legal challenges resulted in significantly broadened rights to protest. The 1960s cycle of protest tested the limits of these rights and led to their further elaboration.

The 1930s cycle was dominated by labor issues and their distinctive forms and targets of protest (Piven and Cloward 1979). The existing law did not provide the wide freedoms to engage in public protest that characterize the present period. Equally important, few legal restraints were placed on authorities or their police agents, nor was there much appreciation among authorities or the police for the rights of dissidents to protest (Brecher 1972). It was not unusual for workers who attempted to leaflet, picket, rally, or march to be harassed, beaten, driven out of town, or jailed (Lens 1969). Taft and Ross, (1969 pp. 270–71) say in this regard:

> The United States has had the bloodiest and most violent labor history of any industrial nation in the world. . . . The precipitating cases have been attempts by pickets and sympathizers to prevent a plant on strike from being reopened with strikebreakers, or attempts of company guards, police, or even by National Guardsmen to prevent such interference.

In addition, legal restraints against protest were readily available to authorities acting on behalf of property owners during the 1920s and 1930s. This was manifest in the wide use of the "labor injunction," a mechanism to prevent picketing, boycotting, and a variety of other protest tactics by striking workers. Frankfurter and Greene's (1930) extensively researched attack on such mechanisms uncovered hundreds of successful appeals by owners for relief from protesting workers during the 1920s. The resulting injunctions specifically prevented workers from engaging in any form of collective protest (including marching, picketing, leafleting, or posting notices) within a three-block radius of the targeted business.

The American Civil Liberties Union spearheaded a collaboration with Frankfurter and Green that culminated in the 1932 passage of the Norris-LaGuardia Act restricting the use of labor injunctions. This law reversed existing policy and established workers' rights to freedom of association and self-organization. Whereas earlier precedents allowed the barring of public protests in *anticipation* of disruption or violence, the courts were now required to provide evidence of *actual* violence before such activity could be restrained. This law "was a historic step toward ending the wholesale denial of rights of freedom of speech and assembly for millions of American workers" (Walker 1991, p. 87). The Wagner Act (1935), also known as the National Labor Relations Act (NLRA), guaranteed workers' right to organize and bargain collectively. Although the Taft-Hartley Labor Act (1947) and the Landrum-Griffin Act (1959) restricted these rights somewhat, the effect of the NLRA was to reduce labor violence greatly (Taft and Ross 1969). However, the basic legal protection of the right to organize still did not provide protesters with the broad access to public space that would subsequently evolve in the United States in the 1970s and 1980s.

Public Forum Doctrine

The current legal doctrine that defines the rights of protesters, and also enables and shapes the extensive regulation of protest by U.S. authorities, is known as "public forum law."[1] The doctrine evolved over the past five decades from a series of Supreme Court decisions pertaining to the First Amendment rights of free public assembly. Public forum doctrine relies on a series of distinctions between physical places; these are the "traditional public forum," the "limited" or "designated public forum," the "nonpublic forum," and private property (Post 1987). Traditional public forums include public streets, parks, sidewalks, and other spaces that, " 'by long tradition or by government fiat,' " have come to be used for expressive activity (An 1991, p. 638). First Amendment activity in these areas can only be limited by reasonable time, place, and manner restrictions that are independent of the content of protesters' messages and can be shown to be narrowly drawn and unavoidable if "compelling state interests" are to be served (Smolla 1992, p. 208). Content-based restrictions are forbidden in public forums, as they aim at the communicative impact of speech activity, restricting expression because of its subject matter, form, speaker identity, or viewpoint. Content-neutral restrictions are accepted only if they aim at the noncommunicative impact of speech and even if they may incidentally limit speech. Such restrictions are justified only under the strictest scrutiny in the case of traditional public forums and are more readily accepted in other forums (Tribe 1988, pp. 789–90).

Limited public forums consist of government property that has been opened for the purpose of expressive activity after reviewing "evidence of express governmental interest" in providing such a forum. Limited public forums include places such as airports, university meeting spaces, and municipal theaters, where speech restrictions must be justified along the same lines required in traditional public forums. The third category, nonpublic forums,

> includes governmental property that is not a public forum "by tradition or designation"—such as post offices and jails. Restriction on speech in nonpublic forums need only be reasonable and "not an effort to suppress expression merely because public officials oppose the speaker's view." (An 1991, pp. 633–36).

Private property is excluded from the right of public protest.

This tiered structure of forum designations has spurred extensive Court activity in the last several decades aimed at establishing clearer standards for placement of classes of government property (e.g., airports, post offices, schools, and state fairgrounds) as well as the semi-public classes of private property (e.g., shopping malls and sports arenas), in one or another of the fora categories. The process of clarifying definitions of, and behaviors permitted in, each forum has been defined by a series of exchanges between policing authorities and protesters in the U.S. courts.[2] Many of these rulings have been provoked by the Hare Krishnas' aggressive proselytizing in public places and have been vigorously litigated when the Krishnas have been denied access to certain of these places (see Rochford 1985; Austine 1982; Paterson 1982–83).[3] The Court has tended to place these newer "limited public spaces" farther away from the traditional public forum, hence allowing greater restrictions to be placed on protest in the newer places than the traditional one. This has led some to argue that the effective public space for protest has been diminished, since more and more of citizens' public lives are spent in these newer categories of public space rather than in the older, traditional public forums such as parks and city squares (see Rybczynski 1993; Opperwall 1981). The issue of limited public fora, however, will not be a main focus of our discussion, since our primary concern is in describing and analyzing the permitting and policing systems that have been developed to regulate protest in the public forum. We return in our conclusion to a consideration of limited and nonpublic fora.

The 1994 U.S. Supreme Court decision *(Madsen v. Women's Health Center)* on blockades of abortion clinics rests directly on the public forum doctrine and was stated in those terms by Chief Justice Rehnquist in his decision. The substance of the issues was whether a state court could, by injunction, set distance limits on pro-life protesters intent on denying access to abortion clinics. The Court ruled that the sidewalks in front of the clinics were in the public forum.

Balancing the right of patients and employees to unimpeded access to the abortion clinic against the protesters' right to free speech, the Court upheld a buffer zone of about 36 feet around the clinic in Melbourne, Fla., that kept protesters away from the entrance and parking lot and off a public right-of-way. (Greenhouse 1994, p. A1).

This Supreme Court decision restricts the place of protest under the strictest principles of the public forum doctrine.

Operational Principles Governing Public Forum Access

The principles embodied in legal rulings governing public forum access are put into practice through governmental regulations, permit application forms that protest groups submit to authorities before their protests, manuals that are written to guide the behavior of government functionaries, and the actual behaviors of those functionaries, all of which may influence the behavior of both protesters and authorities.

Publicly available documents typically announce the most basic principles governing protest in the public forum. Usually authorities provide copies of these documents to prospective protesters who make application for demonstration permits. The principles include (1) commitment to the rights of citizen protest; (2) commitment to content neutrality; (3) time, place, and manner restrictions; and (4) advance permit requirements.

The Rights of Protesters

The common public commitment of authorities to these rights is reflected in the 1989 statement published in the journal of the International Association of Chiefs of Police (IACP):

> [The police] are . . . the first line of defense for the First Amendment rights to assemble peacefully and speak freely. Few unpopular ideas would ever get a public hearing unless the police were on hand to ensure the speaker's safety and maintain order. . . . The recognition of the police role as guardians of civil liberties and civil rights is one of the welcome fruits of the professionalization of law enforcement over the last several decades. The IACP gave that recognition tangible form in 1989 by establishing a committee on civil rights, and held its first workshop on the subject [in 1991]. (Burden 1992, p. 16)

Content Neutrality Guarantee

This principle guarantees the same rights to protesters regardless of the content of their dissent. The public commitment to content neutrality in the message of protesters, common in such statements, was stated as early as 1959 in the National Park Service (NPS) regulations:

> In passing upon requests for permits to speak or meet in such park areas, it is expected that the Superintendent will adhere to established departmental policy to exclude absolutely from his consideration any agreement or disagreement with the political or economic views of the proposed speaker. (U.S. Government Printing Office 1959, p. 9963)

Time, Place, and Manner Restrictions

One of the most elaborate sets of regulations specifying these restrictions is embodied in the 1993 NPS regulations. The following excerpts clearly illustrate how time, place, and manner restrictions are translated into specific rules. First, regarding time:

> (v) The Regional Director may restrict demonstrations and special events weekdays (except holidays) between the hours of 7:00 to 9:30 A.M. and 4:00 to 6:30 P.M. if it reasonably appears necessary to avoid unreasonable interference with rush-hour traffic. (U.S. Government Printing Office 1993, p. 126)

Regarding restrictions on place:

> (I) *White House area.* No permit may be issued authorizing demonstrations in the White House area, except for the White House sidewalk, Lafayette Park and the Ellipse.

With regard to manner, particularly structures, signs, and sounds, the regulations were formulated through a long series of negotiations with affected parties. They state:

> The following are prohibited in Lafayette Park:
>   (A) The erection, placement or use of structures of any kind except for the following: (1) Structures that are being hand-carried are allowed. (2) When one hundred (100) or more persons are participating in a demonstration in the Park, a temporary speakers' platform as is reasonably required to serve the demonstration participants is allowed [with certain restrictions as to size]. . . . (3) When less than one hundred (100) persons are participating in a demonstration in the park, a temporary "soapbox" speakers' platform is allowed [with certain restrictions]. . . . (4) For the purpose of this section, the term "structure" includes props and displays . . . ; furniture and furnishings . . . ; shelters . . . ; wagons and carts; and all other similar types of property which might tend to harm park resources, including aesthetic interests.

Advance Permit Requirements

The NPS regulations explicitly state as do most municipal jurisdictions around the United States, the requirement of advance permitting for large demonstrations:

(2) Permit Requirements. Demonstrations and special events may be held only pursuant to a permit issued in accordance with this section except:

(I) Demonstrations involving 25 persons or fewer may be held without a permit *provided* that the other conditions required for the issuance of a permit are met and *provided further* that the group is not merely an extension of another group's availing itself of the 25-person maximum under this provision or will not unreasonably interfere with other demonstrations of special events. . . .

(3) *Permit applications* . . . Applicants shall submit permit applications in writing on a form provided by the National Park Service so as to be received by the regional Director at least 48 hours in advance of any proposed demonstration or special event. This 48-hour period will be waived by the Regional Director if the size and nature of the activity will not reasonably require the commitment of park resources or personnel in excess of that which are normally available or which can reasonably be made available within the necessary time period. (p. 124)

During the 1996 Democratic National Convention, the Chicago authorities, relied on a permitting system and a set of rules governing the boundaries of protest very similar to those we have described in this section to channel the time, place, and manner of protest. These rules are embedded in larger systems of public order management.

Public Order Management Systems

By this concept (hereafter POMS), we refer to the more or less elaborated, more or less permanent organizational forms, their guiding policies and programs, technologies, and standard policing practices that are designed by authorities for supervising protesters' access to public space and managing them in that space. Our description of the basic principles of these systems draws heavily on our observation of authorities in Washington, D.C. It is also corroborated by extensive investigation of the operations of similar systems in other U.S. jurisdictions. These systems display three important principles in their operation: (1) negotiation between affected parties, (2) planning by authorities, and (3) the encouragement of planning on the part of protesters. The aims of these systems are to achieve as much predictability about a protest event in advance of its occurrence as possible and to create effective lines of communication between affected parties that can be used by authorities if an event fails to follow its agreed-on course.

Negotiations and Communication with Affected Parties

Once alerted to a prospective protest event, the typical management practice of authorities is to begin negotiations with the group or groups intending to protest, as well as with affected parties and counterdemonstrators if and when they become known. For large protests in Washington, D.C., over the last several decades, our evidence suggests that the larger the protest, the more meetings are held between the protest organizers and the authorities. The main concerns are negotiations of time, place, and manner of the proposed protests. In addition to march routes and rally areas, the placement of sanitary facilities, stages, and sound amplification equipment are also subject to negotiation. For instance, organizers of the massive 1993 gay and lesbian rights demonstration in Washington, D.C, were persuaded to locate several massive video screens throughout the rally site so that participants could see and hear without bunching near the stage as often occurs during large rallies (R. Robbins, personal communication, 1993). In heavily used public fora, like the Mall area in Washington, D.C., these negotiations can sometimes require adjudicating requests by more than one protesting group for the same space, or even adjoining spaces, for an event.

The New York City (NYC) Police Department recently went though a contentious set of negotiations over parade routes for rival gay and lesbian groups celebrating the twenty-fifth anniversary of the Stonewall Riot (McKinley 1994). This situation illustrates that one of the most fundamental issues in the negotiation process between police and demonstrators concerns rally sites and procession routes. Demonstrators may request sites and routes based on symbolic significance, ease of access, visibility and audibility to onlookers and passers–by, or some combination of these and related considerations. The police are concerned with the number of demonstrators proposed for those sites and routes by virtue of the implications for the disruption of routine traffic flow, the potential requirement for additional personnel (including overtime pay for off-duty personnel), and the implications for routine policing away from the demonstration of concentrating large numbers of police personnel in the demonstration location. The negotiation of these issues is no small matter between one group of demonstrators and the police; when there are competing groups of demonstrators, the problems escalate.

Stonewall 25, a coalition of international gay and lesbian rights advocacy groups, successfully negotiated with NYC officials for a permit to parade up First Avenue past the United Nations en route to a destination rally site in Central Park. A second set of local gay and lesbian rights advocacy groups sought a permit to march to Central Park by way of Fifth Avenue. They wanted to begin at Sheridan Square, near the base of Fifth Avenue and the symbolic Stonewall Tavern site where the 1969 homosexual rights revolution began. Furthermore, Fifth Avenue is the traditional and symbolic route of protest marches in New York City, and this route also passes St. Patrick's Cathedral, whose presiding cardinal has been a long-standing antagonist of local gays and lesbians. NYC officials allocated 4,000 police officers to the First Avenue route granted Stonewall 25; a second route would have required an additional 2,500 officers. On the one hand, two simultaneous routes would have paralyzed traffic, and the police payroll costs would have mounted into millions of dollars. On the other hand, the Gay and Lesbian Americans (GLA) coalition said it would march with or without a permit even if it resulted in a confrontation with the police, a development that neither NYC officials nor police wanted. The permit was not granted for the second route; officials urged motorists to avoid this section of New York City on the Sunday of the demonstration, and NYC police were charged with the responsibilities of managing the actual turnout of the GLA demonstrators. Fortunately for the police, the number of GLA demonstrators who actually pursued the alternate march route was sufficiently small that traffic was not blocked, a confrontation with the police was avoided, and the "rump demonstrators" met up with their brothers and sisters at the rally site in Central Park.

Communication and negotiations are not restricted to the officials and the demonstrators (and counterdemonstrators) alone but can include many other parties that might be affected by the proposed events. These can be targets of protest, other governmental agencies (including police), or commercial and other private groups. These communications range from the mere notification of intent to protest to negotiations about the roles and responsibilities of the other parties. For large demonstrations in Washington, D.C., during recent years, many other agencies are regularly notified about upcoming protest events. Our analysis of Washington, D.C., data shows that the larger the anticipated event, the more agencies are notified and brought into the negotiation process.

The notification and negotiation process is also evident in the preparations that were made by the local police in Wichita, Kansas, in the summer of 1991 for dealing with Operation Rescue, the pro-life group noted for its use of civil disobedience tactics in blocking access to abortion clinics. "Department representatives also talked with Wichita's own anti-abortion and pro-choice groups. In hopes of averting confrontations altogether, the police had secretly convinced the three abortion clinics to close for vacation" (Burden 1992, p. 19). This strategy did not prove effective: Operation Rescue simply waited for the clinics to open again. Nevertheless, the authorities' behavior illustrates the broad role that negotiation with contending parties can play in protest management.

The behavior of the Aurora, Colorado, local police in the face of a Ku Klux Klan march in 1991 similarly illustrates the notification/negotiation process. "During the month before the big day, police planners held innumerable meetings with the Klan leaders, counterdemonstration planners, the parks and recreation department, street department, other city officials and neighborhood and business groups" (Burden 1992, p. 17). Knowledge that the Klan draws vigorous counterprotests explains why these authorities cast their consultation net so widely. A similar situation was seen in the notorious incident of the march by American Nazi Party members through Skokie, Illinois, in the 1980s.

Planning by Authorities

Police agencies typically develop highly elaborate planning processes to guide their preparations for policing a protest event. For instance, the City of San Francisco crowd management manual first suggests dividing planning into three stages:

> Pre-event Planning: . . . If event sponsors do not come forward to obtain needed permits . . . the Event Coordinator will . . . attempt to locate them and set up meetings.
> [Within-event Planning:] during the event, the Event Coordinator will act as staff to the Event Commander.
> Post-Event Management: After an event, the Event Commander may schedule a formal critique meeting with members of all appropriate public and civilian entities involved in the event. . . . The critique meeting should consider both positive and negative aspects of the way the event was handled. (San Francisco Police Department 1989, pp. 8–10)

The manual goes on to list the steps to be followed in such planning:

A.   Evaluate the situation to be policed. . . .
B.   Meet with sponsors.
C.   Plan Command Post(s).
D.   Plan for Perimeter Management.
E.   Determine the number of officers needed to police the event.

F. Obtain Information.
G. Write a plan.
H. Formulate an enforcement policy and communicate it to affected Department units.
I. Consider possible scenarios which may occur and pre-think your responses and actions.
J. As time permits, conduct drills and exercises to test the operational plan. (p. 6)

The commitment to planning is seen clearly in the response of the City of Wichita Police Department when it was confronted with the reality of massive civil disobedience by Operation Rescue.

In June 1991, Operation Rescue announced plans for six days of protests to begin July 15 at Wichita's three clinics. That gave the police department six weeks to get ready, but there was a lot to do. "In our city and our department we have very little experience in dealing with crowds and crowd control situations or major demonstrations," Police Chief Rick Stone [said]. . . . "We immediately began the development of operational plans to make sure that we were as well prepared as possible for the protesters' entrance into our city and the possibility of violence."

As part of the planning process, the department conferred with other law enforcement agencies that had handled previous Operation Rescue demonstrations and checked with the organization's national office.

The three-inch-thick operational plan for what the department dubbed Operation Safe Protest described each officer's assignment every moment of the six days the demonstrations were to last. All officers were also given intensive training, including basic crowd control formations, as well as media control and relations. . . . As part of the training, officers were tested to see how they would react in stressful situations. . . . As the demonstrations dragged on through the summer, the training was reinforced every day at roll call. (Burden 1992, p. 20)

Encouraging Planning among Protesters

It is the standard practice of authorities to discuss, educate, and encourage protest groups' use of the institution of marshaling (see Mc-Phail 1985). The use of marshals is an almost universal practice in large U.S. protests. The organizers of such protests designate selected participants (the rule of thumb is one marshal for every fifty demonstrators) as marshals and invest them with responsibility to communicate organizers' intentions to the mass of protesters during the protest event. Marshaling is usually discussed during negotiations so that police may both assess the capacity of the group to manage itself and provide advice and assistance to strengthen this capacity, in effect encouraging the development of a command structure within the protest group.

This approach is evident in the current NPS regulations governing protests across the street from the White House in Washington, D.C., which conveys the authorities' view of the importance of marshals for internal group control among protest groups:

> (iii) No permit will be issued for a demonstration on the White House Sidewalk and in Lafayette Park at the same time except when the organization, group or other sponsor of such demonstration undertakes in good faith all reasonable action, including the provision of sufficient marshals, to insure good order and self-discipline in conducting such demonstration and any necessary movement of persons, so that the numerical limitations and waiver provisions . . . [are met]. [Applicants must furnish] ". . . at least ten days in advance of the proposed demonstration, the functions the marshals will perform, the means by which they will be identified, and their method of communication with each other and with the crowd." (U.S. Government Printing Office 1993, p. 126)

Experienced protest groups are well aware of the utility of creating marshaling structures and typically invest effort in training marshals and providing them with distinctive costumes—armbands, hats, or T-shirts—that will identify them to other protesters as well as to the police.

The Transformation of Protest Policing

Donatella della Porta (1995) has insightfully suggested that we cannot understand protest repertoires and their evolution without understanding the interaction between protesters and the police. There had been significant changes in U.S. police-protester interaction over the past four decades. Elsewhere (McPhail, Schweingruber, and McCarthy, 1997) we have developed a systematic picture of these changes from an extensive review of police literature that reports perspectives, policies, training programs, and problem-solving procedures developed by municipal, state, and federal policing agencies. These changes are embedded in the context of the trends we have described earlier and constitute the other central feature of POMS.

We contrast U.S. protest policing practices in the 1960s, characterized as "escalated force" (typified by the behavior of the Chicago police during the 1968 Democratic National Convention), with those of the present period, characterized as "negotiated management" (typified by the behavior of the Chicago police during the 1996 Democratic National Convention).[4] From our investigations of protest policing over the past four decades, we have identified five key characteristics of policing practices along which changes have occurred. We refer to them as dimensions of protest policing because each is a continuum along which the policing practices of any particular policy agency regarding any particular demonstration can be placed. These dimensions are (1) the extent of police concerns with the First Amendment rights of protesters and police obligations to respect and protect those rights, (2) the extent of police toleration for community disruption, (3) the nature of communication between police and demonstrators, (4) the extent and manner of arrests as a method of managing demonstrators, and (5) the extent and manner of using force in lieu of or in conjunction with arrests to control demonstrators. For each of the five dimensions, we will describe police practices under both styles of protest policing.

First Amendment Rights

In escalated force–style policing, First Amendment rights were either ignored or disregarded as mere "cover" for demonstrators. The right to protest was denied, and permits were not issued. Under the negotiated management style of policing, the protection of First Amendment rights is a primary goal of the police, equal in importance to protecting property or lives (Burden 1992; Sardino 1985). Even the most provocative speakers are permitted and protected as the courts have ruled that the threat of counterdemonstrator violence is not a legal reason for withholding a permit (*King Movement Coalition v. Chicago* 1976).

Tolerance for Community Disruption

Under escalated force policing, only familiar and "comfortable" forms of political protest were tolerated, those police described as "peaceful rallies" and "polite picketing." Police showed no willingness to tolerate the disruption caused by civil rights (and subsequently antiwar) demonstrations, involving unfamiliar forms of protest, disruptive tactics, violation of social norms, and often illegal (although usually peaceful) activities. Even the disruption of normal traffic patterns was often seen as unacceptable, and civil disobedience was equated with anarchy (LeGrande 1967; Whittaker 1964, 1966). Under negotiated management policing, an "acceptable level of disruption" is seen by police as an inevitable byproduct of demonstrator efforts to produce social change. Police do not try to prevent demonstrations but attempt to limit the amount of disruption they cause. They recognize that large demonstrations almost invariably involve disruptions of traffic patterns and other normal routines in the community. Police attempt to steer demonstrations to times and places that minimize disruption, a limitation allowed by public forum law. Even civil disobedience, illegal by definition, is not usually problematic for police; they often cooperate with protesters when their civil disobedience is intentionally symbolic. Such cooperation even extends to prenegotiated mass arrests, such as those that occurred at the U.S. Capitol rotunda during an antiballistic missile protest in 1983. The new police goals of protecting First Amendment rights while keeping disruption to acceptable levels required changes in protest policing tactics, which we take up in our examination of the final three dimensions.

Typical of the tolerance of disruption characteristic of negotiated management policing style was the reaction to the recent traffic blockade by "Justice for Janitors" in San Francisco.

> After a brief rally, the crowd took up banners and red and black picket signs, broke off into four large contingents, then marched off in different directions, blowing whistles and chanting. At several key intersections, the groups sat down, blocking traffic. Police twice ordered the crowds to disperse, declaring the protests "unlawful assemblies," but the police were heavily outnumbered and no action was taken and no arrests were made. Eventually, the demonstrators got up and moved on. (Carlsen 1996, p. A14)

Communication

Communication between police and demonstrators was minimal under escalated force policing. The principal exception was undercover police infiltration of demonstrator groups to secure information with which to thwart the demonstration efforts or to act as *agents provocateurs* to entrap demonstration members (Marx 1974). Police did not confer, let alone negotiate, with demonstration organizers before or during the demonstration. This lack of communication often caused misunderstandings, which inconvenienced both demonstrators and police, and which could result in the use of force as police attempted to enforce their interpretation of demonstration requirements (Stark 1972). Police did not cede any control of the demonstration to the demonstrators themselves.

Police using negotiated management believe communication with demonstrators is necessary if the former are to successfully protect the First Amendment rights of the latter and keep disruption to an acceptable level (Kleinknecht and Mizell 1982; Sandora and Petersen 1980). Extensive interaction between demonstrators and police is part of the permit application, negotiation, granting, and protection process. Applicants are informed of time, place, and manner restrictions, and any conflicts over these restrictions are negotiated. Even civil disobedience arrests may be planned by police and demonstrators (Brothers 1985; Sandora and Petersen 1980). Police also help organizers prepare for demonstrations by consulting with them regarding transportation, rest room facilities, first aid, and so forth. Finally, we have already noted the requirement that demonstrators must have trained marshals who understand demonstrator goals, police responsibilities, and the negotiated plans and procedures. This facilitates knowledgeable internal control of demonstrations by demonstration marshals instead of external control by police.

Extent and Manner of Arrests

Under escalated force policing, arrests quickly followed any violation of the law and sometimes occurred where no law had been broken. Arrests were forceful and used strategically by police to target and remove "agitators." The main exception to the rule of immediate arrest was when police used physical punishment in lieu of arrests (Stark 1972). Under negotiated management policing (Chandler 1986; Sardino 1985), arrests are used only as a last resort, then selectively, and only against lawbreakers. Participants in nonviolent civil disobedience are informed that they are breaking the law (often by trespassing) and given every opportunity to desist (Brothers 1985). Arrests deemed necessary are carried out in an orderly manner, with proper documentation, and are designed to avoid injuring the demonstrators. To promote orderly arrests, efficient booking processes, and quick releases from jail, police often negotiate arrest procedures with organizers before the demonstration. Police provide prearrest forms and request estimates of how many arrestees there will be and whether they will actively or passively resist arrest.

Extent and Manner of Using Force

Escalated force protest policing was characterized by the use of force as a standard way of dealing with demonstrations. Police confronted demonstrators with a dramatic show of force and followed with a progressively escalated use of force if demonstrators failed to abide by police instructions to limit or stop their activities (e.g., Applegate 1969; Momboisse 1967). Police used riot control techniques such as tear gas, batons, fire hoses, electric cattle prods, riot formations, and dogs. Police frequently used force in lieu of arrests. Under negotiated management policing, only the minimum necessary force is used to carry out police obligations to protect persons or property and to arrest law-breakers (Chandler 1986; International Association of Chiefs of Police 1992). Police attempt to avoid the need to use force by cordoning off the demonstration area, especially if counterdemonstrators are present, and through prior negotiations with demonstrators (Burden 1992; Gruber 1990).

The Channeling of Protest Groups

Thus far we have focused our attention almost exclusively on the behavior of authorities in our attempt to account for the institutionalizations of protest in the United States. We have good reasons, however, for believing that the process has also been facilitated by the changing social organization of protest itself. We focus on three general trends in the social organization of dissenting groups in an attempt to show some reasons that they are increasingly likely to be as committed to predictable and orderly protest events as are the authorities. These are the (1) trend toward the professionalization of SMOs, (2) the expanding likelihood that SMOs have formally registered with the state, and (3) the increasing involvement in public protest by legitimate, mainstream groups.

A widely recognized trend among U.S. dissent groups has been to become professionalized (McCarthy and Zald 1973; Walker 1991; Lofland 1996). Such groups increasingly employ full-time managers rather than depending on volunteer leaders. Such employment entangles groups with the state through its tax withholding and employment practices requirements, among other laws. Thus, most groups that financially compensate their full-time leaders are formally incorporated as nonprofit groups at both the state and federal levels. This practice almost invariably indicates that such groups have created formal boards of directors composed of people who, thereby, bear some responsibility for the organization's actions. Some have suggested (e.g., Piven and Cloward 1979) that this process inhibits the use of unruly protest. However, it does not necessarily inhibit the use of protest itself, as shown by Cress's (1996) study of homeless groups across the United States. Minkoff's (1996) analyses of U.S. women's and racial/ethnic groups during the last several decades show that the likelihood of protest by a social movement is increased by the extent to which it spawns formally organized and professionalized groups. We know that most large Washington, D.C., protests are organized by highly professionalized groups. When protests are fielded by such organizations, their leaders will have a strong stake in guaranteeing the orderliness of protest events because they, and the many people with whom they bear responsibility, will suffer secondary consequences of serious public disorder if they can be shown to have been liable for it. We also know that in recent years almost all protests in Washington, D.C. (McCarthy et al. 1996), are rallies, marches, pickets, vigils, or literature distributions. The latter three forms (which constitute the majority of protest demonstrations) are typically employed by very small groups, and almost none of these involve civil disobedience on the part of protesters or any kind of violent confrontation between police and protesters.

Many smaller SMOs, especially in local communities, depend on volunteer leaders but have nevertheless chosen to become formally registered with the state as nonprofit organizations because such registration allows these groups to use the U.S. mail system at substantially reduced costs for communicating with their members and adherents. In addition, such registration guarantees that those who provide financial support for such groups may receive tax benefits for doing so. These mechanisms lead many such groups to formal registration and the creation of governing boards similar in form to the highly professionalized SMOs, with similar consequences for their leaders' commitment to ruly versus unruly protest (McCarthy, Britt, and Wolfson 1991).

Finally, protest events are increasingly likely to include sponsors whom few observers would call marginal or dissident. This pattern suggests that public protest has become a more legitimate political tool, one that even the most hidebound traditional groups may choose to deploy when they calculate that it has positive potential benefits. These groups (e.g., the National Organization for Women, the March of Life Committee, the AFL-CIO), of course, can be expected to have the greatest stake in the predictability of protest events of which they are sponsors or cosponsors. All of these mechanisms suggest that protesting groups are more likely now than in the past to have reasons for agreeing to follow the rules established by POMS, which in turn increases the likelihood that their protest event will be enacted with some predictability.

This does not mean, however, that all protest groups have abandoned the use of more confrontational tactics. A number of movement organizations have specialized in the use of civil disobedience tactics throughout the 1990s. Four such groups were very active between 1991 and 1995: ACT-UP, Queer Nation, Operation Rescue, and the Justice for Janitors campaign of the Service Employees International Union (SEIU). Each of these groups has regularly chosen civil disobedience as a tactic and thereby violated the *concordat* that had been achieved between most protest groups and authorities. By its actions, each created the likelihood of a physical confrontation with police. Many of these protests violated certain features of the POMS, usually by a failure to provide advance notification of when and where protest would occur as well as the manner of the protest. The outcome of encounters between these groups and police provide a portrait of negotiated management style policing even in the face of noncooperation on the part of protest groups.

We gathered extensive newspaper reports of confrontations between these groups and police for the years 1990 to 1995 inclusive with a NEXIS search.[5] Table 4.1 displays the results of our summary of these protest events. Most of the reported protest events involving these four groups can be classified as civil disobedience. ACT-UP protesters employed a wide array of flamboyant and provocative forms of civil disobedience during the early 1990s. These included initiating traffic blockades on public streets and private thoroughfares; protesters chaining themselves to the buildings of targets on private property, to the furniture of targets within pubic (e.g., Center for Disease Control in Atlanta) and private buildings (e.g., dressed as Santas at a Macy's Department store in New York), and to the White House fence; disrupting network television broadcasts (e.g., *Saturday Night Live, Good Morning America, NBC Nightly News*) and public meetings (e.g., pro-life rallies, antigay organizations, churches, and cemeteries); sitting in and/or occupying legislators' offices, legislative chambers, and the

TABLE 4.1

Features of Police-Demonstrator Interactions in U.S. Civil Disobedience Protest Events for Four U.S. Social Movement Organizations, 1991–1995

	Social Movement Organization			
Confrontation Features	*Queer Nation*	*ACT-UP*	*Justice for Janitors*	*Operation Rescue*
Civil disobedience* (%)	71	74	93	99
Police present (%)	96	100	100	100
Events with arrests (%)	50	77	73	99
Arrests* per event	8.5	16.0	33.4	58.8
Total number of arrests	102	862	401	5,996
Police force†	4	20	13	5
Total Events	(24)	(70)	(16)	(103)

*For those events with arrests.
†Coded present if there was any hint of use of force by police in confronting and/or arresting them (including reports of resisting arrest) in original report of protest or thereafter in other press reports.

U.S. Capitol (where thousands of blood-stained pennies were scattered); setting off stink bombs in the U.S. Congress underground subways; illegally distributing hypodermic needles to drug addicts in many cities; and even covering Senator Jesse Helms's house with a giant replica of a condom. Queer Nation protesters used many of the same tactics, but they could be characterized as employing a softer mix that included fewer acts of civil disobedience, such as their many "kiss-ins." Justice for Janitors groups used traffic blockades almost exclusively, and Operation Rescue groups mostly used their signature clinic blockade tactic.

Police were reported as having been present at most of the protests, and except for Queer Nation events, arrests were reported at the vast majority of events. For each group except Operation Rescue, a number of protest events included reports of civil disobedience that did not result in the arrest of protesters. We referred to a Justice for Janitors traffic blockade earlier, for example, that saw the police wait for the civilly disobedient protesters to disperse rather than arrest them. Most relevant to our present purpose, however, is the incidence of reported use of force by police. We used a very inclusive criterion for such reports that included any newspaper's direct mention of the use of police force or of a protest group's report of the use of police force (including follow-up stories after the protest event) as well as any reports of protesters resisting arrest. The most striking feature in these data is how rarely any report of the use of police force is made. It is most frequently reported for ACT-UP protests, although police force was more likely to have been reported early in the cycle of ACT-UP protests. In the three cities where much of that protest was located (Los Angeles, New York, and Philadelphia), an early incident of the use of police force resulted in a local court requiring the city to pay large financial damage settlements to protesters who were the object of that force. Some of the decline in the use of excessive force over the ACT-UP cycle, then, can be attributed to increasing police restraint that followed court sanctions.

These newspaper reports thus show that the four groups engaged in extensive confrontational protest over a five-year period, resulting in many arrests. However, these arrests, typical of negotiated management police practices, usually were carried out in very orderly ways. The orderliness of the arrest procedures appears to result from the typical police protest management repertoire we have described earlier, but also from a pervasive passive resistance on the part of demonstrators, the exception being a minority of protestors at the ACT-UP events. This observation suggests that even the most disorderly protesting groups now choose to conclude their attention-getting disorderliness with ritually enacted arrests.[6] This pattern, too, supports our contention that dissenting groups increasingly choose to interact with authorities in more highly predictable ways than was common during the 1960s cycle of protest.

POMS Diffusion and Adoption within a Population of Police Organizations

Public order management systems are institutionalized solutions to the recurring problem of protests that threaten the domestic tranquility that the police are responsible to maintain. The 1960s cycle of protests and urban disturbances, illustrated by the 1968 Democratic Convention protests, created serious problems for many U.S. police agencies. When a POMS is developed or adopted by any one police organization, it can be seen as a rational bureaucratic solution to a recurring problem. Within such a organization, routinized solutions are regularly tested and often must be modified or adjusted to deal with subtle or substantial variations in the problems for which those solutions were initially devised. Purposive actors within such an organization engage in rational problem identification analysis and solution development to modify existing solutions or to identify and adapt new solutions.

However, when most organizations within a population of similar organizations adopt a very similar solution to the same problem, we are led to believe other influences may be at work. This appears to be the case in the population of U.S. police organizations. During the past four decades, the vast majority of these organizations adopted some version of the POMS we have described. It is precisely this phenomenon of similarity in institutionalized solutions, "institutional isomorphism," which has captured the imagination of students of formal organizations and spawned the "new institutionalist" perspective (Powell and DiMaggio 1991).

DiMaggio and Powell (1983) argue that similarities in organizational adoption of routinized solutions are a function of one or more processes that are to a greater or lesser extent external to the organization: coercive constraints on the organization, normative constraints on the organization, and mimetic processes when the organization adopts solutions of external exemplars. All three of these sources of institutional isomorphism are illustrated in the development, diffusion, and adoption of POMS within the population of police organizations in the United States. We will briefly discuss each of the three, but first we must summarize several additional factors that we have ignored here that were important in the diffusion of the POMS.[7]

The widely noted breeches of domestic tranquility that occurred during the late 1960s and early 1970s led to the constitution of several presidential commissions, each of which resulted in criticism of police practices and recommendations aimed at changing them. During the same period, protesters also brought many legal challenges to police behavior, many of which led to decisions in federal district courts and the U.S. Supreme Court that established the broad outlines of the current First Amendment protections of protest and the public forum doctrine we discussed earlier. It was in this climate that the U.S. Army Police School began developing courses in public order management that in its final form incorporated most of the principles of negotiated management policing. More than ten thousand police officers from civilian jurisdictions all over the country went through the training, which was subsidized with federal resources through the Law Enforcement Assistance Act. Figure 4.1 displays, on the left-hand side, our conception of the causal influences of these three factors in contributing to the creation and diffusion of the standard POMS repertoire. Direct influences are noted by solid lines and indirect influences by broken lines. The right-hand side of the figure displays the three factors that we have emphasized in this chapter as responsible for POMS creation and diffusion. We place our discussion of the patterns displayed in Figure 4.1 within the framework of general sources of institutional isomorphism.

If a population of organizations is arranged hierarchically with centralized authority at the top, this authority can be used to direct the adoption of changes. These directions can result in widespread, if not uniform, adoption throughout the hierarchy. Populations of military and paramilitary organizations are classic examples. It was in this manner that POMS were introduced and rather extensively diffused and adopted by police organizations throughout the British colonial empire (McCarthy, et al., forthcoming). Contemporary parallels exist in the nationalized police systems of France and Japan.

The United States, however, has a highly decentralized policing system. Nevertheless, its many police organizations are also subject to various constraints. The foremost example of this process has been the consequences of the development of First Amendment and public forum law by the Supreme Court. Since the U.S. Constitution, as interpreted by the Supreme Court, is the highest law in the land, police organizations were constrained to adopt and enforce those constitutional principles it enunciated. The consequences of this process can be seen in the standard protest permit procedures across U.S. police

FIGURE 4.1. Some Direct and Indirect Factors in the Development of U.S. Public Order Management Systems

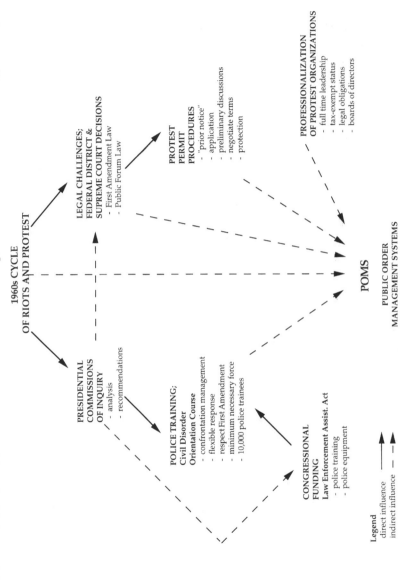

jurisdictions. Moreover, the Law Enforcement Assistance Act, passed by the U.S. Congress following the riots and demonstrations of the 1960s and 1970s, and the recommendations of the presidential commissions of inquiry for police reform together created incentives to adopt the emergent POMS. Whether local and state police agencies qualified for and received financial assistance for the purchase of communications equipment, firearms, and other hardware was made in part contingent on making their policing policies and practices consistent with commission recommendations.

There are other circumstances in which populations of organizations are subject to normative constraints to which they voluntarily adapt. For police organizations, such norms include recommendations for change that have the support of public opinion and new standards advocated by professional associations to which police officers and organizations belong. What is involved in each case is that new standards for policy and practice are advocated by external agencies, but they must be adopted voluntarily by individual police agencies. In the U.S. case, police organizations adopted recommendations from the three commissions of inquiry, which were made up of distinguished and respected senior members of the law enforcement community appointed by the president. Furthermore, these recommendations carried with them the weight of favorable public opinion. In turn, national and international associations of law enforcement officers (e.g., the IACP) endorsed the recommendations of these commissions of inquiry and advocated their adoption and implementation by their members and their members' organizations. These norms were incorporated into the U.S. Army Police School's public order training courses and thereby indirectly influenced local police practices.

Individuals acting alone, as rank-and-file members or as executive decision makers in organizations, learn from the consequences of their own actions as well as from observing the actions and consequences of others' actions. Thus, in the attempt to solve problems with which an organization is confronted, various members of the organization are looking at and listening to the actions and consequences of other organizations confronting similar problems. This is akin to Walker's (1969, p. 889) analysis of state officials observing and learning from other states in the course of formulating or modifying their own structures, policies, and procedures:

> The rule of thumb they employ might be formally stated as follows: look for an analogy between the situation you are dealing with and some other situations, perhaps in some other state, where the problem has been successfully resolved.

But police organizations do not observe and adopt new practices from other police organizations at random. They are more likely to adopt from organizations to which they are already connected through memberships in professional associations, organizations in geographic proximity with which they have established working relationships (e.g., mutual assistance pacts, shared communication systems), distant organizations that are similar in size and resources, organizations in communities with comparable public order environments, or organizations that have developed successful solutions to problems similar to those faced by the adopting organization. The IACP has played an important part in providing communication channels among local police jurisdictions seeking to elaborate their local POMS in response to unusually heightened levels of protest (Burden 1992).

Conclusion

The rights of protesters are now more broadly protected in the United States, but these protections have been institutionalized along with broad powers granted to authorities to restrict the time, place, and manner of protest. Protest now takes place in a highly elaborated institutional arena, for both protesters *and* authorities, that prescribes their behavior. The police can be expected to try to accommodate their practices to the plans of protest groups, to negotiate with them about those plans, and to be restrained in their use of force even in the face of provocation by protesters. On the other hand, protest groups can be expected to be cooperative in negotiating the details of their protests and nonviolent in their confrontations with police, even when their protests involve civil disobedience. As a result, the vast bulk of protest today is more orderly and routinized than in the past. What are the implications of those changes for the role of protest?

Protest has long been perceived as "politics by other means," a social form that provides the less powerful an alternative way of influencing public decisions. Its power is seen as deriving, importantly, from its ability to disrupt normal routines, which thereby requires authorities to attend to protesters' demands. From such a view, the institutionalization process we have described banalizes protest by making it routine and unremarkable—now just another way of influencing public decisions and one that is widely used by all social groups. On the other hand, the highly institutionalized nature of the protest arena can be seen, alternatively, as offering wider opportunities for disruption for those protesters inclined to disrupt.[8] When a group refuses to seek a protest permit and/or to negotiate the details of the time, place, and manner of a protest, it engages in disruptive behavior that is more likely to call attention to its protest than if it had quietly abided by the institutional rules we have depicted.

POMS serve to channel protest in several ways beyond its disruptiveness. The channeling of place occurs at two distinct levels. Within the management systems themselves, some locations in the public forum are off-limits to protesters, but this is a comparatively inconsequential restriction of protest. In contrast, the consequences of the tiered system of fora that we have described represent a far more consequential channeling of the place of protest. As fewer and fewer citizens spend time in "traditional" public places, like town squares, and more and more time in "modern" public places, like shopping malls, sports stadia, and airports, the effective availability of face-to-face public audiences for protesters is narrowed, since they have been excluded from the public fora. Restrictions on dissident speech are both potentially and actually greater in those places. This broader channeling of protest location has the consequence of increasing protesters' dependence on communication media for conveying their dissent to the "public," since protesters have less and less access to large numbers of people in public places. Our research in Washington, D.C. (McCarthy et al. 1996), shows that the media are more likely to cover larger protests and those protesters whose claims are of interest primarily to the media itself. These indirect and interacting but subtle consequences of the channeling of public protest may, in fact, have even more serious implications for the broad social impact of protest than its increasing orderliness.

Nevertheless, the consequences of the institutionalization of protest are not all gloomy. Much of the motivation behind the efforts to institutionalize the protest arena stem from a common aim to reduce the extent of "unintended violence" between authorities and protesters. Most authorities prefer less violence since its occurrence is problematic for them from the level of police on the line to those with ultimate authority.[9] Protesters prefer not to be the recipients of violence and therefore have a stake in a system that reduces its likelihood. By this criterion, the institutionalization process we have described appears to have been successful. Unintended violent confrontation between protesters and authorities appears to have declined dramatically under this system as protest has been incorporated as a normal part of the political process.

Notes

1. Wagman (1991) and Gora et al. (1991) provide useful summaries of the "Public Forum" doctrine.

2. For example, U.S. Park Police, whose responsibility includes the majority of Washington, D.C., protests, have sought what are, from their perspective, legitimate and necessary restrictions on protesters to protect both park space and natural resources as well as the usage rights of the majority of park visitors (Robbins, n.d.). Those regulations have been challenged through the courts, where decisions are made about what constitutes legitimate speech. Park Service officials complain that the courts "should not attempt to administer the parks themselves," and U.S. Park Police should be granted the authority to make decisions in "good faith" without having their decisions constantly challenged. This tension accompanied the system's emergence and remains today.

3. The Jehovah's Witnesses served the same role by their aggressive public proselytizing during the 1940s and 1950s (see Walker 1991, pp. 107–8).

4. The key features of this system imply that "on the ground" policing of protest has evolved to a point where, by della Porta's (1996a, p. 6) criteria, it is now tolerant, diffuse, reactive, soft, and lawful.

5. For ACT-UP, Queer Nation, and Justice for Janitors, we searched the entire NEXIS newspaper database for stories that mentioned the group's name and any indication of a public protest. For Operation Rescue, we limited our search to the *New York Times* only. We make no claim that this sample of protest events is representative of those that occurred during the period across the United States that were covered by newspapers. We read each story, identified discrete events, and then coded each protest event along a set of dimensions, displayed in Table 4.1.

6. The processes of institutionalization of protests we have described here refer to public, collective protest rather than clandestine individual acts of protests that are certainly not governed by the same processes. We are well aware of the extensive property destruction and violence toward individual operators and employees of abortion clinics that have accompanied the intense conflict over abortion in the United States during this same period. The National Abortion Federation reports 5 murders, 17 attempted murders, and 196 death threats for the 1990–1995 period, in addition to 58 incidents of arson and 372 of vandalism over the same period (National Abortion Federation 1997). The leading pro-life SMOs have disavowed these acts, and perpetrators who have been apprehended have mostly been unassociated with organized groups. Consequently, the likelihood of the occurrence of these events cannot be expected to be shaped by the processes we describe in this chapter.

7. We discuss the 1960s cycle of protest and urban disturbances and these additional factors in systematic detail elsewhere (McPhail, et al., 1997).

8. We thank our colleague, John Lofland, for this insight.

9. Waddington's (1994) analysis of protest policing in contemporary London illustrates striking similarities between U.S. and British POMS on this point and others.

5

Policing Protest in France and Italy: From Intimidation to Cooperation?

Donatella della Porta, Olivier Fillieule, and Herbert Reiter

One important aspect of state response to protest is the policing of protest, which we define as the police management of protest events. This response affects protest activists, both symbolically and practically. Because "police may be conceived as 'street-level bureaucrats' who 'represent' government to people" (Lipsky 1980, p. 1), police intervention influences protesters' perceptions of the state reaction to them (della Porta 1995). Waves of protest, in turn, have important effects on the police; protest policing seems, in fact, to be a key issue for police reorganization as well as for the professional self-definition of the police (Morgan 1987; Winter 1997).

Recent research suggests that since the 1960s important shifts have occurred in the mix of different strategies to control public order. In particular, the cycle of protest that developed in Europe and the United States in the second half of the 1960s has produced long-lasting effects on the policing of protest, which is now characterized by growing tolerance for minor violations of the law, large-scale collection of information, and increasing interest in bargaining and negotiations between police and protestors (della Porta and Reiter 1996, 1997a). In what follows, we will analyze some of these developments in two countries, France and Italy, whose police forces have similar historical and institutional characteristics.

The social science literature has always emphasized the presence of different state strategies to deal with opponents. Research on state building and democracy indicates that states with an equilibrium of power among different social classes, new nation-states, and small states facing a strong competition in the international markets developed integrative styles of protest policing, whereas other kinds of states tended to be exclusive (see, e.g., Marks 1996; Kriesi et al. 1995). As far as traditional police styles are concerned, the "civilized" British "bobby"—unarmed, integrated into the community, and essentially autonomous from the political power—has been contrasted with the militarized continental police, living in barracks and dependent on political authorities. By the nineteenth century, the London Metropolitan Police was regarded by the liberal press on the continent as an example of what a police force should be like (Katscher 1878). However, as Robert Reiner (1997) shows, "the British police model was not a reflection of some natural, built-in harmony or order in British society and culture"; on the contrary, "a low-profile, legalistic, minimal force strategy was encouraged because of, not despite, the bitter political protests and acute social divisions of early nineteenth century Britain.

In Europe, the countermodel to this "community policing" was constituted by the French tradition of a "King's police"—that is, a state police under the strict control of the central government, with a very wide range of tasks. The French example served as a model for the police forces in other European countries with centralized administrations, Italy among them. In Britain, during the debates about the institution of the London Metropolitan Police, French police practice was used as a countermodel to warn against the antiliberal aspects of this type of law enforcement (Bunyan 1977, p. 63). Myths aside, there seem to be visible differences between the record of the English police in protest policing the "old" challengers—progressive and labor movements—and the record of continental police forces. On the continent the police seemed to defend not only a general system of power but the interests of a particular government. The protest policing styles that dominated on the continent were more "brutal," more repressive, more confrontational, and more rigid than those of England.[1]

Significant differences developed within the framework of the continental police systems, both over time and between countries. Latin police styles, based on the unconstrained use of force, can be distinguished from the Central European style, characterized by respect for the *Rechtsstaat*. Even between the two Latin countries, France and Italy, which can be classified as the "most similar cases" on the European continent, a closer look at the history of their police forces shows important long-term differences. In the last decades of the nineteenth century, the indiscriminate use of the army to protect internal security came under increasing attack in both countries, and a modernized and professionalized police force evolved as the dominant agent to ensure the public order. In Italy, however, professionalization was far less pronounced than in France, and the intervention of the security forces against protesters remained highly selective, featuring, for instance, frequent deployment of the army to control peasant mobilizations in the south.

Of even more significance was the period between the two world wars. In France the police became increasingly familiar with demonstrations and, within the framework of the law, developed formal and informal rules about intervening in protests, combining strategies of intimidation with a search for cooperation that would allow them, in advance of a demonstration, to set clear limits of what they would accept. In Italy the possibility of such a development was cut short by the advent of fascism, with a far from negligible involvement of all the police forces in fascist violence.[2] The Italian police did not degenerate to the extent of their German counterparts, and they largely maintained their traditional police style.[3] Nevertheless, a very broad conception of "public order" and excessive powers of the police to intervene against protesters survived well into the postwar period (Corso 1979, p. 133 ff.).

Do these historically deep-rooted differences survive in contemporary policing? Or do recent developments in policing reflect a harmonization of the previous different models for policing? Did the social movements of the 1960s and their spin-offs produce a general trend towards a more "civilized" policing? In our analysis, we will try to answer these questions by comparing our two examples of "King's police" with research conducted in the Anglo-American world. In doing so, we will focus on one specific range of strategies of dealing with protest: persuasive strategies, defined as all attempts to manage protest by prior contacts with activists and organizers.[4]

Research in the Anglo-American countries reports the development of complicated procedures of negotiation, which in the United States found a significant expression in the development of a protest permit system (McCarthy, McPhail, and Schweingruber 1997). Looking at the London police, P. A. J. Waddington (1994, p. 69) observed, "The principal method of securing compliance was through negotiation with the organizer of the protest." Keeping in mind the traditional similarities and differences in the development of national police, we will examine whether similar developments occurred in our two Latin cases. In doing so, we will distinguish among different subtypes of the "persuasive" strategies: *intimidation,* based on the menace of an active use of police power in order to discourage protest; *minimal bargaining*—that is, the discussion of the logistics of a demonstration with organizers with very small room of maneuver; and *cooperation,* in which police officers and protest organizers collaborate in the development of a peaceful demonstration. In analyzing these substrategies, we will emphasize the types of resources available to the police, and police perceptions of the external reality that lead them to deployment of different protest policing styles.

In the final section, cross-national similarities and differences between the two Latin models of policing, as well as between them and the Anglo-American model, will be identified. As we will suggest, the developments in police strategies for the control of public order in these countries reveal a significant change in the way police view, and consequently handle, protest and protesters; these changes indicate the emergence of a new conception of the role of the police, the state, and the citizens and, ultimately, of democracy on the part of the police. For France and Italy, this means a move away from their traditional model of a "state police," concerned above all with the defense of constituted political power, toward a police model oriented more to the protection of the citizen and his or her rights, and therefore closer to the Anglo-American tradition.[5]

Persuasive Strategies in France

Historically, the maintenance of public order in France relied on a strategy of consistent intimidation to prevent all political gatherings (principally by the left) and including even demonstrations by unions and interest groups. At the same time, since before World War II, the authorities sought to combine this strategy of intimidation with a search for cooperation to set the limits of what the police would allow. It is only in the 1970s, however, that the strategies used by the French police changed from a coercive model to a cooperative one. We will show in this section how police procedures have gradually moved from a confrontational approach to one that is oriented more to negotiation and crisis management. These changes in police strategies coincided with the broadening of the spectrum of protest constituencies, with more and more people, from a wider spectrum of occupations and/or social classes, employing social protest as a mode of political expression (Fillieule 1997a).

The French law on demonstrations, passed in 1935, permits a strict application of what was then the dominant strategy of *intimidation*. It required organizers to declare their intention to protest at least three days before the proposed date of the event. This law in no way constitutes a right to protest but rather provides the authorities a legal basis to exert pressure before all protest events, either by imposing itineraries and dictating the modalities of the march when permission is given or by formally banning an event and heightening the risks to demonstrators.

After World War II, the culture of resistance colored political demonstrations up to 1953, sometimes in combination with a Cold War culture. On the one hand, the authorities reckoned they were able to allow demonstrations to take place; yet, on the other hand, when they considered that taking to the streets might constitute an attack on the regime, they did not hesitate to resort to a high level of violence. In these cases, one notes reliance on two strong persuasive tactics: (1) the preliminary control of the ground and (2) preventive arrests. At the announcement of any demonstration, the presumed demonstrators were systematically rounded up by the police as soon as they reached the location of the demonstration. They were subsequently held for some hours at police stations. At the location of the gathering, large numbers of police officers were concentrated to prevent all access, following the tradition started by prefect Louis Lépine at the beginning of the century.

During these years at the height of the Cold War, the power of the Communist Party and the trauma of the insurrectional strikes of 1947 meant that governments and the police always relied on the two tactics mentioned to control Communist demonstrations. Matters were made increasingly tense from the beginning of the 1950s with the development of virulent anticommunism within the Ministry of the Interior, which was staffed by former collaborators who had been rehabilitated by the authorities in the service of anticommunism. For example, the *préfet* Jean Baylot, then Maurice Papon, former Vichy officials, reorganized the services of the Prefecture of Police in Paris by reintegrating police officers who had been dismissed at the Liberation. The very violent Communist protest against General Ridgeway's visit to Paris on May 28, 1952, illustrates perfectly this application of strategies of intimidation by means of seeking violent confrontation, as much on the police side as that of the demonstrators. On the occasion of this protest, the prefecture's instructions to the police on the ground revealed a logic of "getting even" in the name of a militant anticommunism.[6]

After July 1953, however, protests increasingly involved interest groups such as peasants, tradesmen, and the worker's unions. Protests related more to the social strains of the economy than to large-scale political struggles, and this situation is reflected in public order maintenance. It was at this time that a system of *minimal negotiation* was put in place, with protesters declaring their intentions to the prefecture and the police announcing their intentions, such as imposing itineraries, banning particular locations, and mandating a dispersal time. This slow evolution from a strategy of intimidation into a strategy of minimal negotiation was delayed by a large number of political demonstrations initiated by the Communist Party and the emergence of protests over decolonization, notably over the war in Algeria. Protests linked to decolonization were subject to extremely severe treatment (e.g., on October 17, 1961, more than two hundred people were killed in Paris).

The movement of May 1968, by its scale and, above all, by the entry on the protest scene of students, contributed to a modification of the rules of the game. Faced with the political risks of repressing French youth, the authorities and the police chose to reduce their recourse to coercion as much as possible. Since then, protests by interest groups are always subject to minimal negotiation—indeed, the beginnings of cooperation—especially when they involve union demonstrations of categories of workers touched by economic crisis (steel workers, miners, shipbuilders) or farmers. This point can be understood if one considers that the large majority of police officers charged with maintaining public order in the 1960s and 1970s came from the working class or the countryside. From 1968 to 1974, under the rule of Minister of the Interior Raymond Marcellin, threats and intimidation remained prominent police strategies, particularly for political protests by left-wingers (Fillieule 1997a). Relying on a restrictive interpretation of the provisions of the law of 1935, the prefects had at their disposal the means to ban all street protest likely to disturb public order, controlling locations of preliminary meetings and making preventive arrests of protesters. For all that, throughout the 1950s and the 1960s, the relations between police and peaceful demonstrators were marked by a certain degree of cooperation. The police sought to impose in advance their advice on the demonstrators, who in turn sought contact with the authorities to make sure that the event took place unhindered. The practice of prior declaration was in this way a means, albeit minimal, for the protagonists to get to know one another.

It was only later in the 1970s that those in charge of the police systematically sought to encourage *cooperation* with protest organizers, as much prior to events as during the demonstration itself. Soon the legal provisions allowing the banning of demonstrations were no longer applied, the authorities preferring procedures of informal negotiation. Since the end of the 1970s, the practice of banning demonstrations has become rare. Technical compliance with the maintenance of public order laws was gradually disregarded. Today, it is very rare that protest organizers even comply with the obligation to declare, and, in numerous cases, they are not even aware of the legal requirement. In the provinces, prior notification is even less common. For example, only 8.5 percent of events recorded in the archives at Marseilles had been registered with the prefecture or the central police commissariat (Fillieule and Jobard 1997). In Paris, where prior notification of demonstrations is much more frequent than in the provinces, rather than stick to the strict provisions of the law, directors of public order try to establish negotiations with the protesters. The goal of the negotiation is to make the demonstrators think that the restrictions are offered in friendly advice, in the best interests of the protesters. As one official explained:

> If there is some small problem, perhaps with the route, I try to make them aware of it before they arrive at the Prefecture. So they can think about changing their route. If, for example, they want to go down the Champs-Elysées, this is not possible. But rather than tell them it is not possible, I would explain to them that they have to park 1,500 coaches [buses], which is an enormous number. A coach is twenty meters long. You need dozens of streets in which to park them. They have not thought of that. So, I suggest to them rue Saint-Augustin, since they can park their coaches in the Boulevard Malesherbes, and so they agree and go away satisfied.

Organizers must always feel, after the meeting, that negotiation helped them in organizing their march. That is why the chief of the Parisian police headquarters presents his requirements in the form of helpful advice. For instance, in dealing with inexperienced demonstrators, senior officers frequently give the organizers some instruction in ways to organize and instruct parade marshals. In fact, the police have an important advantage: they usually hold a monopoly of expertise, which they use to a greater or lesser degree to advise and assist organizers, who are unfamiliar with practices and procedures. In so doing, they guide organizers along a path acceptable to the political authorities.

Police always act so that the organizers feel they maintain responsibility for the demonstration. They ask about their marshaling plans, pointing out potential dangers in this kind of event (and even exaggerating them a little). Their goal is to induce the organizers to be as cooperative as possible and to ensure that they recognize the importance of the "liaison officer" who will be the link between them and the police on the day of the event. Additionally, if the organizers fear some dangerous or violent acts from their own participants or some external group (e.g., hooligans invading student demonstrations), this view encourages a shared interest between the police and the organizers and a shared perspective about identifying and containing potential troublemakers.

Finally, the purpose of negotiation is to establish a climate of mutual trust: to convince the organizers that the police will respect their undertakings. To fulfill this aim, the chief of the police headquarters may reveal some part of the means at his disposal, in a spirit of openness but also to exclude the possibility of ambiguous situations or surprises on the day of the event.

Clearly, these informal principles are applied to varying degrees in negotiations, depending on the nature of the groups involved; the extent of cooperation can vary greatly. On the one hand, for the huge demonstration on January 16, 1995, in Paris in defense of state schooling, during which more than 800,000 people gathered, negotiations lasted for more than a month. Police representatives directly assisted organizers in planning the details of the march, including such matters as developing an effective marshaling plan. On the other hand, when demonstrators show no readiness to cooperate, and even refuse to meet with the police face-to-face, the chief of the police headquarters may content himself with a simple telephone negotiation, with the itinerary and conditions of the march issued by fax.

Beyond the preparation of the protest, once the event is under way the police seek to maintain permanent contact with the organizers. Whereas previously the doctrine of public order rested principally on the idea that the forces of law and order should undertake no contact with the populace for fear of the risks of their fraternization with demonstrators and collusion between officers and the bourgeoisie, today's conception consists, on the contrary, in ensuring that police commanders remain in contact with those in charge of the protest throughout the event. To this end, in every protest, a liaison officer is appointed who is required to maintain a permanent contact with the organizers.[7] During very large protests, this liaison is always a senior police officer.

This process of permanent negotiation in the field will very often produce close cooperation between police forces and parade marshals, since they share common interests. As one police officer said:

> If there is a procession of more than eight hundred meters, we must be able to isolate troublemakers from the crowd, and protect those that have a right to be there. This works very well with the CGT [Confédération Générale du Travail, the Communist-led union] and other professional organizations. They have marshals in place who know that we will isolate those who shouldn't be there. They will put up barriers and if necessary will stop the march, speed it up or cut it short. Sometimes, they will come to us and tell us that they are going to lead the troublemakers up a certain street. And we can be waiting at the other end of the street to greet them! But for student demos, the marshals do not like to do it, because it is seen as collusion with the police.

Beyond these interactions between police and demonstrators, the importance of other actors, particularly the media, has increased considerably in France since the middle 1970s. Mass media presence at demonstrations has a double and somewhat contradictory effect on contemporary social protest. On the one hand, the police are extremely attentive to how journalists analyze their role and responsibilities in violent events. As the chief of the police headquarters in Paris stated, "To know if we did a good job, I wait for the AFP [Agence France Presse] wire news. The *préfet* only calls me after he had read it." For this reason, one could assume that the presence of the media during demonstrations has a calming effect on police behavior. For groups without popular legitimacy, however (e.g., immigrants' demonstrations), such media "protection" does not seem to apply.

On the other hand, protesters seek media attention to publicize and legitimize their cause, and they generally know that violent events have a good chance to be reported. This seems to be corroborated by our own findings on French demonstrations in the 1980s (Fillieule 1997a): the presence of the media often escalate political conflict, even if well-established groups (mainly civil servants) and organizations (such as political parties and unions) consider violence "bad news" for their image in public opinion.

To summarize, police handling of protest has largely evolved in France since World War II. Broadly speaking, we find that persuasive strategies have developed that rely more on mutual negotiation and partnership than on the menace of repression. Yet, one should keep in mind that, beyond that general trend, the way the authorities, whether those in the political arena or the police in the field, perceive protest groups dramatically affects the treatment they give those groups. Some groups, in some situations, still face repressive police tactics, especially those groups that are perceived as a threat within the police subculture (e.g., foreigners, immigrants, young people, the extreme left).

Persuasive Strategies in Italy

Because of the considerable degree of submission to the political power characteristic of the Italian police forces, the dominant "state police" conception was often translated into a "government-controlled police" practice. After the fall of the fascist regime and the liberation of the country, the maintenance of public order and partisan political control, with the police lined up at the side of the government, prevailed over the fight against crime (Canosa 1976; Corso 1979, p. 57). Several documents (e.g., Fedeli 1981, Medici 1979) show a police force isolated from the population and close to political power. If we compare the strategies used by the Italian police for controlling of public order in the immediate postwar period with those practiced in the 1980s, the most visible change is that coercive strategies were increasingly limited to situations in which the security of the citizens was at risk. The most significant development, however, regards the quality of persuasive strategies, with a passage from mediation based on intimidation to a logic oriented to cooperation between the police and protesters based on a common goal: the peaceful course of a demonstration.

In the Italian collective memory, coercive strategies were by far the preferred methods of the Italian police forces for controlling public order. Police in postunification Italy were characterized by "an extreme harshness in the performance of public order services, with very rapid recourse to the use of firearms" (Canosa 1976, p. 83). This tradition was reaffirmed in the immediate postwar period. Only a brief interlude following the fall of the fascist regime was marked by a certain level of tolerance toward protest events, although not uniformly or without contradictions. This tolerance, however, was more the result of material difficulties of the police and their lack of legitimacy than of democratization. Neither the political forces nor public opinion challenged the police's self-image constructively, even though the latter was visibly shaken by the fall of the fascist regime. Already during the first government led by the Christian Democratic leader Alcide De Gasperi (December 1945–July 1946), the police began to reinforce their military and offensive capacity for public order, above all against spontaneous protests and demonstrations organized by associations lacking political legitimacy.

From 1947 on, Minister of the Interior Mario Scelba gave the police a clear political direction, identifying the parties of the working-class movement and their mass organizations as the internal enemy to combat. Popular protest and public demonstrations were framed in a "cold" civil war logic. Decisions concerning the equipment and the training of the police were taken with a "hot" civil war scenario in mind and with the police being considered an integral part of the armed forces. The police thus developed into a force including considerable paramilitary elements, which intervened brutally, without any apparent qualms about offending a substantial part of the population. Their "cold" civil war approach was characterized by strong central control by the Ministry of the Interior; by constant surveillance that habitually used methods of espionage against an internal political enemy; and by the deployment of heavily armed paramilitary units used for intimidation and reactive, but also proactive, repression. The early tests for Scelba's police and their tactics were the elections of April 1948 and the general strike after the assassination attempt against Communist leader Palmiro Togliatti (Reiter 1996, 1997).

The fact that in collective imagination the Italian police of the Cold War years were connected with forceful intervention in the streets, however, does not mean that they did not also employ other strategies. Even in these early days, there was a tension within the self-image of the police between the explicitly paramilitary way in which they presented themselves (evident, e.g., in *Polizia Moderna*, the official monthly of the state police) and their own conception of the protection of public order, which was supposed to take place "with observation and prevention, i.e. with surveillance, and with occasional recourse to repression" (Roddi, 1953, p. 59). In particular, Scelba's model emphasized "observation and prevention," a fact often obscured by the dramatic news of clashes in the streets.

In the immediate postwar period, the Italian police used persuasive strategies initially as a technical-legal routine: before a coercive intervention, police officers had to perform "persuasive work," although it normally did not go beyond mechanical fulfillment of the law. According to law, before charging demonstrators, the commanding officer had to order the crowd to break up. This could take the form of intimidation, with the alternative posed either to "clear the streets" or bear the consequences of "resisting" the orders of the police.

More characteristic for the Italian police in the Cold War years was another variation of a persuasive strategy, suggesting the police found themselves in the service of a "limited" democracy. Against the internal political enemy, the different police forces used methods of *intimidation*, based on the traditional "possibility to utilize practically at will a whole spectrum of administrative measures which could be applied on the basis of simple suspicion" (Canosa 1976, p. 83). These powers of intervention were defined in the most extensive way in the Police Law of 1926, still in force in the 1950s.[8] In clear violation of constitutional rights, these "preventive" measures were used to stifle social protest. One particularly problematic instrument was the *diffida* (intimidation), used by the police forces with the clear intent to intimidate activists who had managed not to break any law or rule.[9]

One indicator of the progressive democratization of the police, from the "police of the government" to the "police of the citizens," is the role citizens in contact with the police have with respect to persuasive strategies. In the "preventive" methods that we have classified as intimidatory, the "civil" interlocutors of the police were reduced to the role of messengers, who had to transmit the direct or indirect threat to the other activists. Not very different seems to have been the role reserved for the organizers of "official" demonstrations of the left during the Cold War years. In arranging their deployment, it was normal for the police to make contact with the organizers of the events, who, for their part, had to ask for the approval of the *questura* (the provincial police headquarters) for their initiatives. During the Cold War years, these interactions officially did not go beyond a purely *technical-legal character*, never challenging the logic of ideological confrontation. Based on their utility from a professional and technical viewpoint, the contacts between the police and their "civil" interlocutors did present the potential to move toward normalizing their interactions. Already in the 1940s and 1950s, in fact, the police "knew" that contacts on a "professional" level would facilitate their work to control public order, especially if they could trust their interlocutors to keep their agreements and respect the "rules of the game," knowing that in exchange they would be respected as *envoys* of an enemy army.

The Cold War polarization between left and right limited even this information normalization. Up to the middle of 1947, the police in moments of difficulty had regularly called on the leaders of the parties and organizations of the working class to calm situations over which they had lost control; after the exit of the left-wing parties from government in 1947, however, the Ministry of the Interior's instructions discouraged this practice (Reiter 1997). Moreover, the attitude of police facing possible interlocutors was guided more by political opportunism than pragmatism. One example of this opportunism was the attitude of police during and after the assassination attempt on the Communist leader Palmiro Togliatti on July 14, 1948, initially determined by pragmatic considerations and later by instructions arriving from political powers. Numerous national and local leaders, especially those of the Parti Communisto Italiano and the Confederazione Generale Italiana del Lavoro ("CGIL, a left wing trade union), played an important deescalating role in working with the police in the control of the spontaneous protests that erupted on this occasion. The case of Piombino, where police repressed the general strike of 1948, demonstrates how the same leaders, following clear indications from above, saw themselves later accused of "armed insurrection against the powers of the state" (Grillo 1994, p. 69 ff).

The polarization of the 1940s and the 1950s continued to have effects in the following decades. If a temporary increase in police tolerance during the experiences of the center-left government of the early 1960s helped to facilitate the emergence of a cycle of protest (Tarrow 1989), the tradition of repression reemerged in reaction to new challenges, produced a radicalization of at least part of the social movements active in the 1970s (della Porta 1995, chap. 3). It was only in the 1980s, after ideological polarization softened, that a "pragmatic" and then a cooperative use of persuasive strategies could develop. All our interviewees agreed in defining contemporary strategies of protest policing as oriented toward consensus building, via dialogue, while coercive strategies are considered as a last resort. Since the 1980s, the Italian police have followed a *cooperative* model of protest control based on negotiations with civil spokespersons usually accepted as brokers. The importance of this brokerage function, often emphasized during our interviews, was explicitly acknowledged at the highest ranks of the police.

In Italy, as well as in most democracies, the announcement of large demonstrations is followed by negotiations about the route of the march, its duration, and how it will disperse. As one interviewee observed, "For better or worse there is a great deal of work spent on planning . . . a lot of work done on the route, through informal contacts, at the level of 'we won't go that way, when you go that way.' In the end, what's allowed is a small protest that won't degenerate further than that, there is a lot of work of this kind" (interview, Milan, November 11, 1994).

The negotiation phase is presented as a way of facilitating the realization of a common goal: the peaceful unfolding of the demonstration. According to one chief officer of the Digos, the political police:

> We are also able in some way to give suggestions and ask for clarifications and give them help. Undoubtedly we say, look at those groups who might create a bloody mess, excuse the term; either you isolate them or we'll have to think about doing it ourselves. . . . This works every time, because when a sizable part of the demonstration are workers . . . then it is in fact the workers in these big initiatives who want everything to go well, otherwise the demonstration will fail. These days, well, *the degeneration of a demonstration into violence is seen as a failure of the demonstration itself.* (interview, Florence, November 14, 1994, our italics)

On the basis of previous experiences, police officials try to evaluate the capacities of the protest leadership to control the peaceful development of their demonstrations. Italian police believe, as do their counterparts in England, it is mutually advantageous if marchers police themselves (Waddington 1994, p. 83). Trade union experiences with marches, and therefore the unions' ability in self-policing, favors negotiations with trade union spokespersons, who are accepted by the police as *partners for security.* As one policeman said:

> When it comes to the workers . . . all you need to think about is the political dimension in a demonstration by workers, because all they are doing is asking for their just rights. It's true, yes, in some demonstrations, you do get troublemakers, but most times they warn the police that there are these troublemakers present. Then, *during the route, with their own marshals, they intervene to isolate them.* (interview, Milan, November 21–22, 1994, our italics)

When the police recognize the legitimacy of protest, as in the case here, the understanding of their mediation role extends to offering services to the demonstrators in exchange for less disruption of public order. In particular, in suggesting contacting a politician or media people, the police implement an exchange strategy, oriented to win the confidence of the protesters, as observed in the British case: "By doing favors, they expect organizers to offer compliance in return" (Waddington 1994, p. 86). Taking on this role of mediator now seems to be a routine police practice, as one respondent explained:

> In certain cases, when, for example, demonstrators say that they want to speak with councilor so-and-so, in effect, we undertake this task through our own channels; we contact the secretary of these political figures and tell them that they have asked for them to get involved. Ninety percent of the time they come; sometimes they don't. (interview, Florence, December 12, 1994)

Recognizing the social dimension of the problem, we see that the interaction between the police and demonstrators is bound up with interaction with (and between) other actors, including the press. The presence of journalists at demonstrations is thought to soothe the mood of the "good" demonstrators, offering them a channel of communication for their demands, providing certain visibility—given that "in the end all these people here are interested in is the photographer arriving, or the television people arriving. They give their interview or their photos, then they pack up and they go home" (interview, Milan, November 11, 1994). For this reason, the police officer responsible for the intervention at a protest event may use his or her own connections to mobilize the press:

> Sometimes the people who protest, the people who want to demonstrate, look above all, as we know, for a way to make public opinion aware of their own particular problems. The fact that there is the press in certain cases is very useful, because angry people when they are interviewed, filmed, and attract the attention of the media begin to calm down because their interests have already been attained. (interview, Florence, December 12, 1994)

The implementation of persuasive strategies, as with other protest policing strategies, remains selective. In the case of the radical "autonomous" youth groups, for instance, the probability that the negotiators are committed to positive outcomes is considered to be particularly unlikely. The police perception here is that the opportunity for mediation is something that must be earned; whereas negotiation is considered likely to be beneficial with the workers, it not seen as promising in other cases. "It would be like giving some official status to this rabble," said one policeman (interview, Florence, December 12, 1994). The choice of a "dialogue" then is not a definite one but is instead implemented in an ad hoc fashion and often subject to accusations of "opportunism."

This is all the more the case since, in contrast with other European cases, including France, the negotiation process in Italy is very informal. In fact, mediation is sometimes carried out by officials of the Digos and sometimes by the representative of the police chief, who will direct an intervention. This informality brings with it a confusion of roles, one that can have negative effects. For example, the Digos officials are the same ones who can press charges; and it is the officials of the Questura who decide on the use of coercive means. The informal Italian culture favors an opportunistic approach in which, particularly in situations of uncertainty, both parties might be tempted not to adhere to the agreements they have made. Moreover, this informality allows for a high degree of selectivity in the implementation of cooperative bargaining, with the exclusion of those actors considered illegitimate or untrustworthy by police officers. Police discretion remains substantial.

To summarize, persuasive strategies changed substantially after the foundation of the Italian Republic. In the 1980s and 1990s, the Italian police no longer regard their civil interlocutors as mere "messengers" or even "envoys of an enemy army" but tend to accept them as mediators, or even as partners in security. However, the "strategy of dialogue" is implemented in an informal and selective way, leaving room for opportunistic departures. Even the search for "partnership" is oriented mainly toward the common aim of a peaceful demonstration and not, as a fully developed democratic conception of protest policing would imply, a partnership for the protection of the right to demonstrate and to "be heard."

Conclusion

In this chapter, we described the development of persuasive strategies for the control of protest in two countries that have been traditionally considered typical of a Latin model of policing. We observed in both a shift from persuasion, mainly based on intimidation, to "minimalistic bargaining," to cooperation. In the relationship between police and protesters, a shift occurred from domination to exchange, with negotiation prevailing over coercive implementation of the rules of the game. Increasingly, the police present themselves to protesters' spokespersons as partners in the peaceful development of demonstrations, going so far as offering them their services, not only in the policing of the demonstrators but also in contacting politicians and the press.

The implementation of bargaining techniques appeared, however, to be very selective in both cases. According to police perceptions, negotiation is a "prize" the demonstrators have to deserve. In fact, the dialogue is considered to be fruitful only with "good demonstrators" that is, with demonstrators who, according to police perceptions, are moved by genuine, rational and legitimate aims and, moreover, have the organizational capacity to isolate troublemakers (della Porta 1997a).

In a cross-national comparative perspective, the tendencies we observed in these continental democracies do not differ much from those identified in the Anglo-American world. The traditional peculiarities of the Latin police model are reflected in a particular form of persuasive strategies, with a longer-lasting presence of intimidation strategies, a mainly informal structure for the development of cooperative strategies, and greater selectivity in the implementation of persuasive strategies in general. Despite these differences, the similarities between the continental and the Anglo-American models of protest policing seem to have increased. How can we explain this evolution from intimidation to cooperation? In the presentation of our cases, we suggested some possible causes for changes in the police strategies; in what follows, we discuss these possibilities in a more systematic way.

A first set of explanations locates the causes for strategic transformation inside the police forces themselves. The availability of new technological resources is, for example, often cited in organizational studies, leading to a sort of "technological determinism" (King forthcoming). Although the presence of new technology clearly emerged in our research, we had the impression that the development of technological resources followed strategic choices rather than determining them. More relevant appeared to be the institutional and normative resources—that is, what is normally understood as police powers. The large arsenal of disciplinary interventions administered by the police, from police arrest to compulsory repatriation, from admonition to internment, that allowed for frequent recourse to intimidation in the immediate postwar period in Italy was reduced by the Constitutional Court in 1956 (Corso 1979, pp. 158–59).

Another set of explanations focuses on factors external to the police and refer to the enlargement of the general understanding of democratic rights. First, as we mentioned in the introduction, changes in protest policing are related to waves of protest, in part reflecting a tactical adaptation on the part of the police to protest behavior. In the 1960s and 1970s, for example, attempts to stop unauthorized demonstrations and a law-and-order attitude on the part of the police in both countries in the face of the "limited rule-breaking" tactics used by the new movements maneuvered the police repeatedly into "no-win" situations. As a result, developments in police strategies for the control of public order seem to go beyond a purely tactical adaptation to new challenges, reflecting increasing legitimacy of new forms of collective action (della Porta 1997b).

Moreover, a transformation in the model of policing is related to the shift in the political context in which policing and protest take place. In particular, in both countries there was a growing integration of the left-wing parties into the political system. In Italy, the center-left governments of the 1960s and the growing legitimization of the Italian Communist Party (PCI) in the 1970s, undermined the very rationale for a "Cold War" strategy based on the repression of the workers and the left (della Porta 1995, chap. 3; Reiter 1997). Notwithstanding some initial resistance, in the long run, a full democratic integration of the PCI and the trade unions reduced political pressure for coercive police intervention. Since the 1980s, in both countries, political depolarization coincided with a moderation in protest repertoires and the related acceptance of noninstitutional forms of political participation in the public opinion, as well as by the police. In France, as ideological polarization declined, cooperative strategies developed.

Referring to the differences between the Italian and the French police, we can see that a weak democratic experience increases the strength of intimidation techniques. In Italy, the long presence of an authoritarian regime left a legacy of laws and regulations, which, in conjunction with cultural attitudes, dissipated slowly. In France, in contrast, a longer experience with democratic institutions produced practices of cooperation. Moreover, in France a higher degree of professionalization is reflected in a more formalized structure for bargaining than in Italy. In both countries, a strong dependence on political power and traditional skepticism toward citizen involvement in policing tasks may explain some hesitation in the development of cooperative strategies, which still appear less formalized than in the Anglo-American countries. As noted, this formality allows for a large degree of selectivity in the implementation of cooperative measures, which are applied only to those who are considered "good" demonstrators—that is, those with legitimate political aims and strong internal organizational control.

In Italy and France as elsewhere, increased mass media coverage of protest seems to have contributed, for some groups, to a development toward "softer" police methods (see e.g., on Great Britain, Geary 1985, pp. 129, 130). Media presence encourages self-control among the police. Our research seems to confirm the police acknowledgment of the need to have a "good press"; in fact, "the citizen, if he does not trust the police, would not call them when in need" (interview, Milan, November 11, 1994). This "media check," however, does not apply to marginal social and political groups that lack public support.

All the mentioned transformations in "internal" and "external" resources and constraints for the police produce most of their effects only when recognized by the police, becoming part of what can be defined as police knowledge (della Porta and Reiter 1997b; della Porta 1996a). The social construction of the external reality is all the more important for a bureaucracy that, like the police, has a high level of discretionary power. It is, moreover, a peculiarity of the police that this discretionary power increases at the lower levels of the hierarchy, providing police officers with the power to define the world in which they operate (Jessen 1995, p. 32 ff.).

In our research, we noticed that technological, institutional, and political changes are reflected in a self-definition of the police as "citizens" and "defenders" of the citizenry, exemplified in the words of an Italian police officer: "we work for the citizens. . . . We are people among the people" (interview, Milan, October 17, 1994). The police seem to ascribe growing importance to their role as mediators between the citizens and public administrators. The relevance attributed to this function is connected to the definition of problems that create disturbances to public order as being social problems, whose solution is the duty of the political authorities. In fact, the police leadership seems to be distancing itself from a restricted conception of its role as an agent of "reaction," by which the police ought to limit themselves to intervening when the law is violated, and moving toward a conception of policing that is referred to in Britain as "proactive." In the latter model, police are seen as agents of public service, with a strong responsibility in social control and perhaps also the responsibility to intervene into the causes of criminality. Yet to shift from a reactive conception to a proactive one increases the level of police discretion. And, if the police have discretionary powers of intervention, the problem of their legitimization and control will be posed in a new form.

Notes

1. For a closer discussion of different protest policing styles, see della Porta and Reiter (1997a)

2. On the involvement of all police forces in the fascist violence in the early

1920s, see Canosa (1976, p. 61), Snowden (1989, pp. 96, 198 ff., 202 ff), and Dunnage (1992).

3. The "benevolent" aspects of the Italian police during fascism, however, should not be overestimated. Scientific literature on the fascist police is surprisingly scarce, but see Carucci (1976).

4. The other two types of strategies for protest policing are *coercive strategies*—that is, the use of arms and physical force to control or break up a demonstration—and *information strategies*, which consist of the targeted collection of information with the aim of persecuting crimes, as well as in the "diffuse" collection of information oriented to preventive control (della Porta and Reiter 1996).

5. Our chapter is based on ongoing empirical research on the control of public demonstrations in Europe. For the Italian case, the historical part is based on an analysis of the Florentine state archives; for contemporary policing, our sources consist of thirty in-depth interviews with police officers in Florence and Milan, integrated with participant observation during police intervention in public order situations and a few interviews with activists. For the French case in the contemporary period, we used semidirective interviews with police chiefs in and around Paris, ethnographic observation of many interventions in protest policing, from their planning to their realization, particularly in Marseille in 1993–94; and a database of about five thousand events based on police archives and referring to the 1980s (Fillieule 1997a,b). Unless otherwise noted, interviews were conducted in Paris with officials promised anonymity. For the earlier French history, we rely on documents from the archive of the Prefecture de Police in Paris and secondary analysis of research on demonstrations and the policing of protest.

6. "For the maintenance of public order, the day of 28th May 1952 marks an important moment. Set up by people totally engrossed in the internal Cold War, police action, the measures taken or envisaged over the subsequent weeks and months, translated into a subversion of republican norms. . . . We might add that if the activists of the party, galvanized by the orders of the Party were enthusiastic about the idea of taking their revenge on Baylot's men, a large portion of the latter seemed not to be scared by the fight to come. Pushed by the police hierarchy, an 'independent' union saw the light of day in December 1951 and strengthened the adhesion of officers revoked at the Libération, but reintegrated by Baylot. Its directors held the responsibility for 'communist violence' " (Pigenet 1992, pp. 8–9).

7. This practice originated at the end of the 1970s, when the police prefecture in Paris used to open large processions with police buses placed several hundred meters in front of the demonstration. It was during a demonstration of the steel workers, March 23, 1979, that a police officer was in charge of the link for the first time. Since the student demonstrations in December 1986 in Paris, this method has been systematically employed, sometimes very visibly. During the annual National Front demonstration in honor of Joan of Arc, for example, on May 1, 1988, a car with a sign "liaison police/organizers" opened the procession.

8. On the basis of rules contained in this fascist law, the police could, at their discretion, prohibit bill posting and distribution of leaflets, collection of funds, and the organization of assemblies and demonstrations, even by legal political parties (in particular the PCI) (for examples, see della Porta and Reiter 1996). Almost inevitably, these decisions of the police were upheld by the courts (see, e.g., Canosa and Federico 1974, p. 186 ff.).

9. During a strike of farm workers and sharecroppers in the province of Florence in November 1948, the *carabinieri* station of Rufina, after having learned from *"notizie confidenziali"* the names of those most active in the propaganda in favor of the strike, intimated these individuals on November 25, 1948, to abstain from any kind of direct or indirect action related with the liberty to work and to strike. If only the most insignificant complaint were heard against them, they would be held responsible "for anything which might happen." According to a report of the *Compagnia esterna 1ª* dei carabinieri dated December 1, 1948, the *carabinieri* of Regello intimated three individuals whom they had "surprised . . . carrying out activity toward sharecroppers which, even though not integrating the elements of the crime of criminal coercion, tended however, in a way not perfectly in keeping with the regime of the established freedom, to induce them to suspend work." A report of the same company dated May 5, 1949, contains the information that the subsidiary *carabinieri* stations had always charged all those responsible for attacks against the "liberty to work" and had in this way severely undermined strike participation (Archivio di Stato Firenze, Questura 525, fasc. "Difesa della libertà sindacale").

6

Institutionalization of Protest during Democratic Consolidation in Central Europe

Jan Kubik

The rapid and unexpected collapse of state socialist regimes in East-Central Europe in 1989, followed by economic restructuration and democratic consolidation, is often misinterpreted. The simultaneity of the breakdowns, despite varied political and economic conditions in each country, reinforced the notion that these regimes were basically *similar* and kept in power by the Soviet military presence. Some experts assumed that in the wake of communism's collapse, Central European states faced *similar* challenges and pressures. In brief, before 1989 all East European regimes were often seen as basically identical one-party states. Now they are considered to be democratizing regimes facing the same problems and challenges.

This view is grossly incorrect both with respect to the communist past and the present developments. Despite ostensibly common legacies and challenges, there were crucial differences in the responses of particular countries to the breakdown of state socialism, and their political experiences following 1989 have varied. East-Central European state socialist regimes underwent complex processes of transformation and adjustment during their four decades in power. Domestic politics developed differently from country to country, producing institutional dissimilarities and distinctive relations between the state and society.[1] Thus, each state socialist regime left behind distinct legacies that should be carefully examined if we are to explain the present rapidly diverging trajectories of political, social, and economic changes in the region.[2] Moreover, despite the clustering of regime breakdowns in

1989, there are important differences in the way particular countries exited state socialism and entered the transition process.

Grzegorz Ekiert and I began a study in 1993 entitled "Collective Protest in Democratizing Societies in Hungary, the former East Germany, Poland, and Slovakia."[3] These four countries were selected so we could study the critical differences in the type of challenges faced by each state and the major choices made by their elites at the outset of transition. Our sample incudes two fast reformers (the former German Democratic Republic [GDR] and Poland) and two slow reformers (Hungary and Slovakia). Moreover, we have two countries where the continuity of the state was not questioned (Hungary and Poland) and two countries where the state underwent a fundamental transformation. Slovakia, following the "velvet divorce," acquired independent statehood in 1992. It faced the task of building new state institutions and developing new domestic and foreign policies. The GDR lost its state institutions, following the reunification of Germany in 1991. The entire institutional order of the country was thoroughly transformed, and the West German federal state structure was imposed, creating five new *Leander*.

This chapter is based on data collected for our empirical project. The existing literature accords more prominence to certain dimensions of consolidation and neglects others; the formation of party systems is usually viewed as the most important element in the stabilization and consolidation of democracy (e.g., Pridham 1990; Linz 1992; Kitschelt 1992). In addition to this emphasis on political parties—prominent in the studies of South European democratizations—the works on Eastern Europe tend to focus on the complex interactions between economic and political reforms (e.g., Przeworski 1991; Ekiert 1993; Bresser Pereira, Maravall, and Przeworski 1993).

The preoccupation with elites, party systems, the relationship between political and economic changes, and popular attitudes has resulted in a considerable gap in the literature on democratization. Relatively little is known about societies' activities. Some students of democratic transitions, however, have begun to emphasize the importance of the "resurrection of civil society" and its political role both during the decomposition of authoritarian rule and in its aftermath.[4] It is often noted, for example, that the greatest challenge to the policies of the newly democratized states may come from various social organizations. Yet the development of such organizations and their political role is not systematically documented and analyzed. The study of civil society's role in democratic consolidations has often been reduced to the study of political attitudes, conducted on representative samples of the population. Such studies contribute to our knowledge of public reactions to regime change and are very useful as long as public opinion poll results are not accepted as a substitute for data on actual political behavior. As Tarrow (1989, pp. 7–8) emphasizes, "Unless we trace the forms of activity people use, how these reflect their demands, and their interaction with opponents and elites, we cannot understand either the magnitude or the dynamics of change in politics and society."

Our research project was based on the assumption that event analysis and, specifically, the systematic collection of data on collective action from newspapers can shed new light on the political behavior of nonelite actors during democratization. In particular, we focused on an institutional domain critical for the progress of democratic consolidation: civil society. We adopted a broad concept of civil society to take into consideration organizations embedded in economic relations (trade unions, employers' organizations), voluntary associations, and other organizations of the public sphere. We traced the activities of these nonelite collective actors and their impact on the process of consolidation to counter the existing elite bias in the literature. Furthermore, we focused on protest activities that are the most spectacular mode of public participation within the realm of civil society.[5]

In this chapter, I will deal with one specific problem: the institutionalization of contentious politics during democratic consolidation. According to many observers, protest, particularly institutionalized protest, has become a regular and even desired feature of politics in *established democracies*. By contrast, it is sometimes seen as an undesirable occurrence in *democratizing societies*. For Bresser Periera et al. (1993, p. 4), for example, one of the criteria of "successful reforms must be consolidation of democracy. And if reforms are to proceed under democratic conditions, distributional conflicts must be institutionalized: All groups must channel their demands through the democratic institutions and abjure other tactics." In brief, protest is often seen as "good" for democracy but "bad" for democratization. I will examine this thesis with the help of empirical data derived from our project and a careful conceptualization of institutionalization.

Postrevolutionary situations offer a unique opportunity to study institutionalization of political systems and the formation of their legitimacy ("taken-for-grantedness") *in statu nascendi*. While studying such situations in several different locations, it is possible to (1) determine *whether* and *how* contentious politics is being institutionalized as one of the modes of interaction between the state and society, (2) gauge the pace of such (de)institutionalization, (3) trace the causes of differential patterns of institutionalization, and (4) assess the impact of contentious politics on democratic consolidation.

Institutions and Institutionalization

I define institutions broadly as "any form of constraint that human beings devise to shape human interaction" (North 1990, p. 4). Institutions include "the formal rules, compliance procedures, and standard operating practices that structure the relationship between individuals in various units of the polity and economy" (Hall 1986, p. 19, see also Thelen and Steinmo 1992, p. 2; Crawford and Ostrom 1996). Thus, as Jepperson (1991, p. 145) states:

> Institution represents a social order or pattern that has attained a certain state or property; institutionalization denotes the process of such attainment. By *order* or *pattern*, I refer, as is conventional, to standardized interaction sequences. . . . When departures from the pattern are counteracted in a regular fashion, by repetitively activated, socially constructed, controls—that is, by some set of rewards and sanctions—we refer to a pattern as institutionalized.

To assess the degree of institutionalization of a given social practice or interaction pattern, we must operationalize this definition. I begin with a suggestion that a social practice (or interaction pattern) is institutionalized when one or more of the following six conditions are met:

1. It is carried out according to a set of preexisting procedures (it is standardized).
2. It is used with high frequency (i.e., repeated almost always when a problem or issue it is designed to deal with emerges).
3. It is widely regarded as "normal" or "taken-for-granted" (i.e., it is *legitimate*).
4. Conformity with the pattern is ensured and enforced by punishments and/or rewards; of particular importance is "official" approval (i.e., *authorization*).[6]
5. Its application involves relatively low costs (*low mobilization* of actors and resources).[7]
6. Its application causes *less disruption* of established routines than the application of (most) alternative practices. Disruption occurs when (often unreflectively) accepted and routinely obeyed *rules* that regulate the flow of everyday life are temporarily suspended (i.e., when people cease to act according to generally accepted *routines*).[8]

All six features are continuous variables of increasing/decreasing intensity; institutionalization is thus a *multidimensional quality of varying intensity*. In a complex, modern society, a task or problem can be solved by any of several available strategies; they differ by their degree of institutionalization. In the following analyses, I construe protest as one of several *modes (strategies) of interaction between the state and society* (its segments).[9] Accordingly, to explain the degree to which protest action is institutionalized, we need to compare its "partial" institutionalizations along the six specified dimensions with the relevant institutionalization of other modes of interaction between the state and society. In particular, we want to investigate forms of interaction that involve larger numbers of people.[10]

Conducting an analysis based on six criteria would be unwieldy; thus, I merged criteria 1 (procedures) and 2 (frequency), for usually (if not always) a frequently repeated action is based on established procedures. Criterion 5 (mobilization) can be subsumed within criterion 6 (disruptiveness). Even with these simplifications, we end up with a somewhat cumbersome sixteen-cell matrix (see Table 6.1), with which I begin my analysis.

Table 6.1 helps to order different forms of interaction between the state and society, from the least to most institutionalized. The least institutionalized can be classified as "protest." It also helps to realize that there are different types of institutionalization, and it makes it easier to follow historical changes in the concept of protest.

In different historical periods, different combinations of the four tabulated features were considered protests. To begin, let us consider the least institutionalized (inter)action, characterized by (1) no authorization, (2) the lack of procedures, (3) no legitimacy, and (4) high disruptiveness. Such an action—for example, the first terrorist attack in a given state—constitutes the *purest* kind of protest, though by definition it does not occur very often.[11] Throughout history, however, most protest actions seem to have shared the following features: (1) no authorization, (2) well-developed procedures (repertoires of contention), (3) legitimacy, and (4) high disruptiveness. They have been institutionalized therefore on two dimensions (procedures and legitimacy) and noninstitutionalized on two others (authorization and disruptiveness). In modern democratic polities, protest actions have become increasingly *fully institutionalized;* they are (1) authorized, (2) conducted according to established procedures, (3) legitimate, and (4) relatively nondisruptive (see McCarthy et al. 1995).

The Measurement of Institutionalization of Protest

Institutionalization of the relationship between the state and society in a given polity is measurable. Generally speaking, what needs to be

Jan Kubik

TABLE 6.1
Interaction between the State and (Civil) Society

		Authorized		Not Authorized	
		Procedures	No/Minimal Procedures*	Procedures	No/Minimal Procedures
Legitimate	Low disruptiveness	Full institutional-ization: Negotiations of tripartite commissions, with popular mandate		Repeated hunger strikes, held in churches	
Legitimate	High disruptiveness	Officially sanctioned and popularly accepted protest (e.g., French and Israeli demon-strations)	New Social Movements (NSMs)†	Established "protest industries" under state-socialism (e.g., Poland 1976–1989)	Initial, "first" strikes or demonstra-tions under state-socialism
Illegitimate	Low disruptiveness	Negotiations between the state and civil society's repre-sentatives, conducted without popular mandate		Clientelism	
Illegitimate	High disruptiveness	Communist demonstra-tions of support (e.g., May Day celebrations)		Ku-Klux Klan rallies(?)	Innovative terrorist attacks (Oklahoma City?)

*The way I cross-tabulated the four criteria (variables) allows one to see that sometimes people are willing to *accept* experimentation (the case of legitimacy and no procedures). Moreover, such experimentation may or may not be authorized by the rulers.

†Offe (1990, pp. 236–38) emphasizes that NSMs thrive on "rights of protest" but pro-grammatically reject "the established forms of political conflict as either unnecessary, given the evident urgency of movement's causes and demands, or even manifestly harmful." Legitimacy of NSMs varies considerably across time and space; I place them in the "legitimate" cell for convenience.

measured is the ratio of *institutionalization* to *action* in society's rela-tions with the state. Such a calculation is suggested by Jepperson's (1991) remark that institutionalization should be distinguished from other forms of social reproduction, particularly "action."[12] According to his formulation, "A social pattern is reproduced through action if persons repeatedly (re)mobilize and (re)intervene in historical process to secure its persistence" (p. 148). It is often assumed that the high ratio of action to institutionalization is politically destabilizing. This thought is strikingly similar to Huntington's (1968, p. 79) observation that "the stability of any given polity depends upon the relationship between the level of political participation and the level of political institutionalization." For him, high political participation in a society with a low level of institutionalization of politics is politically destabilizing.

It should be remembered, however, the ratio between action and institutionalization can be reduced in two ways. Consider Wolfsfeld's (1988, p. 23) definitions: "*Institutional action* refers to all types of political action which are organized within the established political institutions of a country. *Mobilized action* refers to all attempts to have an influence which are organized outside of the formal political system." It becomes clear that institutionalization is achieved in two different ways. First, through reducing the magnitude of direct actions and increasing the volume of others, more institutionalized (i.e., carried out within established political institutions) forms of interactions develop between the state and society. Second, institutionalizing direct action (protest) occurs through the expansion (redefinition) of the formal political system in such a way that protest becomes a regular part of normal politics.

To determine the "strength" of institutionalization, its progress (or regress), and its mechanism (one of the two specified earlier), the four dimensions of institutionalization can be measured in the following ways.

Authorization

Authorization has two aspects: formal and informal. Formal aspects can be treated as a nominal (usually dichotomous) variable indicating the (non)existence of official regulations legalizing a given form of action. The informal aspect of authorization would be a variable capturing the level of "unofficial" tolerance of a given form of action. For example, even an officially forbidden form of action may be "tolerated" through the lack of enforcement. This frequently seems to be the case in newly democratizing states.

Procedures

This dimension implies a reconstruction of the history (tradition) of a given form of the state-society interaction. We need to study the invention and diffusion of a given form of protest from an "objective" point of view—that is, separately from the study of its authorization and legitimacy. This kind of analysis was pioneered by Tilly in his work on "repertoires of contention" (for a recent synthesis, see Traugott 1995).

The constancy of a protest repertoire does not depend merely on the depth of historical traditions. Rather, the prevalence of certain methods over others in a given period of time will constitute a compromise between the habituation engendered by history and the choices dictated by immediate strategic considerations.[13] Some protesters will be more constrained by history and employ known and tested strategies of protest; others will abandon familiar procedures in search of potentially more efficacious new strategies (Tarrow 1989, pp. 59–61).

Institutionalization decreases when the ratio between authorized and nonauthorized protest strategies increases. Increased institutionalization, in turn, diminishes the protesters' power-through-heightened-visibility. Therefore, when the authorities legalize existing protest tactics, protesters, to increase the impact of their actions, should try to develop new, as yet unauthorized strategies. It seems reasonable to assume that the introduction of new procedures is designed to increase protest effectiveness at the cost of lowered institutionalization. Under certain circumstances, therefore, the effectiveness and institutionalization of protest are inversely related. To determine the lack of constancy in a protest repertoire (procedures), a researcher may look for (1) changes in protest repertoire that are accompanied by (2) symptoms of a lack of authorization, such as an increased number of police interventions.

Disruptiveness

We should develop measures of disruptiveness based on some "objective" standard(s), independent from the criteria of "disruptiveness" prevalent within a given culture. One can, for example, try to measure such "objective" criteria as the number of people participating, the number of hours lost due to strikes, the number of hours/days traffic was interrupted/stopped, the number of casualties, or the value of property damage. In this case, I will use two measures of disruptiveness: (1) the percentage of protest events that contained violent protest strategies and (2) the ratio of disruptive to nondisruptive strategies. Subjective or culturally relative perceptions of disruptiveness is a separate element and can best be captured as one of the dimensions of legitimacy.

Legitimacy

Legitimacy of various forms of protest can be measured in two ways: attitudinal and behavioral. The first method relies on such indicators of legitimacy as answers to questionnaire items designed to gauge people's approval of a given form of protest. A behavioral method for measuring legitimacy requires determining the fraction of protest actions in a given unit of time that were (il)legal. Illegality can be measured operationally as a number of protest-related police interventions in a given unit of time. A declining fraction of illegal actions in a country with a high degree of authorization of protest would be a partial indicator of the growing legitimacy of protest.

Empirical Findings

Incidence, Magnitude, and Other Main Features of Protest

We defined public protest event in the following way:

1. Public is understood to mean an action that is reported in at least one newspaper.
2. Collective action is an action undertaken by at least three people. Extreme acts such as self-immolation, hunger strikes, or acts of terror carried out by individuals as a form of political protest will also be counted as "collective acts" because of their rarity and political consequences.
3. A collective public event is an act of protest if it is undertaken to articulate certain specified demands, it is not a routine or legally prescribed behavior of a social or political organization, and its form deviates from the routinely accepted way of voicing demands. Certain kinds of action that are constitutionally or legally guaranteed, such as strikes, rallies, or demonstrations, will be considered protest actions because of their radical and disruptive nature.

A simple count of protest events for each country revealed that Poland and the former East Germany had a higher incidence of protest than did Hungary and Slovakia (see Table 6.2).

However, given our definition, the set of protest events in the database included both small, brief street gatherings and several month-long strike campaigns. We needed a more comprehensive measure of protest's magnitude. One attempt to construct such an index produced an unreliable result, partly because of the large amount of missing data.[14] Fortunately, approximating the magni-

TABLE 6.2
Post-1989 Protest Events in East-Central Europe*

	1989	1990	1991	1992	1993	1994	Total
Poland	314	306	292	314	250	—	1,476
Slovakia	—	50	82	116	47	40	335
Hungary	122	126	191	112	148	44	743
East Germany	222	188	291	268	283	183	1,435

*Data for Slovakia, Hungary, and the former GDR in 1994 include only those protest actions held before the elections in each country. (Parliamentary elections were held September 30–October 1, 1994, in Slovakia, and on May 8 and 30, 1994, in Hungary. General elections were held on October 16, 1994, in Germany).

tude of protest by calculating the number of protest days for each country was more successful. The results of this calculation are presented in Table 6.3.

The protest-days index shows Poland with the greatest magnitude of protest, continually rising and confirming our qualitative analysis of our data. Of course, it may be argued that this is an expected result given Poland is the biggest of the four analyzed countries. To avoid the notoriously gnarled debate over "who has more protest," I decided not to use the magnitude of protest as an independent variable in this study; instead, I focus on analyzing and explaining the most important attributes of protest, such as the ratio of street demonstrations to strikes. In particular, I will attempt to determine whether and how the institutionalization of protest differed from country to country and how these differences may be explained.

Authorization

Authorization of protest in post-1989 Eastern Europe was a momentous event. Under state socialist regimes, protest actions were deemed

TABLE 6.3
Protest Days by Year in East-Central Europe

	1989	1990	1991	1992	1993	1994	Total	Protest Days per Year
Poland	2,033	1,684	3,253	3,529	4,382	—	14,881	2,976.2
Slovakia	—	302	532	851	521	213	2,419	551.5
Hungary	893	210	363	254	854	304	2,878	514.8
East Germany	391	544	535	2,733	1,146	727	6,076	1,154.8

illegal by the authorities. Moreover, the word *strike* was forbidden for some time: there could be no workers' strikes in "the workers' state." After 1989, the new governments swiftly passed laws regulating protest activities, which became a regular fixture in the public life of the four countries studied here.

To obtain a precise measure of authorization, we would need to analyze various laws and regulations designed to deal with contentious collective actions, strikes, and street demonstrations in particular. A content analysis of such laws should allow us to determine their level of comprehensiveness, defined as a ratio of legalized (legal) to "illegal" forms of collective contentious action. It seems almost impossible to gather sufficient information on all relevant laws and regulations to measure such a ratio in the volatile context of newly consolidating democracies.

We collected enough data to document that after the 1989 breakthrough most protest activities were tolerated by the authorities (see Table 6.4 for the levels of police and special forces intervention). What is even more important, the major forms of protest, such as strikes and street demonstrations, became legalized and regulated by each country's legislatures and/or executives. In Poland, relevant laws regulating collective bargaining and striking were signed by the president on May 23, 1991.[15] In Slovakia, the right to strike is guaranteed by the Constitution, whose Article 37, Section 4, states:

> The right to strike shall be guaranteed. The terms thereof shall be provided by law. Judges, prosecutors, members of the armed forces, and members of the fire squads shall be disqualified from the exercise of this right.

The Constitution also guarantees the "right to peaceful assembly" (Article 28) and thus legalizes street demonstrations.[16]

In Hungary, the Parliament passed two acts regulating collective action, the Law on Associations and the Law on Assembly, in 1989, even before the end of the communist rule. The laws were very liberal but sufficiently vague to allow arbitrary police interventions. The police, however, exercised restraint and did not disperse any demonstrations during the period studied (Szikinger 1996). Szabo (1994, p. 10) observed, "Traditions of the protest movements of the Kadar regime are still alive, but under the conditions of 'rule of law,' the 'legalization' of protest occurred." The new Labor Code in 1992 recognized the right of unions to organize and bargain collectively and permitted trade union pluralism. Workers have the right to associate freely and, with the exception of the military and the police, a guaranteed right to strike.[17]

As the Federal Republic of Germany "swallowed" the former German Democratic Republic on October 3, 1990, all Germans automatically became subjects to the federal laws and regulations that regulate with great precision citizens' freedom of assembly and protest.[18]

In general, under state socialism almost all forms of collective contentious action were defined as illegal and were unregulated. Hungary, with its gradual dismantling of state socialism, was exceptional, for some forms of protest were officially approved in the late 1980s. Similarly, Polish communist authorities during Solidarity's first legal period (1980–81) tolerated popular protest actions, although they never issued any laws to guarantee the right to strike or to organize street demonstrations. The situation changed dramatically when soon after the "revolutions" of 1989 nonviolent protest in all four states became authorized. Moreover, the decisive majority of protesters began using legal methods; "legalized contentiousness" replaced "illegality."

Procedures

Among the four countries in our study, Poland had by far the most developed tradition of protest politics. Poles were striking and demonstrating in 1956; Polish workers were striking in large numbers in 1970 and 1976 (Bernhard 1993; Goodwyn 1991; Laba 1991; Zuzowski 1992); the massive strike wave in 1980 led to the emergence and institutionalization of the first large self-governing labor organization under communism, Solidarity (Goodwyn 1991; Laba 1991; Ost 1990; Kubik 1994). Thus, large segments of the Polish populace learned and mastered a specific repertoire of contention, dominated by strikes. We wanted to know whether the strike retained its dominant position within the Polish repertoire of contention after 1989 and whether this repertoire was more stable than in other countries, given Poland's longer and more intensive tradition of protest. The answer to the first question is a resounding yes. As the data collected in Table 6.9 demonstrate, the strike was clearly and constantly the dominant Polish protest strategy, in stark contrast to other countries.

To answer the second question, I set out to establish whether there was any pattern in authorized police interventions in the four countries we studied.

In Poland, Hungary, and Slovakia, the level of governmental actions against the protesters remained remarkably stable and, compared with the former East Germany, low (see Table 6.4). Was, however, the unchanging level of police intervention in Poland symptomatic of the constancy of protest repertoire? First, let us examine the ratio of street demonstrations to strikes during the period studied (Table 6.3). The

TABLE 6.4
Authorized Interventions against Protesters
(as a percentage of all protest events in a given year)

	Poland		Hungary		Slovakia		Germany	
Year	No Force	With Force	No Force	With Force	No Force	With Force	No Force	With Force
1989	.6	5.1	2.4	0	—	—	2.2	20.3
1990	3.6	5.6	4.8	2.4	6.0	4.0	1.6	3.7
1991	5.5	5.5	1.6	.5	1.2	6.1	1.7	15.5
1992	4.2	5.5	1.8	5.4	?	?	6.3	11.6
1993	6.8	6.8	1.6	1.6	4.3	0	7.1	11.0
1994	—	—	6.8	0	2.5	2.5	3.2	10.4

Polish protest repertoire, dominated by strikes, remained relatively stable from 1989 to 1993. What is remarkable is the constant proportion of violent protests in Poland. Judging by the constancy of procedures, Polish protest politics during the 1989–1993 period appears to be highly institutionalized.

East Germany offers an intriguing set of contrasts to Poland. German authorities used force against protesters in East Germany more often than their counterparts did in other countries. This correlates with the higher proportion of disruptive protests in this country and signifies that, measured by the criteria of disruptiveness and authorization, protest politics in East Germany was less institutionalized than in the other three countries.

The protest repertoire was also less stable in East Germany than in Poland. Table 6.4 reveals that the most dramatic shifts in the number of official interventions occurred in Germany during the 1989–1991 period. In 1989 police and other forces intervened in 20.3 percent of all protests, in 1990 this number declined to 3.7 percent of all protest actions, and in 1991 it increased to 15.5 percent. Let us see whether these shifts were accompanied by equally dramatic shifts in the protest repertoire. I chose a simple method of calculating the ratio of demonstrations to strikes and strike alerts for each year (see Table 6.5).

Our data clearly reflect that 1989 in East Germany was the year of revolutionary upheaval (Lemke 1996; Lohmann 1994). The method of struggle was street demonstrations, the institutionalization of protest was low (as always in revolutionary situations), and police were extremely active. In 1990 the process of transition commenced, and East Germans began striking much more frequently. The ratio of street demonstrations to strikes and strike alerts fell rapidly. The number of

TABLE 6.5
Ratio of Demonstrations to Strikes and Strike Alerts

Year	Poland	Hungary	Slovakia	Germany
1989	0.34	1.65	—	18.3
1990	1.47	1.68	0.39	1.9
1991	0.54	1.65	2.67	2.6
1992	0.79	1.37	0.48	4.3
1993	0.52	1.00	1.25	2.6
1994	—	1.44	0.63	1.9

police interventions also dramatically declined. But the German protest repertoire remained more volatile than in other countries.

This comparison of protest repertoires and their determinants in Poland, Hungary, and East Germany supports some of the basic claims of historical institutionalism. If the insights offered by this approach are correct, post-1989 Poland, with the oldest and most extensive tradition of protest in Eastern Europe and a protest repertoire dominated by the strike strategy, should have the most stable protest repertoire, dominated by strikes. Indeed, both hypotheses were confirmed by our data: Polish people organized strikes as their weapon against both the communist state and the postcommunist governments. Moreover, the Polish protest repertoire was quite stable throughout the entire period covered by our study. By contrast, the citizens of East Germany, where traditions of protest were less developed, employed a more varied and variable repertoire of protest, dominated, however, by street demonstrations, used against both the communist regime and the postcommunist state.

Disruptiveness

We measured the level of disruptiveness of protest in each in two ways: first, by determining the percentage of violent protest actions among all protests (Table 6.6); second, by establishing the ratio between disruptive and nondisruptive strategies of protest (Table 6.7).

An examination of Table 6.6 reveals two interesting phenomena. First, we see the remarkably constant (albeit higher than in Hungary and Slovakia) level of violence in Poland. This constancy may be construed as an indication of the firmly established protest industry (or sector). Second, we note the relatively high and dramatically fluctuating proportion of violent forms of protest in East Germany. This indicates a volatile and relatively weakly institutionalized protest industry.

TABLE 6.6
Percentage of Violent Protest Actions among All Protests

Year	Poland	Hungary	Slovakia	Germany
1989	6.7	0.8	—	2.7
1990	8.5	8.7	0	6.9
1991	6.8	2.1	4.8	40.9
1992	8.2	1.8	1.7	15.3
1993	8.8	0	0	26.1
1994	—	2.2	2.5	18.6

TABLE 6.7
The Ratio of Disruptive to Nondisruptive Forms of Protest

Year	Poland	Hungary	Slovakia	Germany
1989	2.06	0.50	—	2.02
1990	1.80	0.74	0.35	3.60
1991	0.93	0.49	1.1	2.61
1992	1.07	0.34	0.28	2.25
1993	0.83	0.31	0.40	1.66
1994	—	0.75 (first half)	0.28	1.26

This weak institutionalization seems to result primarily from the strength of right-wing, radical organizations, which often use violence in their protests. Such groups are much more visible and active in East Germany than in the other three countries.

Table 6.7 reports the two most striking findings of this study. First, in all four countries the ratio of disruptive to nondisruptive strategies of protest was declining. Thus, judging by this partial indicator, the institutionalization of protest throughout the region increased during the period studied. Second, East Germany had the highest proportion of disruptive and violent strategies (average index of disruptiveness [AID] for the whole period = 2.23; followed by Poland, 1.34; Hungary, 0.51; and Slovakia, 0.47). Thus, again the German "protest sector" proves to be less institutionalized than that in the other three countries. A partial explanation of this phenomenon can be found in the whole-sale transfer of the West German political scene to the former East Germany. The new German political scene will have, therefore, many features, earlier developed in the western parts of the country. According to Lothar Probst (1995), among these features is the strong predilection to engage in public life through "antipolitical," both "left" and "right," movements that rely on populist forms of mobilization and radical, polarizing rhetorics.

Legitimacy

Unfortunately, I do not have data on the legitimacy of protest for all four countries. The Polish data I found indicate that after 1989, the degree of acceptance (legitimacy) of such forms of protest as strikes and street demonstrations increased from 1989 to 1992 (Table 6.8). Because legitimacy is the final component of institutionalization, this piece of evidence indicates that the institutionalization of strikes and street demonstrations in Poland was rising, contributing to the increase of the overall institutionalization of the protest sector in this country.

Institutional Correlates (Causes?) of Differential Patterns of Protest Institutionalization

The higher incidence of strikes and strike threats in Poland than in the other three countries can be explained through a comparative study of three distinct, though mutually reinforcing, mechanisms:

1. *Cultural-historical.* We expect more strikes in a country with a long and extensive history of institutionalizing such forms of protest as strikes and strike threats.
2. *Rational.* We expect people to engage in protest as a rational, calculated response to the lack of access to policy making through other channels. For example, labor unions are more likely to organize frequent protest actions if the country does not have a tripartite commission that would provide corporatist inclusion of labor into the governmental decision-making processes.
3. *Sociological-institutional.* We expect more strikes if there are many unions competing for the same "audience." Under such circumstances, unions increase their visibility, via protest, to outbid each

TABLE 6.8
Net Approval of Special Forms of Protest in Poland

Forms of Protest	1981	1984	1988	1989	1990	1992
Petitions, letters	39	61	60	50	68	84
Posting posters	−8	1	15	−4	38	41
Strikes	−2	7	−12	−15	22	47
Street demonstration	−50	−3	−24	−35	7	39
Boycott of state decisions	−26	−14	1	−16	4	22
Occupying public buildings	−52	−72	−67	−71	−63	−55
Actively resisting police	−50	−41	−48	−39	−45	−47

Sources: Jasiewicz (1993, p. 131); CBOS (1992).
    Net approval is the difference between those who think that citizens should have the right to use a specific form of action and those who think they should not.

other in wooing potential supporters. As a result, a specific (pro-test-intensive) institutionalization of the interorganizational com-petition develops.[19]

In looking at Eastern Europe, we face the dilemma of more cases than variables, which makes rigorous testing of hypotheses difficult. In fact, a comparison of Poland, Hungary, Slovakia, and the former East Germany provides evidence supporting all three explanations.

First, let us consider the hypothesis that the repertoire of contention is shaped by history (unique cultural trajectories). Among the East Eu-ropean states, Poland has by far the strongest tradition of industrial conflicts (1956, 1970, 1976, 1980–81, 1988). Hungary, in contrast, has a well-established tradition of street demonstrations and struggles (1956 in particular), which played a significant role during the power transfer period (1988–1990). The unions and other protest organizers in the for-mer East Germany should be influenced by the dominant action reper-toire brought over by West German unions and other SMOs, which organize most of the protest actions there. As Kriesi et al. (1995) report, a demonstrative strategy dominated the German action repertoire. Given these facts, the Polish ratio of street demonstrations to strikes should be considerably lower than that in Hungary or East Germany.

The empirical data, collected in Table 6.9, allow us to strongly con-firm this hypothesis. Hungarian protesters chose street demonstrations four times more often than strikes; German protesters demonstrated six times more often than they staged strikes. Poles, in contrast, were almost equally prone to strike and to demonstrate. This is an expected result given the relatively long, established tradition of industrial con-

TABLE 6.9
Protest Characteristics in Four Countries

	Poland	Hungary	Slovakia	East Germany
Strikes (% of all events)	29.3	8.6	7.5	8.9
Strike threats (% of all events)	27.6	20.0	14.3	4.5
Street demonstrations (% of all events)	36.9	39.8	28.1	55.2
Ratio: demonstrations/strikes	1.26	4.63	3.76	6.2
Ratio: strikes/year/million population	2.26	1.18	1.25	1.30
Ratio: demonstration/year/million population	2.85	4.54	4.73	7.40

flicts in Poland. In Slovakia, the most frequently used protest strategy was letter writing. Again, it is not an unexpected result in a state that is a successor to Czechoslovakia, where the anticommunist opposition (Charter 77) used letters as its main tool of pressuring the authorities.

Other explanations also are confirmed by a comparison of the four countries. Hungary, Slovakia, and East Germany instituted top-level corporatist arrangements early in their transitions; Poland did not.[20] Thus, in Poland one expects more strikes. As Wallace and Jenkins (1995, p. 134) note, the institutionalization of neocorporatist bargaining diminishes the likelihood of protest. Countries with a strong social democratic party (Hungary and Poland since 1993) and a centralized labor sector (Hungary, the former East Germany, Slovakia) are expected to have fewer industrial conflicts and strikes than a more pluralistic country with several unions that do not have "direct" access to the political process (Poland).[21]

Third, the Polish trade union sector was more diversified and decentralized than that in other countries; therefore—exactly as sociological institutionalists would argue—Poland had more competition and thus more "competitive" protest actions.[22]

Conclusion

The interaction between state and society in modern democracies has not been institutionalized through the reduction of direct collective action and the increased use of lower-mobilization, less disruptive strategies but rather through the fuller institutionalization of direct action. This is also the pattern in the democratizing states of post-1989 East-Central Europe, particularly Poland. In Poland, the relationship between the state and industrial workers was institutionalized through the channel of a tripartite commission, aided by the well-established tradition of protest politics. Consequently, Poland had the highest intensity of strikes in our sample. In Slovakia, Hungary, and East Germany, other patterns have emerged, although the *increased institutionalization of protest occurred in all these states.*

As one would expect, the institutional context affected the process of institutionalization. In Hungary, modes other than direct contentious action (i.e., tripartite agreements) have governed the relationship between the state and the workers (even before 1989). Not surprisingly, the magnitude of protest was declining, although "in a multi-party system and parliamentary democracy, social movements and their protest culture is a special, but integrated part of the political process, with its own profile and identity" (Szabo 1994, p. 10). In Slovakia, the protest was relatively anemic; the most frequently used strategies of protest were letters and petitions. The main cause of this situation seems to have been a strong tendency toward the *recentralization* of the state, which regained and retained control over many organizations that might be potential protest organizers (Malova 1996).

In the former East Germany, relatively high, though fluctuating, levels of violence accompanying protest actions had both cultural and political causes. According to Lemke (1996, p. 27):

> Right-wing groups already existed in the GDR before the collapse of the communist regime. Second, recent studies indicate that although right-wing extremism is less organized in the east than in the west, it is much more aggressive. Authoritarian and xenophobic orientations which existed in the former GDR, quickly surfaced after 1990, gaining influence among those disadvantaged by the rapid modernization borne by unification.

In summary, our research demonstrated that during the 1989–1994 period in the four Central European states—Poland, Slovakia, Hungary, and the former East Germany—contentious collective action (protest) became increasingly institutionalized. This phenomenon was most noticeable in Poland, where the protest sector was increasingly institutionalized in all four dimensions: authorization, disruptiveness, procedures, and legitimacy.

Thus, what transpired in Central Europe—most clearly in Poland—was a different kind of institutionalization or consolidation of democracy than the one Bresser Pereira et al. (1993) seem to have had in mind. They conclude that for the successful consolidation of democracy, "all groups must channel their demands through the democratic institutions and abjure other tactics" (p. 4). But what if increasingly institutionalized protest becomes a "democratic institution" which functions as part and parcel of the democratizing polity? Is democratic consolidation threatened by such an increased magnitude of contentious collective action, even if it is highly institutionalized? For most observers, the progress of democratic consolidation in Hungary, Poland, and East Germany passed the point of no return; an authoritarian reversal in these states is highly unlikely. Yet, it is precisely these countries, particularly Poland and East Germany, that experienced a high magnitude of protest actions. By contrast, Slovakia, the country with the least disruptive (most benign) repertoire of protest and a low level of strike activity, is commonly perceived as the least consolidated democracy of the four. I conclude that institutionalized protest is not a threat to democratization but rather its significant component. It is worth recall-

ing, with a modification, Eckstein and Gurr's (1975, p. 452) observation
that

> the risk of chronic low-level conflict is one of the prices democrats should
> expect to pay for freedom from regimentation by the state—or by authori-
> ties in other social units, whether industrial establishments, trade unions,
> schools, universities, or families.

I would only replace the term "chronic low-level conflict" with "institutionalized protest." It may well be that the post-1989 Central Europe, again, particularly Poland, became one of the "protest movement
societies" so characteristic of the last decades of the twentieth century.

It is, however, too early to offer any final conclusions. There is evidence that the institutionalized contentiousness of Polish society characterized only a protest wave that ended in 1994, after a coalition of
postcommunist parties won parliamentary elections. After this event,
the magnitude of protest declined, at least temporarily.[23] It should be
noted, however, that the diminished role of institutionalized contentiousness in the repertoire of the state-society interactions resulted
from a general decline in contentiousness; should it be revived, it may
still be highly institutionalized.

Notes

1. For a detailed elaboration of this argument, see Grzegorz Ekiert (1996).
He argues that the institutions and policies of state-socialist regimes have been
shaped by domestic politics—specifically, by patterns of political conflict, mobilization, and demobilization. The incidents of political crisis, institutional
breakdown, and strategies of regime reequilibration left long-lasting political
legacies in East European countries and were the most important determinants
of their recent history. As a result of these crises, fundamental changes and
adjustments were introduced into the political and economic institutions and
practices of these regimes, altering relations between institutional orders of the
party-state and between the state and society.

2. For an exemplary effort to correlate developments under state socialism
and their constraining impact on the current transformation process, see Janos
Kornai (1996).

3. The empirical evidence for this chapter comes primarily from our research project. We developed a systematic database on collective protest during the first years of democratic transition in four countries: Poland, Hungary,
Slovakia, and the former East Germany. The project was funded by the Program for the Study of Germany and Europe administered by the Center for
European Studies at Harvard University, the National Council for Soviet and
East European Research, and the American Council of Learned Societies. It is

directed by Ekiert (Harvard University) and me. We are currently completing a book entitled *Collective Protest and Democratic Consolidation in Poland, 1989–1993* and a booklong comparative study of the four countries, with Christiane Lemke, Darina Malova, and Mate Szabo. Their contributions proved to be invaluable while I was working on this chapter. The main source of inspiration and continuous support for the whole project has been Sidney Tarrow, whose helpful comments on this piece are also gratefully acknowledged. David Meyer's incisive criticism of the first draft helped me to redirect the study in a more productive direction.

4. For the most recent examples of this growing interest in the role of civil society in democratization, see Bermeo (n.d.), Schmitter (n.d.), and Tarrow (1995).

5. Charles Tilly (1986; also see Tilly, Tilly, and Tilly 1975), in his studies of collective action in France and Britain, convincingly demonstrates that over the last two centuries, organizations of civil society were the typical vehicles of protest.

6. Institutions should be distinguished from norms; the former are "self-policing," whereas the latter are not (Jepperson 1991, p. 160).

7. According to Jepperson (1991, p. 146), practices are institutionalized when they require "little 'action'—repetitive mobilization and intervention—for their sustenance." The basic assumption behind this point is that mobilization is *inversely related* to institutionalization: the higher the former, the lower the latter. However, even though an institutionalized strategy may be less costly than direct action, it may be less efficient *than other institutionalized strategies.* This is the problem of the "stickiness" of suboptimal institutions (higher institutionalization does not always imply the highest available efficiency) (see, e.g., North 1990, p. 7; March and Olsen 1989, pp. 54–56).

8. The three features of institutionalization listed correspond to the three dimensions of institutions identified by Crawford and Ostrom (1996, pp. 582–83).

9. Thus, the general model of protest I subscribe to is the *political process* model (Tilly's [1978] *polity model;* Morris and Herring 1987, pp. 165–71).

10. According to Tilly, "The different forms of collective action are part of the regular processes of struggle. The coherent phenomenon is a process that has an orderly side and a disorderly side. The central process is a process of sets of people acting together on their interests, and that is what we ought to be theorizing about" (Morris and Herring 1987, p. 165).

11. Consider the value of "novelty" in protest. "Size, novelty, and militancy are chief elements of newsworthiness" (Rochon 1990, p. 108). See also Tarrow's (1989, pp. 59–61) comments on Zolberg's "moments of madness" and Kriesi et al. (1995, pp. 134–42).

12. The ratio of institutionalization to action will be different in various polities, although its empirical measurement may be extremely difficult for it depends on the availability of very specific data. In the case of labor disputes, for example, one would need to know how many times (in a given unit of time) conflicts were solved by negotiations alone and how many times negotiations

were forced by strikes or strike threats. Often such information is unavailable, and we will only try to approximate the ratio between direct action and negotiations.

13. Each of these mechanisms is analyzed by a specific school of institutional analysis. Historical institutionalism deals with the former, rational choice institutionalism with the latter (Hall and Taylor 1994; March and Olsen 1989, pp. 21–6).

14. Inspired by Tilly's (1978, pp. 162–64) idea of gauging simultaneously several dimensions of protest, we tried to construct such an index, multiplying three variables of our data protocol: (1) duration, (2) number of participants, and (3) scope. Two research assistants, Jason Wittenberg and Matthias Ecker, relying on two different methods of estimating missing values, produced two different indexes. The "Wittenberg" index confirmed our qualitative analysis, that the magnitude of protest in Poland increased during the period studied. The "Ecker" index shows that the magnitude of protest in Poland, East Germany, and Slovakia, after a period of growth, *declined* from 1992 to 1994 (1993 in Poland). More work is needed to resolve this contradiction.

15. Dziennik Ustaw, no. 55, item 236, pp. 732–34.

16. Darina Malova, personal communication. Strikes were legalized even before the breakout of Czechoslovakia. As Malova (1996, p. 14) notes, "In 1991 and 1992 the Federal Parliament [of Czechoslovakia] passed a series of laws which laid down a framework for the organization and role of post-communist labor unions." The rights guaranteeing the freedom of association and demonstration were passed even earlier, in March 1990.

17. "Hungary Human Rights Practices, 1993," January 13, 1994, U.S. Department of State, on-line documents.

18. Article 8 of the German Constitution states, "1) All Germans shall have the right to assemble peaceably and unarmed without prior notification or permission. 2) With regard to open-air meetings this right may be restricted by or pursuant to a law" (Conradt 1996, p. 292).

19. Each of the three mechanisms represents a different version of institutionalism. For an illuminating typology of institutionalisms, see Hall and Taylor (1994).

20. I base my knowledge of this tripartite organization in Hungary (known as the Council for Interest Reconciliation) on Greskovits (1995), Kornai (1994), and conversations with each author. Kornai described the organization as a "second government," dominated by former Communist union officials, which bears the bulk of responsibility for Hungary's extremely high level of social spending. Malova (1996, pp. 13–16) offers an analysis of the Slovak Council for Economic and Social Agreement.

21. We need more studies on these patterns, given Greskovits's (1995, p. 11) observation that "the extremely low level of strike activity cannot be interpreted as an indication of union strength."

22. "The labor continued to be dominated by postcommunist federations (mostly MSZOSZ—The National Federation of Hungarian Trade Unions)" (Greskovits 1995, p. 10).

23. Kazimierz Kloc, personal communication, June 1996, Warsaw.

7

Democratic Transitions as Protest Cycles: Social Movement Dynamics in Democratizing Latin America

Patricia L. Hipsher

In many respects, the 1980s was the decade of the social movement in, Latin America. In a climate of greater political openness provided by the transitions to democracy, shantytown dwellers' movements, feminists, organized labor, student confederations, and human rights groups mobilized in protest across Latin America. The movements called for an end to the military dictatorships and advanced group-specific claims, such as increased spending for education and urban services, protection of women's and workers' rights, and prosecution of human rights abuses.

How should we conceive of protest movements that emerge during transitions to democracy? Are they examples of the growth of the "social movement society," or do they represent a more cyclical phenomenon? If the latter, how does the institutionalization of these movements during the period of democratic consolidation affect their abilities to represent groups, put new issues on the agenda, and bring about democratizing reforms?

In this chapter, I use a political process approach to examine two distinct social movement processes: the development of cycles of protest and the institutionalization of dissent. The political process approach conceives of social movements and their protest activity as cyclical phenomena, which rise and fall as a function of political

I would like to thank the editors of this volume and David Blatt for their helpful comments on an earlier draft.

changes external to the movement, and expects that transitions from authoritarian politics to democracy will be accompanied by dramatic shifts in social movement strategies and forms of collective action, usually in the direction of greater institutionalization. From a political process perspective, the impact of institutionalization on movements and the broader political process varies from case to case and primarily depends on the political setting.

The Argument

In Latin America, cycles of democratization have generated cycles of protest. The explanation presented here is that as authoritarians liberalize the political process and permit greater freedom of action, selected social movements emerge in protest. These early mobilizers are likely to push the transition farther and faster than it otherwise might have gone and create the conditions under which other groups may emerge, generating a wave of mobilization. During the latter stages of transitions, when political parties return to the fore and confrontation is replaced by democratic cooperation and compromise, movements tend to decline and become institutionalized, thus completing the cycle.

The institutionalization of movements during the latter stages of transitions has variable impacts on movements and the larger political process. These variations are explained in terms of two factors: the nature of parties and party-movement relations, and the openness of the political system. In situations in which political parties and party structures are relatively open and movements have a degree of autonomy from political parties and in which the political system is open, institutionalization tends to result in greater incorporation of social movements in decision-making processes. In settings in which parties are relatively rigid and closed and organizations enjoy little autonomy from parties, and in which the political system is closed, institutionalization tends to result in the marginalization of movements.

In this chapter, the cases of Brazil and Chile are used to demonstrate both the cyclical nature of social movements during democratic transitions and the variable impact of institutionalization on movements and the political process more generally. Brazil and Chile represent cases of Latin American transitions that, initially, were accompanied by high levels of protest mobilization; however, the consolidation of these democracies has brought about movement institutionalization. This institutionalization has had different effects in Brazil and Chile. Generally, institutionalization has allowed Brazilian movements to become more integrated into the decision-making process, whereas in Chile the institutionalization of movements has resulted in their marginalization. In the next two sections, I will show that protest cycles emerge as a consequence of changed political opportunities and that institutionalization produces different movement trajectories that depend on the openness of political parties and the state structure.

Protest Cycles: Defining Concepts and Identifying Causes

Of the contemporary theories of social movement development, the political process model best explains the dynamics involved in cycles of protest and their outcomes. The political process model is based on the premise that the development of social movements is dependent on political institutions, configurations of power, and other factors external to movements (Kitschelt 1986; Kriesi et al. 1992; McAdam 1982; Tarrow 1994; Tilly 1978). These exogenous variables have come to be known as the political opportunity structure (POS). Three aspects of the POS that have been connected with the appearance of social protest in transitional Latin America are the opening (liberalization) of the political process, the presence of allies and support groups, and divisions within the regime.

The opening of the political process during transitions is one element that has encouraged movement mobilization in Latin America (O'Donnell and Schmitter 1986). Transitional political systems, by their very nature, are characterized by a mix of open and closed elements, the most favorable situation for movement emergence (Eisinger 1973; Kitschelt 1986). Although protest under authoritarian governments is not unheard of, it is much more likely to occur during transitional periods. Guillermo O'Donnell and Philippe Schmitter (1986, p. 48) argue that the "resurrection of civil society" will not occur until the costs of collective action are lowered and some contestation is permitted by the regime.

The presence of allies and support groups has also encouraged movement development in the Latin American transitions. In many Latin American countries, the Roman Catholic Church has been an important ally for social movements (Mainwaring 1986; Oxhorn 1995; Schneider 1995). Following Vatican II, in 1965, the Church began to pursue a preferential option for the poor. This preferential option translated into official Church condemnation of the authoritarian regimes, the development of Christian Base Communities (CEBs), and creation of solidaristic organizations to aid victims of the military regimes.[1]

Conflict or divisions within the authoritarian regimes is the final condition that has encouraged social protest (Schneider 1995). Most writers on transitions agree that important divisions within the author-itarian regime are connected with the outbreak of mass protest. The emergence of cleavages between hard-liners *(duros)* and soft-liners *(blandos)* creates a situation in which movements may be able to pres-sure soft-liners to "get off the fence" and to demand greater liberaliza-tion of the regime (Przeworski 1991, p. 61). In a more liberalized system, movements will have greater facility of action, and the likeli-hood of repression will diminish.

In most cases of democratic transitions, the initial upsurge of popu-lar protest, encouraged by changes in the POS, evolves into a massive wave or "cycle of protest" (Tarrow 1994, p. 153). In transitional Latin America, cycles of protest have been characterized by the following: (1) the diffusion of protest from older, more mobilized movement sec-tors to newer, less mobilized movement sectors (Alves 1985; de la Maza and Garcés 1985); (2) geographic diffusion from central regions to more peripheral regions (Alves 1985; de la Maza and Garcés 1985); (3) an increase in the number of protest events and protest participants (Alves 1985; Salazar 1990); and (4) intensified interactions between movements and authorities (Arriagada 1988; Schneider 1995).

These cycles of protest develop, as specially placed movements—movements with access to greater resources, better organization, per-haps a history of contention—test the waters and demonstrate the vulnerability of the regime to heretofore reluctant movement sectors.[2] O'Donnel and Schmitter (1986, p. 49) write that the early acts of exem-plary individuals and "privileged sectors," particularly those of human rights movements, provoke or revive collective identifications and actions, thus serving as the basis for the generalized explosion of civil society during transitions. Additionally, the early acts of protest "undermine attempts by the regime soft-liners to perpetuate them-selves in government" and "raise the perceived costs of the coup that . . . . the hard-liners would want to make" (O'Donnell and Schmitter 1986, p. 53). In these ways, early mobilizers lower the costs of collective action for those who follow.

Regardless of the protest cycle's intensity or scope, it must ulti-mately come to an end. One factor that may lead to the decline of transitional protest cycles is the increasing intensity and violence of protest, which has the effect of driving many moderates off the streets.[3] As protest intensifies and becomes more violent, and as the govern-ment becomes more repressive, many movement activists retire from street actions and begin to pursue more moderate goals and use more institutionalized forms of action.

Another important factor in the decline of transitional protest cycles is the return of political parties and the internal divisions over partisanship. The return of parties affects movements by diverting their time and energy from the actual goals of the movement to issues of autonomy and party-movement relations, by accentuating existing divisions within movements, and by weakening movements' capacities to wage unified campaigns.

Finally, important in explaining the decline of movement cycles in transitional countries are the intentional efforts made by elites to demobilize movements for the sake of a peaceful, successful transition (Cotler 1986; Gillespie 1986; Gunther 1992; Hipsher 1996). Usually, demobilization from above does not require extreme coercion on the part of elites. This is because movement activists frequently perceive a certain long-term rationality in demobilizing; by demobilizing, they are "helping" the democratic transition to succeed (Hispher 1994, p. 427).

Institutionalizing Dissent

One of the ironies of democratization cycles is that the social movements that lead the push for democracy tend to become institutionalized once democracy becomes a reality. Institutionalization is a process that involves a shift toward more standardized, nonthreatening forms of collective action that entail less mobilization and less disruption. The key indicators of institutionalization are changes in the forms of collective action. Institutionalization involves greater reliance on negotiations, the electoral process, and working through government institutions and agencies.

Institutionalization has variable outcomes. One outcome of institutionalization is movement marginalization. Another outcome is greater incorporation of movements into the decision-making processes of government and political parties. These variable trajectories depend on the nature of political parties and party-movement relations and the openness of the political system.

During transitions to democracy, social movements are not the only groupings to reemerge. Political parties also resurface during transitions. As political parties reassert their role as principal interlocutor between civil society and the state, social movement influence becomes much more dependent on the relations between parties and movements and parties' willingness to include movements. In systems in which political parties are more democratic and open to outside groups, movements are likely to have greater access to the political process and experience greater success in influencing party positions and practices than those in systems in which political parties are closed and dominating.

The impact of institutionalization on movements also depends on the openness of the political systems. As authoritarianism gives way to democracy, the political process will naturally become more open. However, even democracies can vary in terms of their openness, affecting movements' abilities to influence or develop a working relationship with government institutions.

Political "openness" refers to the organization of power within the political system that facilitates or hinders groups' efforts to gain access to the decision-making process. The degree of territorial centralization and distribution of power among branches of government are dimensions of political openness. These may be formal, constitutional dimension (federal versus unitary systems, separated versus "fused" powers) or informal dimensions. "Open" systems allow movements greater opportunities to become part of the decision-making process than "closed" systems (Kitschelt 1986); thus, they are more likely to be receptive to democratizing pressures than "closed" systems.

The Chilean Protest Cycle, 1983–1987

On May 11, 1983, tens of thousands of Chileans responded to the call by the nation's Copper Workers' Confederation (CTC) for a national day of protest against the Pinochet dictatorship. Organized labor, student movements, shantytown dwellers, and middle-class professionals stayed home from work and school, engaged in work slowdowns, and participated in loud and massive street marches and demonstrations.[4] National days of protest, like this one, were called on nearly a monthly basis until 1987, fueling one of the most intense cycles of protest in Latin America in the 1980s.

Emerging in 1983, the Chilean protest cycle was facilitated by an opening in the political system and divisions within the regime, generated by the economic crisis, and the support of political parties and the Catholic Church. The cycle peaked in 1986 and thereafter quickly declined as increased violence, government repression, and efforts by opposition party leaders to ensure a peaceful, stable transition forced a shift toward more institutionalized forms of social movement activity. The institutionalization of dissent, beginning in 1987, has facilitated a relatively successful and stable transition from authoritarian rule; however, it also has involved the marginalization of movements and has resulted in a somewhat limited democracy.

In the early 1980s, Chile experienced a severe economic crisis, brought on by heavy foreign indebtedness and lack of investment during the late 1970s. At the height of the recession in 1983, unemployment reached 30 percent (Arriagada 1988, p. 51). Although much of the research on the Chilean protest cycle identifies economic grievances as being key in the development of protest, Cathy Schneider's (1992, pp. 262, 263) research on the shantytown movement clearly dispels this notion. Her research indicates that the economic crisis generated a political crisis and, in this way opened up the political opportunity structure (Schneider 1992, 1995). The Cabinet divided over economic policy, rifts developed within the military, and right-wing and centrist supporters moved into open opposition to the regime (Schneider 1995, pp. 155, 156). Evidence emerged of divisions within the Chilean armed forces and *carabineros* (uniformed police), in the form of a communiqué calling for the replacement of the regime's leader (Casa Chile 1984, p. 24).

External support for the protests was a second important factor in the eruption of the protest cycle. The Church was an important ally for the protesters (Oxhorn 1995; Schneider 1995). In the late 1970s, the Church began to lend its support to neighborhood movements, human rights movements, and the labor movements. Priests and layworkers allowed shantytown movements to meet in the neighborhood parishes and provided them "with a certain legitimacy that helped overcome their initial fear of participating in any organization" (Oxhorn 1991, p. 75). The Church also created the *Vicaría de la Solidaridad* to provide a protective umbrella for organizing groups and legal counsel to victims of the regimes.

Centrist political parties began to lend their support to the opposition movement in the early 1980s. Before 1981, the Christian Democratic Party (PDC) had been led by former president Eduardo Frei, a relatively conservative figure in the party. Although he opposed the dictatorship in principle, under his leadership the party did not move into direct confrontation with the government. Frei's death in 1982 and the election of Gabriel Valdés to replace him shifted the party further to the left, committing it to more mobilization and direct confrontation with the government (O'Brien and Roddick 1983).

When the CTC issued the call to protest in May 1983, Chileans from many sectors mobilized in protest. During the first four months of the protest cycle, middle- and upper-class sectors actively supported the protest movement and participated by banging on pots and pans and honking their car horns in the evenings (Arriagada 1988, p. 56). However, the sectors most frequently cited as being involved in protests in 1983 were students and shantytown dwellers (Salazar 1990, p. 410).[5] Regardless of the makeup of protesting groups, the numbers involved tended to be large, over two hundred people in many cases (see Table 7.1).

TABLE 7.1
Number of Participants in Chilean Protest Events, 1982–1987

Year	Size of Group			
	1–3	3–20	20–200	200 +
1982	1	3	1	8
1983	6	16	3	36
1984	1	8	7	20
1985	1	22	13	19
1986	0	20	15	18
1987	0	18	7	14

Source: Salazar (1990, p. 409).

The forms of collective action used during these early protests were numerous and varied. In the early protests, Genaro Arriagada writes (1988, p. 56), the repertoire of collective action was dominated by non-violent forms of action:

> The first few protests consisted of non-violent activities, such as banging on pots and pans at a specified hour, honking car horns, boycotting all stores and markets, and keeping children home from school. Political and social leaders held unauthorized meetings in public plazas . . . and industrial workers staged work slowdowns.

Initially, protest was limited to a few central cities; however, in the weeks that followed, protest spread throughout the country. On the first day of protest, May 11, protest events were reported in only the largest cities—Santiago, Punta Arenas, Valparaiso, and Concepción. By July, protests had spread to most of the provincial cities. By the fourth national day of protest, in August, demonstrations were being reported everywhere, from Antofagasta in the north to Punta Arenas in the south (de la Maza and Garcés 1985).

In 1984, protest temporarily declined when the government imposed a state of siege. However, once the state of siege was lifted in August 1985, the cycle resumed, this time with greater intensity. In 1985 and 1986, the number of protest events returned to their 1983 levels (see Table 7.2), and their intensity, measured in terms of repression, was much greater than in 1983 and 1984. Ariagada's (1988, p. 63) data show that the number of arrests rose from 1,213 in 1982 to 4,537 in 1983, 5,291 in 1984, 5,314 in 1985, and 7,019 in 1986. According to the *Vicaría*, the arrests were intended to create "a general atmosphere of fear in the shantytowns and to discourage the eventual recurrence of collective dissidence or protest" (Arriagada 1988, p. 63).

TABLE 7.2
Number of Protest Events in Chile, 1982–1987

Year	Number of Events
1982	13
1983	61
1984	36
1985	55
1986	58
1987	39

Source: Salazar (1990, pp. 406, 407).

During the 1985–1986 period, participation by the middle sectors declined, such that shantytown dwellers and youth appeared more dominant and violent protest more visible. As middle sectors fled the streets, the remaining protesters used greater violence to make their point. Beginning in 1985, organized national days of protest became infrequent, and the repertoire of collective action came to be dominated by more violent, confrontational forms of collective action. In 1985, only five national days of protest were called, as compared with ten in 1983 and seven in 1984. And in 1986, there were only two national days of protest. Taking their place were demonstrations, armed attacks, and armed confrontations (Salazar 1990, pp. 406, 407). Additionally, the number of events involving large masses of people declined, while the number of events involving smaller groups increased (see Table 7.1).

The protests reached their apogee in July 1986. In April 1986, the moderate political forces of the Democratic Alliance (AD)[6] and the leftist parties of the Popular Democratic Movement (MDP)[7] united to form the Civil Assembly (AC). The AC drew up a platform, calling for the resignation of Pinochet and free and fair elections, and "notified the regime that it had 30 days to respond to its demands, threatening a national strike on July 2 and 3 if there was no satisfactory response by May 31" (Petras and Leiva 1988, p. 98).

Pinochet rejected the proposal and refused to negotiate with the members of the Assembly, setting into motion preparations for a massive nationwide strike. On June 2, 1986, the opposition initiated a sustained and increasing campaign of mobilization, which climaxed in a general strike on July 2 and 3. The July 2 and 3 strike was a success for the AC in the sense that its forces managed to paralyze activities in Santiago for forty-eight hours. However, the government's use of force and repression against the protesters had tragic results. During the two days of protest, ten people were killed by government forces. In one shantytown, two teenagers were detained by a military patrol, doused with kerosene, and set on fire (Schneider 1995, pp. 184, 185).

Following the July 1986 general strike, the cycle of protest quickly declined. The total number of protest events fell by half in 1987 (see Table 7.2). Students abandoned the streets to participate in the Campaign for Free Elections (*Cauce* 1987), and shantytown dwellers shifted their activities away from illegal land seizures and barricades to enrolling in housing subsidy programs and formulating proposals for emergency housing (Hipsher 1996).[8]

One reason for the decline of protest was the escalation of left-wing violence, as exemplified by the following two events. The first event was the August 12 discovery of a clandestine arsenal of weapons brought into the country by the Manuel Rodriguez Patriotic Front (FPMR), an armed group associated with the Communist Party. The second was an assassination attempt against General Pinochet by the FPMR on September 7. These events horrified moderates and drove a wedge between them and the left, making unified mobilization difficult (Constable and Valenzuela 1991, p. 294). These incidents also led Christian Democrats, Socialists, and other moderate opposition forces to accept Pinochet's offer of a dialogue concerning the return to democracy.

A second reason for the decline of the protest cycle was repression on the part of the government. Schneider (1995, p. 186) argues that government repression, especially in its more extreme forms in 1986, "convinced the vast majority that the risk was simply too great" and encouraged a shift toward more institutionalized forms of action.

Once opposition forces made the choice to pursue a negotiated route to democracy social movement mobilization became increasingly rare. In an attempt to ensure that the transition to democracy succeeded and was not thwarted by provocative violence, opposition parties of the center and center-left discouraged protest by movements and encouraged them to get involved in the Campaign for the "No"[9] and to work through the proper institutional channels (Hipsher 1996).

The Brazilian Protest Cycle, 1978–1982

On May 12, 1978, 2,500 metalworkers at the Saab-Scania truck and bus factory in São Bernardo do Campo punched their time clocks, went to their work stations, and sat down, initiating one of the largest waves of strikes and protest activities in decades.[10] Sebastião C. V. Cruz and Carlos E. Martins (1983, p. 59, cited in MacRae 1992, p. 185) said of the 1978 strikes, "With the strike in the ABC,[11] and with the movement that it precipitated, an enormous space was opened in the field of ideas and in the political imagination. Suddenly, the realm of the possible was expanded, the new began to sprout." A cycle of protest had begun.

The Brazilian protest cycle that was initiated in 1978 by workers and, to a lesser degree, neighborhood movements was facilitated by the liberalization of the regime, divisions between hard-liners and soft-liners, and the support given movements by the Catholic Church. The decline and institutionalization of the protest cycle in 1981 can be explained in terms of government repression of the workers' movement and the factionalization engendered by the return of political parties. The institutionalization of dissent has permitted many movements to become more incorporated into government decision-making processes via commissions, councils, and informal negotiations, creating a more inclusive polity.

The origins of the 1978–1982 cycle of protest can be traced back to the mid-1970s. After ten years of military rule, in 1974 the regime initiated a slow and gradual liberalization. At the beginning of the *distensão* (decompression), few social movements or organized groupings existed, and those that did were relatively quiet, fearful of state repression and lacking resources. However, as the *distensã* unfolded, movements began to reemerge, benefiting from the opportunities created by the new political environment.

The Catholic Church provided resources and leadership for social movements. Popular women's groups and neighborhood associations met in local parishes, and the dioceses provided indirect financial support. Additionally, the Church organized hundreds of base-level communities (CEBs) in neighborhoods, parishes, and factories. The CEBs allowed women and men to develop self-confidence and establish networks of solidarity that would serve as the basis for movement organizing in the late 1970s and early 1980s (Mainwaring 1986).

Another factor that encouraged the reemergence of social movements was the state's inability to respond in a unified fashion to the opposition. The state was divided by an internal power struggle between the security community and the core leadership of the government and by a coup attempt by General Sylvio Frota, Minister of the Army (Stepan 1988, pp. 30–53). By 1977, the struggle within the Geisel government between hard-liners and moderates had intensified to the point that Geisel was forced to dismiss Frota, one of the key hard-liners within the regime. Geisel then introduced a series of political reforms to phase out certain authoritarian elements of the political system. *Habeus corpus* was reinstated for political detainees, prior censorship was lifted from radio and television, and political exiles were allowed to return to the country (Skidmore 1988, pp. 18, 19). It was in this context that Brazilian civil society erupted in protest.

The first major strike wave in a decade occurred in May 1978. The strike movement began among auto workers in the ABC region and spread quickly to other regions and economic sectors. During the first and second weeks of the industrial strike wave, the activity was limited to three cities: Santo André, São Bernardo, and São Caetano. By week 3, strikes had spread to São Paulo and Osasco. Ultimately, the actions encompassed twenty cities in seven states. By the end of 1978, over half a million workers from fourteen sectors had gone on strike (see Table 7.3).

Between 1978 and 1979, new movement sectors emerged, joining the labor and slum dweller movements. Having begun to organize in the mid-1970s, the women's movement became a much more active and contentious actor beginning in 1979. Sonia Alvarez (1989, p. 212) writes that during the period 1979–1981, the "political action of feminist groups centered on protest actions—petitions, protest marches, mass media denunciation of sexist government policies, etc."

Despite the importance of feminism in the burgeoning protest movement, Thomas Skidmore (1988, p. 212) finds that the increased intensity and strength of the protest cycle is best explained in terms of the development of a strong solidarity network. In 1978, workers had gone on strike with little outside support. However, in 1979, the workers benefited from the presence of a broad support network, which included the Church, its CEBs, and the neighborhood movements. Catholic clergy and layworkers donated money, food, time, and meeting facilities to keep the strike alive (Skidmore 1988, p. 213), and, in São

TABLE 7.3
Industrial Strikes in Brazil, May 12–July 13, 1978

Week	Number of Factories on Strike	Number of Workers on Strike	Number of Cities Affected	Total Number of Workers on Strike
1	24	60,500	3	60,500
2	12	17,450	3	77,950
3	21	17,990	5	95,940
4	27	29,470	9	125,410
5	38	39,694	9	165,104
6	32	22,967	9	188,071
7	17	23,441	9	211,512
8	21	19,803	9	231,315
9	21	14,620	9	245,935

Source: Alves (1985, p. 196).

Paulo, the Friends of the Neighborhood Movement (MAB) participated in a solidarity movement with auto workers and teachers and sent representatives to local demonstrations (Mainwaring 1989, p. 174). The solidarity shown the workers by the Church, its lay groups, and middle-class professionals created a sense of optimism and strengthened activists' claims that a real multiclass mobilization was under way.

The strike activity of 1979 began in mid-March, again in the automobile factories of the ABC region. Whereas the 1978 strikes involved some 350,000 auto workers, in 1979 nearly a million auto workers struck, managing to shut down every automobile factory in the nation (Alves 1985, p. 199). The strike activity spread beyond the auto industry and the ABC region to encompass over three million workers in fifteen states (see Table 7.4). Also interesting is that in 1979 a larger

TABLE 7.4
Number of Strikes and Strikers in Brazil, 1978–1980

Sector	1978 Strikes	1979 Strikes	1980 Strikes	1978 Strikers	1979 Strikers	1980 Strikers
Auto	5	27	2	357,043	958,435	244,500
Port	1	0	1	1,200	0	0
Transport	1	19	0	170	443,160	10,000
Construction	0	8	1	0	303,000	0
Mills	0	1	0	0	1,500	0
Tobacco	1	0	0	400	0	0
Glass	1	0	0	450	0	0
Textiles	1	2	0	5,390	3,350	0
Baking	0	1	0	0	500	0
Food	0	1	0	0	1,500	0
Clubs	0	1	0	0	3,000	0
Ceramics	1	1	0	2,000	1,050	0
Grave digging	0	1	0	0	1,000	0
Gasoline	0	1	1	0	3,000	2,000
Gas	0	1	0	0	8,000	0
Chemical	1	0	0	2,750	0	0
Paper	0	1	0	0	2,000	0
Garbage	0	4	0	0	10,000	0
Mining	0	4	0	0	34,600	0
Electric	0	1	0	0	10,000	0
Commercial	0	1	0	0	40,000	0
Health	1	1	0	7,500	10,000	0
Banks	1	4	0	10,000	105,000	0
Security	0	3	0	0	20,000	0
Teachers	3	16	3	138,634	752,000	111,000
Professors	1	4	26	800	14,139	39,200
Public	0	5	0	0	387,998	0
Medicine	5	1	15	11,500	2,400	6,500
Journalism	0	1	0	0	1,500	0
Rural	1	3	1	1,200	90,162	240,000
Total	24	113	50	539,037	3,207,994	664,700

Source: Alves (1985, pp. 196, 198, 202).

number of the striking sectors called more than one strike, indicating the increasing intensity of the movement. In 1978, only three of the fourteen striking sectors called more than one strike. However, in 1979, twelve of the twenty-six striking sectors called more than one strike (Alves 1985, pp. 199).

Strike activity fell dramatically in 1980, as government forces repressed the strikes and the economy worsened (Keck 1992, p. 169). The number of strikes fell to fifty, involving only 664,700 strikers. Additionally, the number of sectors involved dropped to eight, of which only four called more than one strike (see Table 7.4). This point signaled the decline of labor as an active sector in the protest cycle.

The decline of strike activity did not mean the end of the cycle of protest. Other movement sectors, especially feminists and neighborhood movements, remained relatively active and contentious in 1980. Feminists demonstrated in support of prostitutes, in solidarity with the Argentine Mothers of the Plaza de Mayo, and marched with the gay movement and the black movement to condemn the São Paulo police chief's effort to rid the downtown area of "undesirables" (Alvarez 1994a, pp. 32, 33). Neighborhood movement organizations were popping up everywhere. In the state of Rio de Janeiro, it was reported that a new neighborhood organization was founded every week in 1980 (Alves 1985, p. 175). Finally, new identity- and issue-based movements began to organize. These included black movements, homosexual movements (MacRae 1992), and environmental movements (Hochstetler 1993; Goldstein 1992). Overall, however, the cycle of protest was entering a phase of decline.

The downward turn in the protest cycle is explained by two factors: government repression of the labor movement in the 1980-strikes and the return of political parties. During the 1980 strikes, troops occupied the city of São Bernardo, and the government placed the union under intervention. Union leaders were jailed, purged from office, and charged with violating the National Security Law (Keck 1992, p. 169). The repression caused the movement to abandon large-scale strikes and to increase its use of institutionalized collective bargaining at the plant level (Keck 1992). It also made obsolete the emerging multiclass solidarity networks for striking workers. In both ways, the decline of labor protest weakened the wave of mobilization.

The return of political parties had an even greater weakening effect on the protest cycle. Since 1966, only two political parties, the Alliance for National Renovation (ARENA) and the Brazilian Democratic Movement (MDB), had been allowed to exist and compete for electoral office. ARENA was seen as the government party and MDB as the opposition, but, in fact, there was little difference between the two. In

1979, a new electoral reform law was passed, permitting the formation of new parties beginning in 1980.

Until the return of parties, social movements had been united in opposition to the dictatorship. However, this unity broke down with party reorganization. Renato Boschi (1987, p. 193), in his discussion of neighborhood organizations in Rio de Janeiro, writes:

> Competitive party politics tended to work against uniting people around common local objectives. With a multiparty system created in 1979, and with the opposition beginning to fragment as a consequence (and as the government intended) this tendency became more pronounced.

Related to this, the assertion of partisan loyalties within movements stimulated debates over party-movement relations. These debates further divided movements and diverted their time and attention away from local concerns. In the neighborhood and women's movements, the divisions primarily were between members of the "new left" Workers' Party (PT) and the PMDB (Party of the Brazilian Democratic Movement). PT members advocated a strategy of greater movement autonomy from parties, while the PMDB favored greater movement inclusion in a broad front for redemocratization (Mainwaring 1989, p. 175).

The return of parties also weakened the protest movement by creating greater opportunities for institutionalized forms of activity. A number of women who had been active in the women's movement temporarily left movement activity to participate in campaign activity. Dozens of women candidates, many of whom were activists in the feminist movement, ran for office. Twelve female candidates ran for the national legislature for the PMDB, and twenty-three women ran as candidates for the Workers' Party (Alvarez 1994b, pp. 170, 171).

By 1982, when congressional elections were held, the protest cycle had bottomed out. The labor movement was in a relatively defensive posture, as it concentrated its efforts on building the Labor Party and on creating national labor organizations (Keck 1992, p. 168), and it engaged in no more strikes than in 1980. And, overall, the popular movement appeared to be in crisis. The movements were no longer able to mobilize large numbers of people (Mainwaring 1989, p. 177), and they began to move from a politics of protest to a politics of making proposals.

Institutionalizing Protest in Brazil and Chile

Following 1986 in Chile and 1981 in Brazil, social movements underwent changes in their organizational forms and strategies toward greater institutionalization. In both countries, disruptive forms of collective action, such as demonstrations, strikes, and land seizures, became increasingly rare, and movements began to work within the state structures almost exclusively to try to achieve their goals.

The institutionalization of dissent has produced different outcomes in the two countries. The institutionalization of dissent has resulted in more exclusionary politics in Chile than in Brazil. In Chile, institutionalization has resulted in marginalization. With very few exceptions, Chilean movements have been denied access to the political process since the restoration of democracy, as a strong state and elitist parties have "appeared to displace social movements and leave them diminished" (Foweraker 1995, p. 107). In Brazil, while institutionalization has carried with it the potential danger of movement cooptation, it has served to incorporate movements into the system.

The struggles of the women's movements and urban social movements in the two countries serve as excellent examples of these different outcomes. The institutionalization of the Brazilian women's movement in 1982 has allowed feminists to approach the state and political parties and to advance women's interests by initiating public policies and actions that respond to the specific needs of women. Some of the most successful initiatives of the Brazilian feminist movement have been the creation of the São Paulo State Council on the Status of Women in 1983, the establishment of a women's health initiative known as the Program for Integral Assistance to Women's Health, a National Women's Council in 1985, and of women's police stations. Sonia Alvarez (1994a, p. 44) notes that some feminists were concerned about the possibility of cooptation; however, this tended not to be a problem—at least not until 1986, when nonfeminist party loyalists were appointed to the National Women's Council. Before that, the state institutions were very responsive to the feminist movement. The councils and the feminist health program were staffed by longtime feminist activists who managed to incorporate much of the feminist discourse about population policies and contraception into their programs (Alvarez 1989, p. 222), and they were perceived as legitimate agents of the feminist movement within the state (Linhares 1991, p. 27). In this way, the feminist movement has been allowed a voice in the political process and has managed to bring about democratizing reforms within political parties and the state.

The women's movement in Chile, has experienced fewer policy successes than the movement in Brazil and has been excluded from feminist policy making. The state did create the National Women's Service (SERNAM) in 1990. However, Patricia Chuchryk (1994, p. 88) contends that it is not regarded by those in the women's movement as a strong advocate of women's rights. It has failed to serve as interlocutor for the women's movement in the same way that the Brazilian Women's Councils were able to do in the 1980s. One reason for this failure is its inability (and unwillingness) to incorporate women's organizations into the policy-formulating and policy-making processes. Lisa Baldez's (1997, chap. 7) analysis of Chilean feminism demonstrates that feminist policy making had tended to be formal and nonparticipatory and that feminist nongovernmental organizations (NGOs) exercise very little influence over SERNAM and its policies; rather, they perform services solicited by SERNAM. Another reason for SERNAM's failure to truly represent the feminist movement has been its conservative leadership. During the Aylwin administration, SERNAM was headed by Christian Democratic women who were not prominent in the women's movement in the 1980s, and they acted very cautiously (Chuchryk 1994, pp. 88, 89). As such, the political process has remained relatively closed to what remains of the women's movement.[12]

Lacking indigenous resources, Brazil's urban social movement organizations traditionally have found it difficult achieving their goals without being coopted by clientelistic political parties. The return of democracy has not eliminated this dilemma completely, as corporatist and clientelistic practices continue in many areas. Following the 1982 elections, state and local governments in São Paulo and Rio de Janeiro began to develop channels whereby popular movement organizations could have access to decision makers and input into the policy-making processes (Alvarez 1993; Gay 1994). The result, in many cases, was cooptation. However, the 1986 election of a PT government in São Paulo has allowed movement organizations to achieve their goals through autonomous councils, not state- or party-controlled councils (Alvarez 1993), creating reasons for optimism.

The institutionalization of urban social movements in Chile has tended not to result in movement incorporation but rather marginalization. One of the few institutions created by the Aylwin regime to deal with the concerns and demands of the popular sector was the Division of Social Organizations (DOS). This institution is designed to "moderate popular expectations by reinforcing popular organizations as an alternative to state action" and to channel popular movement organizations into self-help forms of organization (Oxhorn 1995, p. 262). Self-help forms of organization have emerged to deal with a variety of problems, including the shortage of affordable housing among poor people. Seeking solutions to their housing problems homeless people no longer organize to put pressure on or negotiate with the government; instead, they tend to organize "savings committees" whose principal goal is to help their members to apply for housing subsidies offered by the government and fund-raise for members who may have trouble saving enough money to be awarded a subsidy (Hipsher 1994). State and party promotion of self-help forms of organization may respect the autonomy of the organizations, as noted by Oxhorn (1995, p. 263); however, it also marginalizes movements from the government decision-making processes that affect them.

These different outcomes can be explained by variations in the two countries' parties and party systems and in the openness of their political systems. Comparisons of Brazil and Chile reveal greater openness, democracy, and willingness to allow movement autonomy on the part of Brazilian political parties than those in Chile. The Brazilian political party system has traditionally been characterized by multiple, ideologically weak, clientelistic parties. Clientelism carries with it the danger of movement cooptation; however, on occasion, it also allows movements to get their demands satisfied, by engaging in negotiations and making brokered agreements. The emergence of the Workers' Party (PT) in the early 1980s has allowed movements to exert greater influence than ever and with less risk of cooptation. This is because the PT exhibits a strong commitment to "bottom-up" decision making, internal democracy, and the empowerment of civil society (Keck 1992, pp. 91, 121).

The Chilean political party system, on the other hand, is characterized by a system of strong, ideologically distinct parties and an interlocking pattern of relations among parties and social organizations (Garretón 1989, p. 9). Although close relations exist among movements and parties, these relations are not of equals; parties tend to dominate movements. At the national and local levels, movement leaders frequently are party leaders or militants. As a consequence, the parties influence movement strategies, tactics and goals. However, parties are resistant to the demands of social movements and tend to push them aside until the next elections.

The Brazilian state, not unlike the political parties, is corporatist in structure and uses clientelistic strategies to incorporate groups into the political process and to satisfy their demands. The Brazilian state is also founded on a decentralized federal system, which allows the expression and incorporation of demands at more than one level of government. The result is a relatively open system with multiple access points.

The Chilean state, in comparison, is quite closed. Under military rule in the 1980s, decentralization initiatives were implemented. These initiatives increased the responsibilities of municipal governments but did not increase the autonomy of local governments in any meaningful way. The local governments have more money to disperse, but it is the central government that still determines how much money each municipality receives and how it is to be spent. Thus, the Chilean system remains relatively centralized.

Conclusion

The two cases presented here call into question the notion that Latin America is experiencing a growth of the social movement society. Social movements, which emerged during Latin America's transitions from authoritarian rule, have not continued to grow in strength and numbers since the restoration of democracy. Rather, they have adopted more institutionalized forms of collective action.

Whether the institutionalization of protest will serve to deepen the democratization process or, instead, insulate political actors from challenges by social movements, leaving democracy limited and weak, largely depends on the nature of the parties and the structure of the state. Despite the fact that Brazil has had little prior democratic experience, the openness of the state and the democratic nature of the Workers' Party make me optimistic that social movement will have some successes in bringing about democratizing reforms in this country. I am less sanguine about Chile and the role that social movements will play in that country in the near future. The lack of will on the part of the democratic left, particularly the Socialist Party and the Party for Democracy (PPD), to act as a strong advocate for progressive and poor people's social movements has left movements with little outside support. As long as Chilean political elites continue to believe that democracy is best served by subordinating popular participation to the necessity of maintaining stability, and as long as the political system remains closed to the claims of social movements, institutionalization will leave movements marginalized from the political process and democracy rather restricted and restrictive.

Notes

1. There is a large body of literature on the role of the Latin American Catholic Church during the authoritarian and transitional periods. Among the most important works on the political role of the Church are Berryman (1984), Mainwaring (1986), and Smith (1982).

2. Sidney Tarrow (1989, pp. 143–67) refers to these movements as "early-risers."

3. Tarrow (1989, p. 320) found that this was an important cause of movement decline in Italy in the early 1970s.

4. This description of the protests comes from Cathy Schneider (1992, p. 296).

5. See Schneider's (1995) work for a detailed discussion of the processes underlying the reemergence of the shantytown dwellers' and student movements.

6. The Democratic Alliance was a moderate opposition coalition of six political parties: the Republic Party, Radical Party, Social Democratic Party, Christian Democratic Party, Socialist Party, and Popular Socialist Union.

7. The Popular Democratic Movement was an opposition coalition of various left-wing parties and movements, including the Communist Party, the Christian Left, Ad-MAPU, and the Movement of the Revolutionary Left.

8. Schneider (1995, p. 191) notes that there was a brief revival of protest in April 1987, when the Pope visited Chile, but the shift by moderate opposition forces toward a strategy of free elections inhibited the mobilization of sustained protest.

9. In 1988, Pinochet held a yes-no plebiscite on whether he should remain president until 1996. The Campaign for the "No" opposed Pinochet continuing as president, and won the plebiscite with 54 percent of vote. This set the stage for presidential and congressional elections in 1989 and, prior to that, a constitutional reform plebiscite.

10. This description comes from Keck (1992), Seidman (1994), and Skidmore (1988).

11. The ABC region refers to an industrial region outside of São Paulo, which includes the cities of Santo Andre, São Bernardo do Campo, and São Caetano.

12. Despite the demobilization and marginalization of the women's movement following the democratic transition, Baldez (1997, chap. 7) notes that SERNAM, during the Frei presidency, has had some success in putting forth "radical" feminist initiatives. She explains that these feminist outcomes have not resulted from the incorporation of women's movement organizations in the policy-making process or from women's mobilization. Rather, they have been the result of elite negotiations and support from international organizations.

8

A Movement Takes Office

Bert Klandermans, Marlene Roefs, and Johan Olivier

Not very often in history is a movement organization in the position to take office. The African National Congress (ANC)—a core organization of the South African antiapartheid movement—was. The unbanning of the ANC, along with other movement organizations, such as the South African Communist Party and the Panafricanist Congress (PAC) in 1990, and the release of Nelson Mandela later that year marked the beginning of a process that reached a temporary culmination point with the inauguration of Nelson Mandela as president of South Africa and the establishment of a government of national unity (GNU). From an organization that had been banned and persecuted, the ANC moved to the center of the new power configuration. The movement literally took office. Thousands of former antiapartheid activists flocked into positions in the administration, not only at the national level but also at provincial and local levels.

At the same time, the relative position of power of the other players in the South African political arena changed. The former political elite assembled in the National Party saw its position of power weakened, although the party's power did certainly not vanish completely. Ginsburg (1996, p. 18), for example, argues that the reason that the democratic opposition did not press for more was that it was not dealing with a defeated enemy. The balance of power, he argues, "may well have shifted closer to a position of equilibrium, or stalemate, but it had not moved that far to enable the democratic opposition to demand an unconditional hand-over of state power." At the other end of the political spectrum, the ANC's competitor in recent years, the Inkatha Freedom Party, turned out to be less important than hoped by some and feared by others; and the Extreme Right countermovement that for a

173

moment appeared as a real threat to peaceful transition failed in the elections.

This chapter is about the response of the South African population to the political changes. When asking about the people's response to the political changes, we find that some of the questions central to this anthology come to the fore. Political protest in South Africa for decades was the monopoly of the African population. Excluded as it was from the political arena, political protest was the only means it had at its disposal. But, of course, protest was directed at a hostile government. The question, then, is how the African population will react to the new ANC-dominated government. Will Africans continue to use the political means they found to be so successful in the past and thus resort to protest if they want to influence authorities or if they dislike what the government is doing? Or will the institutionalization of the movement lead to a decline of political protest on their part? Will they continue to feel committed to the ANC? Or have they become alienated from the ANC or politics altogether? On the other hand, the new power configuration may lead to diffusion of protest to once-quiescent sectors of the population—the whites, the coloureds, and the Asians. Will these groups use political protest more often now that political powers have changed?

The answers to these questions are far from simple. Having one's allies inside government seems to be a mixed blessing. Kriesi et al. (1995), for example, discuss the changed political opportunities for new social movements in France in 1980, when a socialist government under Mitterand took office. Unlike what one might expect, new social movements rapidly declined in France, while mobilization from the right increased. As for South Africa, Ginsburg (1996) indeed suggests that the ANC in office might actually pursue a policy of demobilizing the movement it is rooted in. Marks's (1996) discussion of the fate of the youth movement in Diepkloof, an important sector of Soweto, seems to underscore this observation. It describes how the majority of those in the youth organizations of Diepkloof felt alienated from the decision-making process of the ANC and powerless in trying to change decisions that had already been made. In Italy and Germany, on the other hand, della Porta and Rucht (1995) observe a radicalization of left-libertarian movements when parties from the left took office or ideologically moved to the center. In a similar vein, it was feared in South Africa that some of the more radical parts of the antiapartheid movement would radicalize as the more moderate parts of the movement became parts of the center of power. Having one's political allies in the opposition is not necessarily an advantage. As observed by Kriesi et al. (1995) for the Netherlands and Germany and Maguire

(1995) for Great Britain, facilitation by political allies in the opposition considerably increases the mobilization capacity of the movement but at the same time reduces the possibility for the movement to have any effect on government policy.

Changed Opportunities

All this concerns profound changes in the political opportunity structure in South Africa. Tarrow (1994, p. 85) defines political opportunity structures as those "consistent, but not necessarily formal or permanent, dimensions of the political environment that provide incentives for people to undertake collective action by affecting their expectations of success and failure." As Tarrow stipulates, political opportunities can be both stable and transitory. In the context of our argument, for obvious reasons the transitory aspects are most important. Political opportunities change in many different ways. Political systems can become more or less open, configurations of power may change, political alliances may fall apart, and political elites may become divided, to mention a few. Opportunities and opportunity changes would not have had any impact had they not been seized. The simple implication is that opportunities must be perceived. A crucial question, then, is how the changed opportunities are perceived by citizens involved. And, perhaps more important, are they perceived in the same way by different sectors of society?

Indeed, the political opportunities *are* changed, but changed in what way and for whom, we may rightly ask. Admittedly, opportunity changes are not zero-sum games, but neither are they indifferent to various societal sectors. One would be inclined to believe that whites' opportunities have declined, that their access to governmental institutions has decreased, and that inversely the opportunities of the other population groups (the Africans, the coloureds and the Asians) have opened up and their access to government has increased; in reality the situation might be more complex. To be sure, the state has become much less repressive in all respects but also weaker. With the ANC securing an overwhelming majority of the votes, the country appears to be heading to a single—rather than a multiparty system (Ottaway 1991). No doubt, then, the political opportunities have changed, but the political reality is too complex to say only that they opened up. Opened up to whom, one may ask, and some may feel that their opportunities have closed. Changing opportunities are not identical for everybody, nor are they perceived alike by every citizen. Much depends, of course, on the positions occupied in the conflict arena (Rucht 1988). Indeed, in South Africa the challengers have taken over government. Naturally, their constituencies consider this as new opportunities opening up, up to the point that they may feel that there is less need for political protest. But both the movement's competitors and the former elite may perceive the new government with suspicion and react with heightened action preparedness.

Demovementization

For decades, political protest has been the routine political manner in South Africa. In a way, South Africa *was* a movement society, although perhaps in a different sense than conceived by the editors of this anthology. Will South Africa continue to be that way, or will the transition to politics as usual result in a demovementization of society? Will, as Ginsburg (1996, p. 20) fears, the new government demobilize civil society by "persuading the masses to participate in politics in the 'correct' way, which is voting every few years for the legislature"? Will the people lose their interest in politics, as politics becomes more distant to the people, as the youth in Marks's (1996) study in Diepkloof seem to have?

The questions that concern us in this chapter thus relate to the profound changes in the political opportunity structure in South Africa—changes that have very different consequences for different sectors of the population. Therefore, we have no reason to assume that those different sectors will react to the changes in a similar way. To what extent have they changed people's political outlook? Do people perceive and seize the new opportunities? And how are their perceptions affected by their positions in the political arena?

Assessing Responses to Changes

There are different ways of assessing responses to changes in a political opportunity structure. As we were interested in the perception of the changes, the strategy we chose is to assess people's opinions about the changes. We conducted surveys in 1994, 1995, and 1996 of random samples of the South African population to monitor changes in the people's perception of government, in political involvement, and in preparedness to take part in politics, both conventional (electoral and party politics) and unconventional (protest behavior). As we expected these responses to differ depending on where people stand politically, we will systematically compare the responses of the constituencies of the country's main political currents.

With a bit of simplification, we can distinguish four main currents in the country's political landscape. First, the *African National Congress* (ANC), previous core organization of the antiapartheid movement, is now the country's largest political party supported by the vast majority of the African population. Second, the *National Party* (NP), is the political party that controlled the state for almost half a century, the party of the former apartheid elite and, as such, is the ANC's natural adversary. As the second largest party in the country, the NP is predominantly white, although substantial proportions of the coloureds and the Asians voted for it in the 1994 elections. The third largest party is the *Inkatha Freedom Party* (IFP), established by Buthulezi, the *enfant terrible* of South African politics. Its constituency is regionally based in Kwazulu Natal; in that province the IFP is the largest political party and the ANC's competitor for the African vote. Outside Kwazulu Natal, however, the party is insignificant. Finally, there is the *Extreme Right*, a conglomerate of tiny political organizations, most not even represented in the parliament. It is composed of frantic opponents of the dismantling of the apartheid state and fanatic defenders of the Afrikaner heritage. In the period before the election, it was engaged in forceful, sometimes violent, protests. Although modest in size, it competes with the NP for the conservative white vote.

In addition to these ideologically distinct political constituencies, we were interested in the impact of diverging levels of political activity. Movements and parties alike have active members and sympathizers. As active members have a high level of political involvement, they may be sensitive to cues and signals that remain unnoticed by the average sympathizer. Therefore, in the pages to come we will compare how in the course of the three years since the transition active members and sympathizers of the four political currents in South Africa have evaluated the political developments.

Respondents

The first interview took place in February and March 1994, just before the elections. The following interviews were conducted in February and March 1995 and 1996. The three waves are based on separate samples of 2,286, 2,226, and 2,228 respondents, respectively. The standard procedures of Markdata, the institution in South Africa that collected the data for us, were applied. Face-to-face interviews were conducted in people's homes by trained interviewers of the same ethnic background who spoke the language of the interviewee. The interviews were based on a structured questionnaire. The respondents were drawn by means of a multiple-stage cluster probability sample design. The population used was all residents of eighteen years and older. We will only describe briefly the sampling procedures used (but see Klandermans, Roefs, and Olivier 1997, for a detailed description). The South African population of persons 18 years and older was stratified according to provinces[1] and a classification of socioeconomic regions. The sampling allocation to these strata was proportional to the 1991 population figures with a few exceptions: provinces were given a minimum of 120 respondents, and the minimum number of Asians was fixed at 120.[2] As a consequence of the sampling procedure, unweighted results are not representative of the South African population. However, for our purposes this is not a problem because the analyses are conducted for the separate constituencies of the four political formations.

Party Preference and Political Activity

Much of our analysis will build on a comparison of sympathizers and active members of the four main political groupings, the ANC, the NP, the IFP, and the Extreme Right. Therefore, we will start with a discussion of party preference and activity levels.

Party preference

In the 1994 elections, an estimated 86 percent of the electorate cast a vote; 62 percent voted for the ANC, 20 percent for the NP, 10 percent for the IFP, and 2 percent for the Freedom Front, representing a coalition of the Extreme Right groups. The remaining 6 percent of the vote was scattered over fifteen parties, of which three secured a few seats in the parliament: the Democratic Party (DP), the Panafricanist Congress (PAC), and the African Christian Democratic Party (ACDP). Figure 8.1 breaks these results down into the four main population groups. In addition to the election results, the figure also provides a breakdown of party preferences in the years following the elections. As these results will be the point of departure for the remainder of the analyses, we will discuss them in some more detail.

Obviously, the vast majority of the African population voted for the ANC. The results of our two surveys indicate that this majority even seems to have grown in the years after the elections. The support for the IFP among the African population decreased slightly, from approximately 10 percent in the election to 8 percent in 1996 survey. The African constituency of the IFP is almost completely Zulu and regionally restricted to Kwazulu-Natal. Small percentages of the African population voted for the remaining parties. As the African population constitutes almost three-quarters of the electorate, the impact of the other

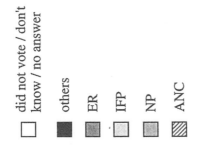

FIGURE 8.1. Election Results and Party Preferences

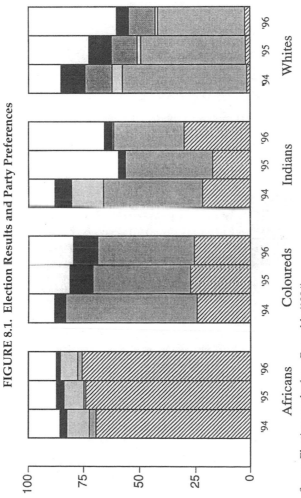

Source: Election results from Reynolds (1994).

three population groups on the turnout is inevitably limited. Yet, the picture there is revealing.[3]

No less than 59 percent of the coloured population voted for the NP, but during the years following the elections this sector of the constituency of the NP seems to have eroded. Interestingly, it is not the ANC that benefits from this decline: the one-quarter of the coloureds that supports the ANC remains stable over time. A preference for the small parties and uncertainty about what to choose are the accompanying features of the erosion of the NP's support among the coloured population. Among the Indians, however, the ANC does benefit from a reduced support for the NP. A fair proportion of the Indians in Durban and Natal voted for the IFP in the elections, a result that did not show up in our surveys. Large proportions of the Indian population no longer knew which party to support after the elections.

The same holds for the white population. Decreasing support for the NP seems to translate into increasing uncertainty about which party to vote for. The Extreme Right, however, enjoys a stable 10 to 12 percent of the white vote. Interestingly, some 6 percent of the whites voted for an African party, predominately the IFP, but in the years after the elections the support for the IFP decreased while that for the ANC increased slightly, although the latter did not compensate for the former.

Activity level

In our surveys we asked people whether they sympathized with a political party and whether they were actively involved in a political party as a member who visited meetings with some regularity or as an office bearer (Table 8.1). Sympathy levels appear to be fairly stable over

TABLE 8.1
Party Preferences and Active Members of Political Parties (%)*

	1994		1995		1996	
	Inactive	*Active*	*Inactive*	*Active*	*Inactive*	*Active*
	(*n* = 2,268)		(*n* = 2,226)		(*n* = 2,228)	
ANC	(32.3)	10.1	51.9	9.4	53.7	5.6
IFP	(3.3)	(.03)	6.2	1.4	5.4	1.0
NP	(14.0)	1.7	16.5	1.9	15.2	1.4
Extreme Right	(5.3)	1.4	3.0	.3	2.6	.1

*In 1994 party preference was asked in a different way than in 1995 and 1996. Active membership was assessed in the same way in all three years. In 1994, at the time of the survey the IFP was still in the process of building a party organization. As a consequence, few active members could be sampled.

the years 1995 and 1996. However, the percentages of actively involved people decreased across all parties, most prominently among the ANC and the Extreme Right.

In combination, these two sets of results suggest that the political landscape is changing, although not dramatically. Perhaps the most striking finding is the indecisiveness among all population groups but the Africans. A decline in support for parties other than the ANC does not translate into support for other parties but in a growing uncertainty about which party to support. Furthermore, there is an intriguing difference in the patterns for party support and those for organizational strength. As a party, the ANC is growing or at least stable among the Africans, Indians, and whites. In fact, it is the only party that is increasing its support overall. The shrinking number of activists, however, suggests that the ANC as a movement organization is on the decline. The Extreme Right seems to have a similar problem. As an organization it almost disappeared, but as a political party it continues to draw a stable proportion of the white vote. The ANC's competitor, Inkatha, is losing both support and organizational strength. The NP is the only party that has managed to maintain its organizational strength, but it has lost substantial support.

In other words, all the parties that originated from movements seem to have declined in organizational strength. The only party that has operated as a party for decades, the NP, maintained its organizational strength at least compared with the others. As far as the movement parties are concerned, this may signify difficulties with the transition from movement into party. Movement organizations tend to formalize and bureaucratize when they turn into parties. After the years of turmoil, being a party activist might be less interesting and exciting than being a movement activist, and people who are motivated to engage in one kind of activism may not be similarly motivated for the other. On the other hand, it may be the first signs of what Ginsburg (1996) foresaw, a process of demobilization. It is difficult to say which of these two explanations is stronger based on our results, but each probably contains a kernel of truth.

Political Involvement

Our first research question concerns possible change in political involvement. We have tried to assess such changes by asking people about their interest in political communication in newspapers, on television or radio, and in interpersonal communication. Not surprisingly, the levels of involvement among active members are higher than those among sympathizers. Furthermore, over the three years since 1994, political involvement evidently decreased (Table 8.2). But there is more. Depending on the party, the patterns of change over time vary. Among sympathizers of the ANC in 1994, just before the election, political involvement was high, but it declined in 1995 to remain approximately the same until 1996. Sympathizers of the IFP and NP, however, revealed a steady decrease in political involvement. Sympathizers of the Extreme Right are the only ones who, after an initial drop, return to the same level of political involvement as before the elections. Among the active members of the ANC, involvement initially even increased a little bit, but then in 1996 it declined. We found similar patterns among the two other movement parties, the IFP and the Extreme Right. The active NP members deviate from this pattern. After an initial decline in the year after the elections, they remain at the same level.

Thus, the movement parties seem to lose political involvement from their sympathizers and active members. This result confirms our previous findings that the organizational strength of the movement parties is weakening. To this finding we can now add that their cadre is also losing its interest in politics.

Perceived Opportunities

Our second research question addresses changes in political opportunities. More precisely, it concerns perceived changes as indicated by such variables as expectations for the future and political cynicism. Elsewhere we have discussed the interrelationship between expectations for the future and beliefs about government (Klandermans et al. 1997). Political cynicism—that is, lack of trust in government and the perception to have no influence on government—supposedly makes people pessimistic about the future. The political transitions in South Africa implied pervasive changes in political opportunities for the anti-

TABLE 8.2
Political Involvement (means)

	1994		1995		1996	
	Inactive	*Active*	*Inactive*	*Active*	*Inactive*	*Active*
ANC	2.8	3.1	2.3	3.2	2.1	2.7
IFP	2.4	2.5	2.2	2.6	1.8	1.8
NP	2.8	3.7	2.6	3.1	2.3	2.9
Extreme Right	2.6	3.3	2.3	3.5	2.5	2.8

Note: ANC: main effect of activism and time, $p<.001$, and interaction of activism and time, $p<.001$; IFP: main effect of time: $p<.001$; NP: main effect of activism and time, $p<.001$; Extreme right: main effect of activism, $p<.01$.

apartheid movement. No longer is a hostile government opposing any movement to improve the situation of the nonwhite citizens ruling, but the movement itself took office. Changes of such magnitude inevitably have a profound impact on beliefs about government and on expectations for the future, as we operationalized perceived political opportunities.

People were asked to estimate what the situation of the people they identify with will be in five years and how just they consider the outcome of that estimation. The answers to these questions were combined into a single measure of exxpectations for the future ranging from 1 (optimistic) to 7 (pessimistic). Indeed, sympathizers and active members of the ANC alike became less pessimistic about the future (Table 8.3). The same holds for the IFP. The NP and the Extreme Right, on the other hand, became *more* pessimistic. This is, of course, what one would expect, just as it will not come as a surprise that the constituency of the ANC is the least pessimistic of all. But there are some interesting, less obvious results. For example, as far as expectations for the future are concerned, we did not find any difference between sympathizers and active members. This is also true of the NP: sympathizers and active members are very much alike in their beliefs about the future. On the other hand, among the IFP supporters and those of the Extreme Right, active members *do* differ from sympathizers but in opposite ways: active members of the IFP are less pessimistic about the future, and active members of the Extreme Right are more pessimistic. Indeed, the latter are the most pessimistic of all four groups.

Trust in government

Such expectations appear to be determined by beliefs about government. In a more comprehensive analysis of the same data, we found that pessimism or optimism about the future to a large extent could be

TABLE 8.3
Pessimism about the Future (means)

	1994		1995		1996	
	Inactive	*Active*	*Inactive*	*Active*	*Inactive*	*Active*
ANC	3.0	3.2	2.9	2.8	2.8	2.7
IFP	3.9	4.0	3.7	3.1	3.4	3.2
NP	3.6	3.9	4.1	4.3	4.2	4.2
Extreme Right	4.2	4.9	4.3	5.1	4.7	6.0

Note: ANC: main effect of time, $p<.001$; NP: main effect of time, $p<.01$; Extreme right: main effect of activism, $p=.01$, and main effect of time: $p=.13$.

explained by trust in and perceived influence on government. The more South Africans trusted government and the more they felt they could influence governmental decisions, the more optimistic they were about the future (Klandermans et al. 1997). Therefore, it is important to look into how these matters stand among the constituencies of the four political currents. Table 8.4 provides results regarding trust in government: in 1994, trust in the last apartheid regime of President de Klerk; in 1995 and 1996, trust in the government of national unity (GNU). For obvious reasons, in 1994 the constituency of the NP has the most trust in government, active members even more than nonactive. However, those white South Africans who support the Extreme Right have much less trust in de Klerk's NP government, with active members trusting even less than the ANC constituency. Not surprisingly, the African population has little trust in the NP government. Note, however, the difference between ANC and IFP supporters. IFP supporters do not trust the NP government at all. This result is certainly related to the fact that the government during the negotiation for the transition (in the so-called Convention for a Democratic South Africa [CODESA] and in informal consultations) continuously gave the impression that it neglected the IFP as a political force (Mattes 1994).

The year 1995 reveals a completely different picture. This time it is the ANC constituency that trusts government (the GNU) most, active and nonactive members alike. Trust among the IFP constituency increased, too, but stayed at a much lower level than that among the ANC constituency, especially among active members. The NP constituency changed positions with the ANC constituency. Trust in the GNU is low among the mainstream white population. Even lower are the

TABLE 8.4
Trust in Government (means)*

	1994		1995		1996	
	Inactive	*Active*	*Inactive*	*Active*	*Inactive*	*Active*
ANC	2.3	2.2	3.4	3.6	3.2	3.2
IFP	1.6	1.0	2.5	1.8	2.4	2.5
NP	3.3	3.7	2.5	2.5	2.4	3.0
Extreme Right	2.6	1.7	1.9	2.2	1.7	1.7

ANC: main effect of time, $p<.001$; IFP: main effect of activism, $p=.13$, main effect of time, $p<.01$, and interaction of activism and time, $p<.05$; NP: main effect of activism, $p<.01$, main effect of time, $p<.001$, and interaction of activism and time, $p<.05$; Extreme right: interaction of activism and time, $p<.05$.
*Answers to the question of "How often do you trust the government to do what is right for people like you?" on a scale from 1 (never) to 5 (always).

levels of trust at the Extreme Right end of the political continuum. Interestingly, trust in government among activists of the Extreme Right increased to a level even higher than that of IFP activists. Trust among the nonactivists, however, declined considerably. In 1996 the levels of trust have consolidated for nonactive supporters of all four political currents. But among the active members some intriguing changes can be observed. Trust in government among active ANC supporters decreased, while that among IFP activists increased. At the same time, trust in government among NP activists increased but declined among active right-wingers.

Perceived influence

Beliefs in government also concerned perceived influence (see Table 8.5). Interestingly, in 1994 ANC supporters and NP supporters estimated their influence on government as approximately equal. IFP supporters and supporters of the Extreme Right, on the other hand, both perceived similar and lower levels of perceived influence, and this was even more pronounced among the active members. These findings confirm those with respect to trust in government. The fact that perceived influence among those two constituencies were so much lower is very much in line with the actual power relations. In the eyes of many onlookers, the ANC and NP were doing business with each other while the others were kept on the sideline.

Substantial changes in perceived influence also occurred in 1995. The constituencies of the two African parties perceived increasing influence, although levels remained highest among the ANC supporters. The white parties perceived declining influence, especially among the

TABLE 8.5
Perceived Influence on Government (means)*

	1994		1995		1996	
	Inactive	*Active*	*Inactive*	*Active*	*Inactive*	*Active*
ANC	3.9	4.1	4.4	4.7	4.2	4.3
IFP	3.4	3.0	4.0	3.7	3.8	4.2
NP	4.1	4.2	3.6	3.8	3.6	4.2
Extreme right	3.7	3.4	3.2	2.5	3.2	3.3

ANC: main effect of activism, $p<.01$, and main effect of time, $p<.001$; IFP: main effect of time, $p=.08$, and interaction of activism and time, $p=.10$; NP: main effect of activism, $p<.05$, and main effect of time, $p<.01$; Extreme Right: main effect of time, $p=.12$.
*Answer to the question of "Do you agree or disagree with the statement: people like you can have an influence on governmental decisions?" on a seven-point scale ranging from "disagree very strongly" (1) to "agree very strongly" (7).

Extreme Right. One year later levels of perceived influence remained more or less the same among the nonactive members of the four constituencies but decreased among the active ANC members while increasing among the active members of the three other parties. Apparently ANC activists grew disappointed in the government of national unity, whereas for the active members of the other three parties, it could have been worse.

We assumed that the active members are more sensitive to political cues and signals than is the average member; therefore, the differences between the two groups are worth examining. The diverging patterns of change particularly draw our attention. There appears to be a distinct "white" pattern: among nonactivists perceived influence dropped in 1995 to remain at that lower level; among activists it also dropped in 1995 but returned in 1996 to the level of 1994. The patterns for the two constituencies are more or less the same, although a bit more pronounced among the activists of the Extreme Right. We also found parallel patterns among the nonactivists of the IFP and the ANC: a sharp increase in 1995, followed by a slight decrease in 1996. But the patterns among the activists were completely different: a steady increase among IFP activists but a decline among ANC activists in 1996 after a sharp increase in 1995. The activists of the two parties are now at almost the same level in 1996.

We believe that these patterns reflect some real changes and differences in the positions of the four groups. On the other hand, it may also be an overestimation of the consequences of the changes by ANC and NP activists, and activists of the Extreme Right in 1995, which was then adjusted in 1996.

Coloureds and Indians

The Africans voted predominantly for one of the two African parties, the whites for one of the two white parties. However, both the coloureds and the Indians were split between the African ANC and the white NP. Did that mean that they also differed in terms of perceived opportunities—that is, their expectations for the future and their beliefs about government? In other words, were those who had a preference for the ANC more like the average ANC supporter and those who preferred the NP more like the average NP supporter? Or were they somewhere in between?

Table 8.6 presents the results regarding pessimism for the future, trust, and perceived influence in 1995 and 1996. Because the numbers of active members were too small, we could not compare active and nonactive members; instead, we compared politically uninvolved and

TABLE 8.6
Coloureds and Indians (means)

	1995		1996	
	Uninvolved	*Involved*	*Uninvolved*	*Involved*
Pessimism about the future				
Coloureds				
ANC	3.0	3.1	3.4	3.2
NP	3.6	3.4	3.7	3.7
Indians				
ANC	3.7	3.7	3.6	3.3
NP	3.4	4.4	3.5	4.3
Trust in government				
Coloureds				
ANC	2.9	3.1	2.7	3.0
NP	2.6	2.3	2.7	3.1
Indians				
ANC	3.2	2.8	2.3	2.8
NP	3.3	2.3	2.2	2.7
Perceived influence				
Coloureds				
ANC	3.9	4.6	4.1	4.3
NP	3.8	4.0	3.8	4.2
Indians				
ANC	4.4	4.3	3.7	4.3
NP	3.6	3.6	2.9	3.5

involved people.[4] Comparisons of the results of Table 8.6 with those of Tables 8.3, 8.4, and 8.5 lead to a few observations. ANC supporters among the coloureds in 1995 did not differ much from the average ANC supporter in terms of their expectations for the future, but one year later the coloureds among the ANC voters became more pessimistic, while ANC supporters in general had become more optimistic. As a consequence, these two groups within the ANC constituency have grown apart. The NP supporters among the coloureds were sort of in between the general NP results and the general ANC scores. The Indians among the ANC voters, on the other hand, were much more pessimistic than ANC supporters in general but became slightly more optimistic. Politically involved NP supporters among the Indians were as pessimistic of the future as the average active member of the NP. Politically uninvolved NP supporters among the Indians were less pessimistic about the future than were their fellow partisans.

As far as trust in government is concerned, neither coloured nor Indian ANC supporters reached the level of trust of the ANC supporter in general. The levels of trust among coloured ANC supporters did not change as much as those among the politically involved ANC supporters among the Indians. Among the politically involved NP supporters among both the coloureds and the Indians, however, the level of trust increased to levels much closer to that of ANC supporters in general. Among the politically uninvolved Indians, trust in government declined considerably among both the ANC and the NP supporters. The result of all this is that ANC and NP supporters within the two groups are almost identical as far as trust in government is concerned in 1996. The level of trust among coloureds is at a level somewhat above that of the NP supporters in general; the levels of trust among the Indians was somewhat below that level.

Perceived influence on government among the coloureds in 1995 and 1996 was fairly similar to the general ANC or NP figures, except for the uninvolved ANC voters in 1995, but in 1996 this difference had disappeared. The Indians presented a somewhat different picture. In 1996, politically uninvolved ANC voters perceived less influence than did their fellow partisans in general. This is the result of a decline compared with 1995. NP supporters among the Indians perceived less influence on government in 1996 than did NP supporters in general. Among the uninvolved, this view is because of a decline in perceived influence; among the politically involved, it occurs because unlike NP supporters in general, those among the Indians did not report an increase in the level of influence they perceived.

The net result of all these changes is that in 1996 ANC supporters among the coloureds and the Indians were more pessimistic about the future than ANC supporters in general, while NP supporters are less pessimistic than NP supporters in general. Moreover, ANC supporters of both groups had less trust in government than did ANC supporters in general. NP supporters of both groups, however, were similar to NP members more generally. Finally, levels of perceived influence on government among ANC members from both groups came close to those among ANC supporters in general. The same holds for NP supporters among the coloureds vis-à-vis NP supporters in general, but NP supporters among the Indians perceived less influence than did NP supporters in general.

Protest Participation

Protest participation was assessed by asking people whether they would probably take part in each of two types of action in the future (on a four-point scale from "definitely not" to "definitely"). The distinction was made between peaceful actions, such as signing petitions,

attending rallies, walking in marches or demonstrations, and participating in stay-aways, and forceful actions, such as occupying buildings, blocking traffic, and engaging in all kinds of boycotts, such as
rent, school, or consumer boycotts (see Tables 8.7 and 8.8). As far as
participation in these forms of protest was concerned, the constituencies of the four parties varied considerably, and the patterns of change
over the last three years have also been different. To complicate matters
further, willingness to participate in moderate and forceful action reveal different pictures.

The likelihood of ANC supporters participating in moderate action
has decreased over the last three years, among active and nonactive
members alike. However, the constituencies of the other three parties
reveal a different pattern. For nonactive sympathizers, the first year
(1994–95) brought an increasing likelihood of participation. Subsequently, among the IFP supporters, the likelihood of participation
dropped again, but supporters of the NP and the Extreme Right stayed
at the same level. Among active supporters of the NP, we found a simi-

TABLE 8.7
Likelihood of Participation in Peaceful Action (means)

	1994		1995		1996	
	Inactive	*Active*	*Inactive*	*Active*	*Inactive*	*Active*
ANC	3.6	4.1	3.6	4.0	3.2	3.8
IFP	2.8	2.7	3.3	2.8	2.3	3.0
NP	1.9	1.6	2.2	2.5	2.1	2.4
Extreme Right	1.7	2.4	2.2	1.5	2.3	2.0

ANC: main effect of activism and time, $p<.001$; IFP: interaction of activism and time,
$p<.05$; NP: main effect of time, $p<.001$; Extreme Right: interaction of activism and time,
$p=.10$.

TABLE 8.8
Likelihood of Participation in Forceful Action (means)

	1994		1995		1996	
	Inactive	*Active*	*Inactive*	*Active*	*Inactive*	*Active*
ANC	2.1	2.6	2.0	2.1	1.9	2.2
IFP	2.0	1.7	2.2	2.5	1.9	2.4
NP	1.5	1.4	1.4	1.3	1.4	1.5
Extreme Right	1.5	2.5	1.6	1.0	1.4	1.0

ANC: main effect of activism and time, $p<.001$, and interaction of activism and time,
$p=.05$; Extreme Right: main effect of time, $p<.01$, and interaction of activism and time
$p<.01$.

lar pattern, but those of the IFP showed an increasing likelihood of participation, while those of the Extreme Right revealed a declining likelihood of participation.

As far as forceful action is concerned, IFP activists are the only ones who showed an increasing likelihood of participation. NP supporters stayed at the same low level, and all the others showed a decrease. The changes among the Extreme Right activists are especially revealing. Apparently, the negative experiences with previous forceful actions had taken away any appetite for repeating them.

Coloureds and Indians

Action preparedness of ANC supporters among the coloureds and Indians was higher than that of the NP supporters among these groups but lower than that among ANC supporters in general (see Table 8.9). NP supporters among both groups were similar to NP supporters in general.

Conclusion

We concluded our introductory section with four questions concerning the possible consequences of the political changes in South Africa,

TABLE 8.9
Coloureds and Indians (means)

	1995		1996	
	Uninvolved	*Involved*	*Uninvolved*	*Involved*
Peaceful action				
Coloureds				
ANC	3.0	3.2	2.5	3.1
NP	2.3	2.6	2.2	2.5
Indians				
ANC	3.0	3.0	3.2	3.1
NP	2.6	2.7	1.6	2.6
Forceful action				
Coloureds				
ANC	1.8	2.1	1.5	1.9
NP	1.6	1.3	1.4	1.5
Indians				
ANC	1.6	1.7	1.9	1.7
NP	1.6	1.1	1.0	1.4

questions about the depoliticization of society, the demovementization of society, the diffusion of protest to once-quiescent sectors, and changed political opportunities. We now return to these questions.

Our results regarding political involvement and activity levels within parties suggest that South Africa in the years of political transition has experienced a process of depoliticization. Levels of political involvement declined, and so did the number of active members within political parties. Interestingly, taking into account the loss of active members, the party organization of the NP seems to have survived the first three years in better shape than those of the three "movement parties"—the ANC, the IFP, and the Extreme Right. This does not necessarily mean that the parties weakened or strengthened accordingly. On the contrary, electoral support for the ANC increased and that for the Extreme Right stabilized, whereas electoral support for the IFP, and especially for the NP, declined. Indeed, as we are finishing this chapter the NP seems to face difficulties in surviving and is desperately trying to renew itself to maintain its position in the political arena. On the other hand, the so-called movement parties seemed to have had difficulties in maintaining their organizations during the transition from movement to party. The decline of movement parties may be a temporary phenomenon caused by this transformation. Moreover, let us keep in mind that compared with the other parties, the ANC continues to have a high proportion of active members. Thus, we certainly cannot say that the ANC as an organization is falling apart. Similarly, it is too early to predict the demise of the IFP and the Extreme Right

Do our results, then, signify a demovementization of society? Not really. To be sure, we assessed a declining likelihood of participation in forceful action, but among active members of the IFP, the likelihood of participation in such action increased. And, admittedly, we assessed a decreased likelihood of participation of ANC supporters in peaceful action. This was not, however, a dramatic decline; moreover, supporters of all other parties reported that they were more likely to engage in peaceful action. Indeed, to provide an answer to our third question, it looks like protest is diffusing to other sectors of society that did not protest before. On the other hand, ANC supporters remain the ones who are the most likely to take part in protest, which holds true among the coloureds and the Indians as well as Africans. In fact, their readiness to participate in political protest remained high, nurtured by a hardly shaken faith in the possibilities of success of such action. In other words, there is hardly any sign of a demovementization of South African politics. On the contrary, protest continues to be part of everyday politics, as South African newspapers testify day after day, although it is too early to conclude that movements will be an enduring part of South African politics.

The government of national unity meant a tremendous change in the political opportunities, a change that the actors in South Africa's political arena *did* notice. This transition process has not yet come to a closure, as witnessed by the electoral realignment that is still taking place. The support of the NP is eroding, and an increasing number of whites, coloureds, and Indians do not know what to vote for anymore. At the same time the support for the ANC is growing both among the Africans, the Indians, and the whites, although white support for the ANC remains marginal. Most striking, of course, are the changes in the perceived opportunities as revealed by our results regarding future expectations and beliefs about government. As expected, in the eyes of the Africans, the opportunities have opened up, especially among the supporters of the ANC, but also among supporters of the IFP, who apparently felt that circumstances evolved better than they expected. The opportunities closed in the eyes of the white population, especially among those who supported the Extreme Right. Among NP supporters, the changes have been less discomforting than they feared.

The picture, however, is more complex than that. First, the coloureds and the Indians among the ANC supporters draw a less rosy picture than do the ANC supporters in general, while the NP supporters among these groups hardly differ from their fellow partisans. In other words, as a group the coloureds and the Indians are less persuaded by the government's performance than the Africans. Whether this will eventually generate a "brown" coalition movement of non-African minorities against an African-led government is unclear at this point. But our comparisons of coloureds and Indians with Africans and whites suggest that outcome as a possibility. Additionally, ANC supporters, especially active supporters, seem to show some signs of disappointment in the government of national unity. This may be a sign of alienation by a constituency that experiences that power creates distance and that it has become more difficult to establish rapport with their comrades in office, or perhaps frustration about the limited achievements of the first years, or both. In any event, emerging from our research is a picture more complicated than a simple black-and-white photograph with the former antagonists having traded places.

What happened, then, when the antiapartheid movement that had turned South Africa upside down took office? More than that, what was the effect of it forming a national unity government with its former opponents and competitors? Did its constituency turn away with horror? Did they withdraw from politics altogether? Did the new government repress its enemies from the past, and did these enemies constitute new protest movements? Did the old movements erode to be replaced by new ones? It is too early to give any definitive answers to these questions, but thus far none of these possible outcomes has materialized.

During the time of our study, the majority of the Africans continued to support the ANC. In fact, taking the party preferences into account, support for the ANC among the Africans increased. Yet, except for perhaps the Indians, the ANC failed to establish stronger links to the non-Africans, despite the fact that these groups seem to turn away from the NP. Rather than commit themselves to the ANC, many non-Africans became uncommitted. Indeed, among the non-African population, politically homeless is the most rapidly growing category. This may be a fateful sign that these population groups are turning away from politics. However, as far as our data show, declining political involvement is not an exclusive non-African matter. On the contrary, political involvement declined more among the African than among the non-African population. Political homelessness, then, seems to be due more to a decline of the party that went out of office, the NP, than due to the party that took office, the ANC.

Thus far, there have been no signs that the new regime suppresses its former antagonists. On the contrary, the first years the ANC painstakingly tried not to alienate its former enemies and competitors, and with some success, as our data suggest. Certainly among the IFP supporters and activists, trust in government increased after the power transition—although less spectacular and after an initial decline among the active supporters of the NP. The constituency of the Extreme Right was the only one of the four compared in this article that continued to mistrust government, but that hardly comes as a surprise.

South Africa seems to remain a movement society. A look into a week's South African newspapers supports that conclusion. The fact that the old movement took office did not make that aspect of South African politics disappear. Nor did it bring an erosion of the old movement's networks, although some of that seems to have taken place. Old and new groups alike are prepared to take action, as the newspapers and our data demonstrate. Political protest continues.

Notes

1. The stratification for the black population for the first survey was done differently because at that time South Africa was still divided among the so-called self-governing states, the TBVC states (Transkei, Bophuthatswana, Venda, and Ciskei), and the rest of South Africa. In the first survey, the black

sample was stratified into these areas, on the one hand, and into metropolitan and nonmetropolitan areas, on the other. The regional distribution of the 1994 sample and the later samples, however, is very similar.

2. In the 1994 sample design, no fixed minimum per region was stated. However, numbers *were* fixed for the population groups: 1,252 blacks, 600 whites, 300 coloureds, and 200 Asians.

3. South Africa had an estimated population of 22.7 million inhabitants in 1994, 16.7 million of those were African, 3.4 million coloured, 2 million white, and 700,000 Indian.

4. The two groups were distinguished based on a median split.

9

Stepsisters: Feminist Movement Activism in Different Institutional Spaces

Mary Fainsod Katzenstein

Students of social movements commonly associate institutionalization with demobilization (Piven and Cloward 1971; Kriesi et al. 1995, p. 250; Tarrow 1989, pp. 330–34).[1] The workshop for which many of these chapters were initially prepared was itself entitled "movement societies *or* institutionalization of protest" stipulating an opposition between movements and institutions. Social movements, in this view, are necessarily extrainstitutional: claims voiced by social movements, when incorporated within institutional settings, are thought to be both routinized and depoliticized. Institutional actors (lawyers, judges, politicians, employers, journalists) are definitionally precluded from being social movement activists—except after hours. In the social movement literature, those who wield influence inside institutions are generally denoted as "third parties" called on as allies of, rather than parties to, a movement's effort to effect change (Lipsky 1968).

This presumed inconsistency between movement politics and institutional politics is based on a frequently drawn linkage of location, form, and content. When social movement actors doing street politics (location) opt for or ally themselves with those who use conventional modes (form) of political activism such as lobbying or voting, a social movement is generally deemed to have crossed the threshold separat-

I owe a large debt of thanks to David Meyer, Heidi Swarts, and Sidney Tarrow for their very helpful close readings and their exhortation to greater clarity and development. Some of the material in this chapter is drawn from my book, *Protest from Within: Feminism in the U.S. Military and American Catholic Church* (1998).

ing protest politics from institutional politics, and the result is presumed to be deradicalizing (content).

This location-form-content distinction between movement and institutions invites judgments that are too readily overdrawn. It is too easy to presume that what occurs on the streets is disruptive and what occurs within institutional contexts is accommodative. But what does "disruption" really mean? Is a demonstration outside the White House or a snake dance around the Pentagon that causes security to be deployed and that may temporarily interrupt traffic and block the entry of people trying to reach their place of employment more disruptive than the presence of self-acknowledged feminists at the workplace who make known their expectations about changes in language, sexual behavior, and office hierarchies? Disruption needs to be distinguished from "interruption." Disruption is about challenges to power that have the potential of compelling change.

I see three hazards worth avoiding in specifying the relationship between movements and institutionalization. One is the tendency to elision, blurring political space, political method, and political claims. Their linkage needs to be demonstrated, not implied, and the conditionalities that shape their connections specified. The second is the tendency to presume a dichotomous distinction between outsiders and insiders. One need not go the full distance of Michel Foucault's claim that modern-day power does not emanate from the sovereign (or state) alone to recognize the way all locations in society are implicated in issues of power and to understand that, as with the solar system, it is hard to stipulate where the inside ends and the outside begins. Third is the presumption that what holds for one social movement applies equally well to others. Whatever definitional distinction is made between movement and institution is likely to elucidate the political iterations of some social movements better than others. Freedom fighters in nationalist movements staged violent protests or civil disobedience and then joined legislatures. If this trajectory also somewhat satisfactorily captures civil rights history in the United States, it does a less successful job of describing the women's movement. Constrained by traditional gender role stereotypes and by political choice, feminist activists' arsenal of political activism has drawn only fleetingly on demonstrative protest activities and even more rarely on violent activism. This raises the question of whether the very definitional distinction of conventional and unconventional political forms, then, is situated in the experience of freedom movements and, most particularly, of the 1960s male-dominated new left and civil rights movements.

The 1990s provide an ideal moment to study the intersection of movement and institution. Their encounter (the marriage of movement and institution) has by now produced a generation of offspring who are no longer toddlers, or even adolescents, but old enough to have developed identities of their own. This is a study of two stepsisters: born of a common feminist mother (the women's movement), the institutionalization of feminist protest in two organizational environments imparts a tale of siblings whose lives are both different and the same. Feminist activism in the military is well behaved—behavior that belies its sometimes defiant character. Feminist activism in the Catholic Church is openly rebellious but not in the short run, I think, any more threatening to the institution.

Institutionalization as Habitats

I define the process of institutionalization in spatial terms. The institutionalization of feminist activism, in this study, refers to the establishment of organizational habitats of feminists within institutional environments. Such habitats are spaces where women advocates of equality can assemble, where discussion can occur, and where the organizing for institutional change can originate. In the military, such habitats would include, for example, the Women Military Aviators (WMA) that pressured for the opening up of combat aviation positions to women or the Defense Advisory Committee on Women in the Services (DACOWITS) that monitors women's situation throughout the armed services. In the Catholic Church, such habitats include many long-established religious orders that have become protected spaces for women who would challenge hierarchy within the institutional Church as well as organizations such as the Women's Ordination Conference founded explicitly for that purpose. In universities, such habitats comprise women's studies programs and women's student or staff organizations that aim to make the institution more receptive to feminist concerns. By contrast, the National Organization for Women is a more autonomous organization, spatially situated outside an institutional environment to which it is directly accountable.

My point is that the significance of financial or institutional accountability *for* feminist activism within the institution is not preset. Any *a priori* assumption that organizational location mandates a particular set of political forms or political claims obscures that which needs to be elucidated. A variety of things happen within institutional habitats. The purpose of this comparison of feminist activism within the military and the Church is to offer a description of the different versions of feminist politics within institutional spaces and an account of why activism takes such different forms in different institutions.

In this study, to clarify further, I am eschewing two common meanings of the term *institutionalization*. The first usage is often deployed to denote a shift in movement strategies. Costain (1992, p. 2), for example, depicts the women's movement as engaging in a confrontational strategy in the 1960s, an organizational strategy in the 1970s, and an electoral strategy in the 1980s. This portrayal suggests a purposeful redirection from disruptive to rule-abiding behavior. Although Costain is surely right that there is less overt confrontational expression in what feminist organizations do now compared with the placard-bearing demonstrations of the 1960s, it is too easy to read such a schema as a narrative of deradicalization. Feminist activists persist in challenging existing practices around institutional policies ranging from reproduction and sexual orientation to day care and employment. It is important to leave open to consideration the possibility that feminist activism in some of its 1990s manifestations demands as much or more in the way of societal change even as it does so less overtly. Any definition that equates institutionalization with deradicalization assumes that which should be subject to interrogation.

A second usage of the term *institutionalization* describes a process by which movement goals become integrated into the rules, policies, and practices of an institution. In any given institution, for instance, the transference of feminist protest, by such a definition, would imply greater equality, say, in hiring practices and the development of policies that seek to discourage sexual harassment. This usage emphasizes policy success or failure. I am chary of such a definition partly on pragmatic grounds. To judge the degree of feminism's institutionalization would require the nearly impossible—estimating the movement's impact law by law, policy by policy, enforcement measure by enforcement measure. At best, it is possible (and indeed worthwhile) to attempt this kind of scrutiny for individual issue areas. But any attempted appraisal of the institutionalization of the movement as a whole, by a rule/policy-based standard, would be daunting.

A definition of feminism's institutionalization as "habitat," rather than as acceded-to rules and policies, makes particular sense in the context of an analysis of *American* feminism. As distinct from the state-driven feminism of much of Europe, the success of American feminism is dependent, at the very least, on strong organizational efforts in civil society (Tarrow 1997). What those organizational projects look like within institutional contexts is crucial. No decision-making elite in the United States is going to institute feminist policies that feminists do not mobilize to claim.

Pressure Group Activism in the U.S. Military

Law and Opportunity

To tell the "story" of feminist activism in the military over the last several decades is to relate a three-part narrative about how (1) women's claims making has been institutionalized; (2) how the law has instigated activism by providing opportunities for feminist pressure politics; and (3) how the law has contained this activism by shaping the ways activists see themselves (their political identities), thus influencing what activists think to want politically.

Now in her forties and recently a mother, Rosemary Mariner became in 1990 the United States Navy's first female jet squadron commander. She spent the initial twenty years of her career "operational"—not behind a desk but behind the controls of anything she was allowed to fly, from helicopters to high-performance jets, racking up over 3,500 flight hours. Flying was a childhood dream for Mariner, a dream she announced early on to the principal of her Catholic girls school. Along with becoming a crackerjack aviator (testing planes and training male aviators for combat missions that she was not by law permitted to perform herself), Mariner became an activist promoting gender equality in Navy aviation. She hadn't always been outspoken. In the mid-1970s, Mariner was asked to join in the *Owens v. Brown* class action suit in which women were suing the service to open up Navy ships to uniformed women. At the time, Mariner was establishing herself as an up-and-coming young aviator in a fighter community. Going it on her own seemed smarter than calling attention to herself as part of a cadre of discontented women. "I basically wimped out. Because I had it good, I didn't want to get in trouble with the Navy. And I consider that moral cowardice on my part" (Zimmerman 1995, p. 121).

By the late 1980s, however, the military had changed and so had Mariner. Equality of opportunity was official institutional orthodoxy, at least at the level of rhetoric. A Southern Californian product of parochial schools and Orange County Republicanism, Mariner had become a feminist. This was a shifting of identity if not a metamorphosis. Losing none of her dyed-in-the-wool patriotic love of country, Mariner, nonetheless, became an unrelenting advocate of women's career advancement. As squadron command leader, Mariner worked self-consciously to support women seeking training and promotion. In the late 1980s, Mariner became the head of Women Military Aviators, an organization of six hundred that networked in support of equal opportunity. As with most women activists in the military, this was not a feminism Mariner brought with her into the armed forces. It was a commitment to gender equality that Mariner discovered and made her own *in* the military, itself.

The Women Military Aviators arrived on the scene later than several other groups that sought to support women's equality in the armed forces. Other habitats also existed that supported women activists: WOPA (the Women's Officers' Professional Association) began as an informal network of Navy women in 1978, incorporating in 1984. Both organizations brought women officers together to network, to attend talks, and in informal ways to create a sense of mutuality and strength in numbers. Other civilian organizations "worked the issues." The Defense Advisory Committee on Women in the Services, founded in the early 1950s as a public relations arm to facilitate military recruitment, was by the late 1970s an active lobbying force for military women operating from an office in the Pentagon, pressuring decision makers to reconsider a range of discriminatory policies. The Ford Foundation–funded Women and Military Project housed in the Women's Equity Action League was directed in the early 1980s by an ex-army officer, Carolyn Becraft, a woman who was to become for the next ten years a one-person social movement, monitoring the services, networking, strategizing, coordinating, and ultimately leading the lobbying efforts to change discriminatory practices and law. These civilian groups were a crucial lifeline to the uniformed women who wanted to be active but could not assume all the burden of speaking out themselves.

Even more important to the survival of feminism within the institution was the legitimation that came in the 1970s from the courts. Given the pressures on military women (and on all members of the military) to support the "party line," or at least to seek redress for any grievances they might harbor but without making waves, it is astonishing that even some military women chose to identify themselves as advocates for women. They could afford to do so, however, because throughout the 1970s, coinciding with the early days of the all-volunteer force, the courts sided with women who sued the military for sex discrimination. This judicial sponsorship—despite its reversal in the 1980s—was vital in supporting uniformed women together with their allies in nonprofit and lobbying organizations who entered the fray to struggle for equal opportunity. Although the courts pulled back from equality of opportunity norms in the 1980s, by that time, military women and their lobbyist confederates were already invested in the promises of equal opportunity.

The 1970s tell a remarkable tale. Time after time the courts, which had generally allowed the military broad leeway to set its own standards of conduct, refused to allow the services the autonomy to practice sex discrimination. During this decade the court was prepared to instruct the military to begin to make good on the transgressions of sex discrimination even as, in *other* arenas, the court demonstrated consistent deference to military sovereignty.

In what Stephanie A. Levin (1990, pp. 1010–61) calls the *Stanley* line of cases, the Supreme Court articulated a highly deferential standard of judicial review with respect to First Amendment claims. In 1987, *Stanley* capped a series of cases in which the Court refused to impose the same standard of review used in assessing civilian claims. In *United States v. Stanley* (1987, pp. 669, 671), a slim majority of the Court refused to uphold a suit brought against the Army by a sergeant who had been given LSD without his knowledge in an experimental program designed to test protective clothing and equipment.[2] In the *Stanley* set of cases, Levin suggests, the Court majority repeatedly asserted that "military life calls for a different standard of constitutional review than civilian life" (Levin 1990, p. 1014). Under this higher standard, the Court failed to protect First Amendment rights not only in situations where combat engagement and military mobilization were immediately at issue but even in situations where combat readiness or military discipline was a much more distant concern. In 1974, in *Parker v. Levy*, the Court declined to overturn the conviction of an Army captain and chief of dermatology who refused to train Special Forces aides for service in Vietnam, claiming his conviction was a violation of First Amendment rights. With the Vietnam conflict ongoing and in light of Levy's explicit opposition to the war and his declared support for those who might refuse orders to deploy, the Court's deference to the military is not surprising.[3] But two subsequent 1980 cases continued the separate standards perspective even in a situation that was neither wartime nor fully pertinent to combat readiness.[4] In 1986, the Court went on to rule that an Orthodox Jewish air force captain had no First Amendment right to wear a yarmulke while in uniform (*Goldman v. Weinberger* 1986). Under both Constitutional standards and also tort law, claimants have had little success in suing the military.[5]

In light of this history of judicial deference toward the military, it is striking that the courts in the 1970s required the military in numerous instances to dismantle sexually discriminatory policies (Goodman 1979, pp. 243–83; Stiehm 1989, pp. 108–34). Rather than exempting the military from equal protection claims, as might be expected given the courts' record of holding the military immune to First Amendment claims in the *Stanley* line of cases, the courts time and again in the 1970s upheld claims of sex discrimination against the armed services.

This readiness to support equal protection claims was evident in the 1970s decisions of both the Supreme Court and the lower courts. In

1973, the Supreme Court ruled that policies requiring military women but not men to prove spousal dependency to qualify for family allowances was unconstitutional (*Frontiero v. Richardson* 1973). In 1975, the Court denied an equal protection case brought by a male Navy officer but, rather than holding that the military was immune to equal opportunity challenges, found that the Navy's promotion system that treated men and women differently (allowing women extra time in rank) was justified by the different situations of male and female service personnel in the Navy (*Schlesinger v. Ballard* 1975).

The willingness to impose equal protection standards on the military was evident in lower court cases as well. In 1974, the D.C. Circuit Court overturned a lower court ruling that had upheld the prohibition against women's admission to the military academies (*Waldie v. Schlesinger* 1974).[6] In 1976, following an abundance of cases challenging military policies that required pregnant women to be discharged, the second circuit court ruled that the automatic separation from the military of pregnant servicewomen was a violation of equal protection and due process guarantees.[7] In 1978, the D.C. District Court held that an absolute bar on the assignment of Navy women to sea duty was a denial of equal protection (*Owens v. Brown* 1978). In contrast to the First Amendment *Stanley* line of cases, in which military deference was the standard of the day, in all of these 1970s sex discrimination cases the courts paid surprisingly little deference to the military.

Feminism in the military, then, played by the rules. Far from taking to the streets, they formed organizations to try to influence policy in the services and when that seemed to fail, they took to the courts. The law created opportunities for feminist activism in two ways. First, it provided direct authorization for military women who felt compelled to take their charges of discrimination outside the chain of command and outside the institution. When uniformed women did so, at least in the 1970s, the courts listened. Although the courts went on to play a more restrictive role in subsequent years, following the Court's determination to hold the line on all-male conscription with *Rostker* (1981), the courts' reversion was in some senses too late.[8] By 1980, the courts had transmitted the message to women that in certain basic respects, under the Constitution, they were entitled to equal treatment. Second, not only did the law directly affirm women's claims by providing a hearing outside the perimeters of the military, but the law also invested women with ammunition for their battles inside. The courts' endorsement of equal opportunity, although less than wholehearted, spawned a shift in institutional norms. As the belief in equality of opportunity spread, it provided women with an ideological resource to use in their internal efforts to argue for policy change. As Brigadier General Evelyn

P. Foote (1993), one of the most forceful advocates for military women, put it, "It is simply far easier to challenge a policy that has a basis in law."

Law and Identity

But women's activism in the military—its simultaneous boldness and reticence—cannot be explained simply through an analysis of the opportunities the law afforded for women to challenge discriminatory practices. What must also be understood is how the law, in subtle ways, shaped feminist identities. What the law stipulated—reflecting its fundamental roots in liberalism—was that those the law deemed "the same" would be treated the same. What this meant for feminist activism was that the less attention they called to difference (differences in gender, race, or sexuality), the more chance they saw of being accepted within the institution.

Sameness rather than difference was the legal norm that the court decisions and legislative actions of the 1970s promulgated. Before the 1970s, the decade in which the courts began to hold the military accountable to equal opportunity legal strictures, military women who saw themselves as champions of women's interests based their efforts largely on their sense of themselves as different from men. The leadership of the women's line components had worked hard over the previous decades to look after women's concerns, to ensure women proper training and good housing, and to win women respect and status in the services. They assumed, however, that women's interests were best served by supporting a military structured on gender difference rather than gender similarities. Women were differently trained and differently assigned to "support" jobs that were intended to free men to fight.

By the 1970s, however, the law privileged gender sameness over gender difference. The dismantling of the women's components (the WACs, the WAVES) and the shift to the All Volunteer Force (AVF) set new terms for women's participation in the military. The women who were moved to the forefront of the ranks of women leaders—Major General Jeanne Holm, Brigadier General Evelyn Foote—were people who stressed the desirability of gender-blind, merit-based recruitment and promotion, leaving behind leaders like General Elizabeth Hoisington who thought women did not belong in the academies and who belonged to a different age. (Paradoxically, difference advocates such as Hoisington believed that pregnancy and abortion should disqualify women from military service, whereas the new equality advocates largely argued that equality required women to have pregnancy leave, child care, and abortion services.) The new advocates for women were leaders who sought to integrate women into a single unified military stressing women's capabilities and talents and the imperative that jobs and careers be based on individual ability not gender.

But if gender sameness could be interpreted in ways that could take account of reproductive difference supporting women's claims to equality in the military, the same room for maneuver did not exist on the issue of sexual orientation. The law no longer declared pregnancy incompatible with military service, whereas the law has continued to declare homosexuality as inconsistent with the right to serve. The message that women activists in the military then receive from both their own peer environment and the higher authority of the law is "You can be a woman in the military—but only one kind of woman." Women can be recognized as servicewomen; they cannot be recognized within today's military as also lesbian.

The consequences of the law's differential treatment of uniformed lesbians and gays is that women activists in the military try hard to avoid linking gender issues to issues about homophobia. In 1990–91, as the issue of the combat exclusion began to heat up, the question of the homosexual exclusion was becoming simultaneously politicized. Most of the women who were trying to push for the reform of combat exclusion were concerned that the two issues not be intertwined. In anticipation of the lobbying on Capitol Hill, the group preparing to lobby met to hash out a political strategy. One of the issues that needed to be settled was whether they would approach Congress exclusively around the issue of the combat exclusion or whether the gay issue would also be posed. All but one in the group adamantly resisted organizing around the issues simultaneously.

The law, thus, plays a dual role. It encourages feminist activism by opening up certain kinds of political opportunities, and it discourages certain kinds of activism by conveying identity-constructing messages about the kind of political person one can be as a feminist within the military. The relationship of the military to the law simultaneously incites and limits protest within the institution.

Discursive Activism in the Catholic Church

If an account of feminist activism in the military can begin illustratively with a profile of an individual Navy aviator and crackerjack pilot-head of the women's aviator organization, the contrast of feminist activism in the Catholic Church can be captured by a description of the Women's Ordination Conference held in the fall of 1995 in a suburban hotel just outside Washington, D.C. About a thousand women were gathered to discuss issues related to women's ordination. Each session was peppered with singing, interspersed often between speakers as well as at the beginning of every plenary session. In both Spanish and English, the refrains brought back some of the rousing militancy of the 1960s with a feminist difference:

> *Rompe, rompe, hermana el silencio yal*
> *Rompe, el silencio y greta la verdad*

and then in English:

> Say it . . . Say it . . . Sister . . . Don't hold nothin' back
> Say it . . . Say it . . . Sister . . . Don't hold nothin' back

Then another song by c. marsie silvestro:

> I'm crossing the lines for justice
> Crossing the lines for liberation
> Crossing the lines for you

In Spanish, Rosa Martha Zarate, a Mexican woman and nun who had once lived and worked (until she was dismissed) in the Los Angeles Diocese, sang with spine-tingling emotion:

> *Por nada me devuelvo . . . (For nothing will I go back)*

No person could better signify the different institutional lives of women activists in the church and in the military. Sister Rosa Martha Zarate was one of a tiny number of women who, with little public fanfare or attention, sued the Church on grounds of race and sex discrimination when she was dismissed from her diocesan job. She lost.

To tell the story of feminist activism in the American Catholic Church is to relate a very different three-part narrative: (1) As with the military, feminist claims making in the Church has been institutionalized. (2) Unlike the military, in which the law affirmed the legitimacy of activism, the absence of such legal legitimation for women activists in the Church means that the sources of affirmation or condemnation of feminism in the Church are largely institutional. (3) The opportunity- and identity-forming power of the Church, in contrat to the military, has radicalized feminism within the Church.

The habitats which came to house feminist activism in the Catholic Church were of several types. Religious congregations themselves constituted one such space where women who were rethinking their lives in relationship to the Church came together, debated, reflected, explored, and refashioned their life and spiritual missions.[9]

Church renewal and social justice organizations provided a second habitat for the development of a feminist voice within the Church. One of the first organizations to be established was the National Assembly of Women Religious (NAWR), later to change its name to the National Assembly of Religious Women (NARW) to reflect the participation of laywomen. Founded in 1968, NARW endeavored to give voice to a more grassroots expression of views by religious women than was at that time possible in the Leadership Conference of Women Religious, and it remained until its demise in 1995 one of the groups most actively involved in tackling class and race issues within the movement of Catholic feminism.[10] The National Coalition of American Nuns was formed in 1969 with the intent of speaking out on a range of social justice and human rights issues.[11] Also in 1971, Las Hermanas, an organization of Hispanic sisters and laywomen engaged in the struggle against poverty and discrimination, was also founded. Numerous other organizations were founded throughout the decade that addressed issues about ordination, reproductive rights, homosexuality, and a range of poverty and antiracist concerns.[12]

A third habitat for feminism within the church has been academic institutions housing feminist scholars. By the 1980s, feminist theologians, historians, and sociologists had secured, in fairly significant numbers, tenured places in American universities.[13] These positions have provided sometimes safe and sometimes highly contentious (as with Mary Daly's tenure fight at Boston College) spaces from which feminist scholars have been able to produce hundreds of volumes about church teachings and church history. It was of no small importance to feminism's institutionalization that feminist theological writings found outlets in prominent commercial presses (Harper and Row, Simon and Schuster, Beacon) in addition to the presses that carry largely religious publications.[14] It is also telling that by the late 1980s, women were one-quarter of all students enrolled in American Roman Catholic theological schools (Baumgaertner 1989, pp. 90–92, as quoted in Wallace 1992, p. 5).

Many feminist organizations within the Church gained a visibility surprising in light of their tiny staffs and limited budgets. Skilled in the arts of communications and media, all the renewal organizations, no matter how small, ran workshops, organized conferences, and produced quantities of literature—newsletters,[15] resources for workshops, liturgies, and press releases, not to mention fiction, poetry, plays, posters, tapes, and extensive dramaturgy of all sorts. The spokespersons for the organizations were also spending large amounts of time on the road, interacting with others in projects, meetings, and educational endeavors. Feminism in the Church was above all discursive, engaged as it was in a project of reinterpretation and meaning making (Katzenstein 1995).

The agenda of these groups was both discursive and radical. Feminists worked at knowledge producing that questioned some of the basic precepts of the contemporary institutional Church. Substantial numbers of feminists, for instance, have argued against women's ordination as merely underwriting the hierarchy of the Church itself. Many have questioned the structural basis of inequity and injustice in state, in society, and in the Church. Activist nuns and laywomen have worked in prisons, in shelters, with refugees from Central and Latin America, with babies (often born drug addicted) and children of poor mothers. A number have worked on issues about homosexuality within the Church. A few, supported by outside funding (principally the Ford Foundation), have worked on issues about reproductive rights. The agenda is not monolithic—with important debates recurrently flaring up over Christology in a renewed Church, Catholic feminism's own racism/classism, and the accountability of women to their orders and to the hierarchy. In comparison with feminism in other institutional contexts, women activists in the Church stand out as overtly, vocally committed to a restructuring of the society according to principles of equity and inclusiveness.

Opportunity and Identity

The explanation for the rise and endurance of this spirit of insurgency is found within the history of the institution itself. Unlike women activists in the military, women religious could not turn to the law. But in certain ways they were able to turn to the Church itself. Not all would-be activists were ready to do this. In the face of Vatican intransigence, some chose conformity and silence. Others chose to leave the Church. But many stayed within the Church and opted to challenge its hierarchy, making abundant use of the discursive resources of print, speech, and song.

What activist women found in the Church was both opportunity and identity. The opportunity came with the declarations of Vatican II. By asking what role the Church should assume in the modern world and by inviting the active participation of the laity in the construction of a lived faith, Pope John XXIII and Pope Paul VI catalyzed vast changes. The call for renewal invited all religious orders to examine their constitution, directories, ceremonies, and prayers—indeed, their entire mission and self-understanding (see Ware 1985; Curb and Manahan 1985). When, in response to Vatican II, nuns rewrote their orders' constitutions and recomposed their rituals, they exchanged the old standardization of behavior based on rigid rules of obedience and conformity for new rules that provided at once for greater community and greater individual autonomy. Gone were the requirements to ask the mother superior for permission to take a bath, to use a needle and thread, to read the newspaper, to go outside, to consult a book other than the Bible. No longer were letters between the eighteen-year-old postulant and her mother or father or erstwhile boyfriend opened, read, and maybe not delivered. Gone were the ban on "particular friendships" and the arbitrary assignments to jobs and locations arrived at through closed deliberations to which the nun assignee was not privy.

The opportunity Vatican II provided, then, came in the form of the injunction: that the church was to be understood as the people. But in the successor years in which Pope John Paul II reasserted strict centralized control over Church affairs, Vatican II was reinterpreted by many increasingly exasperated feminist sisters and laywomen to mean "If the church is the people, and we are the people, then the church is us—womenchurch."

Vatican II had opened the way. But Vatican II cannot explain the American feminist reaction in full. The council's injunction to activism was sent out from Rome to all corners of the globe, and the reaction of lay and religious was certainly not everywhere the same. Why the America feminist response took the form it did—profuse in its printed expression, readier to challenge the clerical hierarchy, and, as elsewhere, committed to egalitarianism in the church and in society— cannot be explained without understanding the way the institution shaped the identities of women activists within the Church.

As an institution, the Catholic Church in some ways nurtures the possibility of defining oneself as in dissent. One word that is often used to legitimize dissent within the Church is *prophetic*. One cannot exactly be "prophetic" in the military—disagreeing with those higher in the chain of command. In the Church, there is at least the possibility of appeal to the tradition of prophets and to the call of moral conscience. But this would not explain a readier tendency to insurgency among American religious than among their female counterparts in many other parts of the world. To understand the American "exceptionalism" means turning to the way American women in the Church came to be influenced not only by the social movements of the time (the civil rights, peace, and women's movements) but by the specific migration of ideas to North America from the ecclesial neighbors to the south.

Beginning in the 1960s, Latin American liberation theology exerted a powerful influence over many women religious in North America. At least some of this influence was transmitted through the presence of United States sisters who were sent to work throughout Latin America.

Already by 1961, the Church hierarchy had appealed to religious communities in the United States to send 10 percent of their community members to missions in Latin America (Prevallet 1995, p. 91).

The Loretto experience, as related by Elaine Prevallet (1995), vividly depicts one process by which ideas of liberation theology migrated north. As Loretto sisters became exposed to the Latin American interpretation of Vatican II that was embodied in liberation theology, their view of their own role shifted from a more traditional understanding of "mission" work to a belief in a broad, populist coming to faith in a common struggle for justice. Even before 1961, the Lorettos had been planning on establishing a site in La Paz, Bolivia. After some deliberation, a school for girls was opened in 1961. Colegio Loreto drew from the privileged strata of society—the military, politicians, and professional families. But very soon, the sisters who were running the school began to reassess its purposes. A 1963 meeting of Latin American bishops in Cuernavaca exhorted religious orders to link education to social justice work. The 1968 Medellin conference was further to reaffirm the "preferential option for the poor" that defined the Latin American reaction to Vatican II.[16] By the latter part of the 1960s, the La Paz sisters were also in touch with Loretto projects in Chile and Peru. Several of the sisters had studied in Cuernavaca under Ivan Illich, and the debates about renewal in North America had reached an intense pitch. At the Colegio, Loretto sisters were divided over the degree to which the school should be made over in a more democratic mode with tuitions scaled and curriculum planned to include experiential learning that would expose students to the realities of inequality in Bolivian life. These debates between radicalism and reformism were brought back into the North American Loretto community where the executive committee and the general assembly of the religious order became involved in considering the future of the school.

By the 1980s, many sisters were traveling to Central and South America. Many worked as teachers and health workers in El Salvador, Nicaragua, and elsewhere in Latin America.[17] The 1980 rape and murder of two Maryknoll and one Ursuline sister and a laywoman who had been working with local communities in El Salvador by members of the National Guard sent shock waves through the religious communities of North America and undoubtedly intensified further the attention that religious groups were directing to events in Latin America (Neal 1990, p. 39; Ferraro and Hussey 1990, p. 197). In the 1980s, Sister Marjorie Tuite, much revered by activist sisters, established the Women's Coalition against United States Intervention in Latin America and the Carribean. She made continuous trips to Central America and Cuba, taking groups of women religious with her to be "present in the struggle."[18] The National Assembly of Religious Women (NARW), which Tuite founded, shared offices with an organization working with Guatemalan women and continued to work in alliance with women like Renny Golden who were active in the sanctuary movement. Network, the Catholic lobbying group in Washington run by sisters, made U.S. policy in Central America one of its central issues. Deeply committed to a common struggle for social justice, the entire Loretto order's assembly voted to spend significant amounts of money on Latin American projects: $30,000 in humanitarian aid to Nicaragua in 1979, $20,000 for two projects in 1980 in El Salvador, $23,500 for aid to refugees from "repressive Central American countries" in 1981 (Ware 1995a, p. 75). But even for those women who had no direct experience in Latin America, the writings of Paulo Freire and the practices of *conscientiazation*[19] were present in the methodologies of discussion and reflection used in meetings of women religious. "Speak outs," breaking up into small groups—methods of deliberation incorporated into the assemblies of many religious orders during the 1970s—were all at least partly a result of teachings that had come to the United States through liberation theology.

Vatican II created the opportunity for nuns to rethink their vocation. But the Vatican call for renewal did not dictate the character of that vocation. Nuns and many laywomen came to see themselves in distinctly radical terms, to redefine their identities, strongly influenced by the social movements outside the Church and by the powerful might of liberation theology whose teachings were transported from Latin American missions to the meeting rooms of American religious.

Conclusion

To see the social movements of the 1990s through the lenses of the 1960s may invite a misreading of the 1990s. The 1960s held out what seemed to be, at least then, a clearer definition of who was (in the language of the time) "inside the system" and who was out. A 1960s student protester could readily define someone inside the system as an adult living in a world the student had not yet had chronological reason to enter. An African American might have readily seen an insider as necessarily white given the near-absence of persons of color in government, in universities, on the television set, running local businesses, or in the courthouse. The boundaries separating protest on the outside and business as usual on the inside seemed clearer than they do today. The distinction between movement politics and institutional life seemed unmistakeable.

The inside/outside of feminism in the 1990s is, in two ways, less distinct. First, in the 1960s, the energy of protest movements could be sapped by young activists opting to enter business, enter politics, become a lawyer, or get a government job. In the 1990s, feminist activists in the Church and military did not leave the movement for the institution; feminists, in particular, came *to* the movement *from within* the institution. Second, by the 1990s, there was protest drama inside and outside institutions. Partly because of the expose-hungry culture of the media, the public has come to witness theatrical "episodes" in once-private spaces—the suites of the Las Vegas Hilton, the living rooms of army drill instructors. The reasons for taking protest into the institution are now vivid and compelling.

But do we see in the 1990s what the 1960s activists feared—that claims voiced from within an institutional milieu must face an inevitable routinization and deradicalization in the face of the controlling rules of institutional life? If the experiences of the military and the Church provide any single answer to this question, it is that feminism runs a different course depending on its institutional location.

On first take, feminism's encounter with the military appears in some ways to be a straightforward exemplification of the deradicalization thesis. After twenty years of equal opportunity, women's numbers in the academies and in the services are nowhere above 20 percent and mostly well below; uniformed women activists are careful to keep their political struggles out of the press and to contain their issues to "women-focused" concerns. Only recently have women's organizations in the military begun exploring the commonalities of race and gender, and, for the most part, they continue to segment their cause from any tarnishing it might suffer by linking issues of gender inequality to the bigotry of heterosexist policy and culture in the armed services.

At the same time, such a narrative, if it is not to be reductionist, must acknowledge additional realities. Military feminists were hardly radicals to begin with. If the institution plays a role in containing protest, it is not to subdue what was there before, as much as to divert what might be there in some future time. Clearly military elites fear change: At each turn military feminists face vehement resistance from within (with the integration of the academies, with their efforts to seek institutional resolutions to problems of sexual harassment, with their insistence on women's inclusion in the combat specialties of military aviation and the naval services.) If the opposition women activists encounter at virtually every turn is any indication, what they seek to change is not easily dismissable as matters that are marginal to the definition of the institution. Reformist, perhaps, but words like *depoliti-*

cization and *deradicalization* are inadequate to describe institutionalized feminism in the military.

Relative to their counterparts in the military, feminism in the Catholic Church is a far more insurgent enterprise. Feminist habitats in the Church are some of the few places, in the 1990s, where a 1960s activist can feel at home. In the face of a Church that excludes women from its hierarchy, that condemns the sin of homosexuality, and in the face of a society that dismisses any defense of affirmative action and welfare rights as evidence of extremism, the words of activist laywomen and women religious in the Catholic Church produce texts in which radicals still "talk the talk."

But this description, too, is oversimplified. It is hard to know what radicalism means in the context of the contemporary age. Much of the radical language of Catholic women activists is that: language— theological writings, newsletters, editorials, workshops, talk, lectures, dance, and song. Far more than others, many activist women in the Church live by their words in the sense of working in prisons, with the homeless, in the inner city, caring for the poor and crack babies. But is this radicalism rather than humanitarianism? Is the rebellious language of Catholic laywomen and religious—language that has been ineffectual to date in changing church policies—any more radical in its contemporary significance than the slow chipping away of institutional hierarchy by their more moderate-minded military stepsisters?

But this ambiguity does not diminish the clarity of the lesson that the Church-military comparison imparts: If the politics of activism inside institutions is to be understood in *both* its radical and more moderate forms, the character of its particular institutional location must be carefully specified. Feminist habitats in the Church and military are nested in very different institutional environments (Aggarwal 1986; Tsebelis 1990; Meyer 1994).[20] Situated in a transnational church and insulated from the law, the Vatican has been able to repudiate the demands of American religious women, paradoxically inviting a rebelliousness born out of foreclosed political options. Military activists, by contrast, occupied habitats in an institution that was situated in a national context that bound institutional leadership to the law and that promised activists at least some rewards for moderately voiced claims. The question for today's activists is perhaps less about whether you are outside or inside institutions than it is about the systems of authority the institution is nested within.

Notes

1. Frances Fox Piven and Richard A. Cloward (1971, p. 456) write, "Protest movements have always been the resort of those who lacked institutionalized

forms of political access and influence." Meyer and Tarrow's introductory essay in this volume speaks of institutionalization as transporting movement actors into a realm of more routinized and established political practices. They do not see institutional actors as abandoning political goals, a perspective that I share. They describe institutionalization, however, as defined partially by the occurrence of cooptation, meaning that "challengers alter their claims and tactics to ones that can be pursued without disrupting the normal practice of politics." I argue, by contrast, that institutionalized activism may or may not be cooptative and can be, under particular circumstances, quite disruptive.

2. Stanley claimed to have been severely debilitated by the LSD— experiencing hallucinations, memory loss, disorientation, and eventually the breakup of his marriage and discharge from the service.

3. The case was decided by a five-Justice majority opinion written by Justice Rehnquist. The dissent expressed dismay at the use of a separate standard of review for the military, different from that which might have been applied in a civilian context. But as Marilyn A. Gordon and Mary Jo Ludvigson (1990) point out, the court did not hesitate to inquire into the constitutionality of military actions. They argue that *Parker* would have been among the cases that women might have cited had the constitutionality of combat exclusion been challenged in the courts.

4. *Brown v. Glines* 444 U.S. 348 (1980) and *Secretary of the Navy v. Huff* 444 U.S. 453 (1980) (per curiam). These cases involved the service requirement that prior approval by a commanding officer be given before petitions could be circulated. Justice Brennan points out in his dissent that this requirement pertained to bases that were not operating "under combat or near-combat conditions" and that the application of such stringent standards to these "rear-echelon" situations should be considered particularly questionable (as discussed in Levin 1990, pp. 1017–18).

5. The *Stanley* case was brought both under constitutional law and as a tort. The Federal Tort Claims Act (FTCA) is the instrument through which the government can be sued for negligence or wrongful acts (see Levin 1990, p. 1011, n. 6). See also the discussion in Stiehm (1989).

6. The appeals court ordered the case to trial, but it was dropped when Congress took action the following year (Morden 1990, p. 320).

7. *Crawford v. Cushman* (1976); *Struck v. Secretary of Defense* (1972); *Robinson v. Rand* (1972); *Gutierrez v. Laird* (1972); *Flores v. Secretary of Defense* (1973). The *Cushman* case did not decide military policy, however. Well into the 1980s, the services continued to debate the issue of whether pregnancy should cause a military woman's discharge. The services have no common policy on the issue of aviators and undetected or diagnosed pregnancy. This is likely to continue to be debated over the next years.

8. In *Rostker v. Goldberg*, the Court was confronted with the issue of women in combat—touching, as Bill Brundage terms it, "the defining nucleus" of the military mission: it drew back. This shift occurred as the Court moved ever-closer to the self-defined essence of the military—the combat issue. Moving from dependency allowances, to the pregnancy issue, to the matter of women's

service on ships, the Court began to approach what many saw as the core definition of a masculinist military—the composition of a fighting force. Justice Rehnquist, writing for a six-justice majority, claimed that draft registration directly related to conscription and thereby to combat. The dissenting judges claimed that women could be registered or drafted without necessarily implicating them in combat duties. And in language that was significant in its absence from earlier sex discrimination cases brought against the military, Justice Rehnquist affirmed the importance of a "healthy deference to legislative and executive judgments in the area of military affairs."

9. Throughout the late 1960s and continuing to this day, many religious orders have held discussions in their regular assembly meetings about gender and race issues. These discussions raised both spiritual and secular issues. They considered the meaning of religious renewal and such specific matters as whether the congregation should support the ERA. What does racism mean in the everyday lives of sisters? What does an inclusive liturgy mean? Should a particular resolution on sanctuaries be adopted? In the case of particular orders (the Sisters of Mercy), there were discussions, for instance, about the responsibilities of Sister-run hospitals for women's gynecological and reproductive health care. Smaller networks were also formed within a congregation. When particular subgroups within an order wished to address themselves to an issue not necessarily involving the whole congregation, measures were taken to constitute community-connected associations. Loretto Women's Network, formed by a group within the Loretto Sisters, and the Network's newspaper, *couRAGE*, are examples; see the essays in Ware (1995a), particularly the chapter by Virginia Williams, "Loretto and the Women's Movement: From 'Sister' to Sister,' " especially pp. 245–46 on the origins of the Loretto Women's Network. The Adrian Dominicans also have a commission for women. Similarly, the Sisters of Charity of the blessed Virgin Mary have a network for Women's Issues—loosely held together through small group discussions, personal contact, and a newsletter.

10. See the final issue of *Probe* for a history of NARW. Vol. XXIII, No. 2. Summer, 1995.

11. For a history of NCAN, see "If Anyone Can, NCAN: Twenty Years of Speaking Out," edited by Margaret Traxler and Ann Patrick Ware and available from NCAN, 7315 S. Yale, Chicago, Ill 60621.

12. The Women's Ordination Conference (WOC) was founded in 1974, the same year that Chicago Catholic Women (CCW) was established. In 1974, Catholics for a Free Choice (CFFC), directed by Frances Kissling, was founded to support the right to legal reproductive health care including family planning and abortion, later to be declared by the Vatican as not an official voice of the Catholic Church. Other multiple-issue groups also date from this period (the Quixote Center, the Eighth Day Center for Justice, Call to Action), all of which work toward the advancement of gender equality as part of their broad agendas. In 1977, Sister Jeannine Gramick and Father Robert Nugent founded the New Ways ministry to work toward reconciliation of Church teachings and gay/lesbian issues. In 1982, Mary Hunt and Diann Neu founded the Women's

Alliance for Theology, Ethics, and Religion, which organizes workshops and resources for an ecumenical constituency. In 1987, Mary's Pence was established to raise and distribute money for women's causes. Peter's Pence collections raise money for the papacy. The feast of Teresa of Avila, October 15, has been selected as Mary's Pence Day, but because many of the fund's donors are not churchgoers, much of the fundraising occurs through other avenues. In 1995, the fund distributed $60,000—a surprisingly high sum given that Mary's Pence has not been approved for entry in the Kennedy Book that lists sanctioned Catholic charities.

13. The writings of feminist historians, sociologists, and political scientists throughout the 1980s were also very important in the creation of an epistemic community. Some prominent examples from the roster of names of present/former women religious include Sister Marie Augusta Neal, SND de Namur, Department of Sociology, Emmanuel College; Helen Rose Ebaugh, Department of Sociology, University of Houston; Ruth Wallace, Department of Sociology, George Washington University, but the literature produced by the vast numbers of women religious with M.A.'s and Ph.D.'s documenting, reanalyzing, and reconstructing (in the 1970s and 1980s) the history of women in the Church is far too great and too important to represent in an endnote. Part of what is extraordinary about some of that literature, which is highly scholarly, is that it was done by women who had neither the salary nor the free time provided by academic institutions. Lay academics have also been significant contributors to this community of scholars, including historians (e.g., Mary Jo Weaver, professor of religion at Indiana University; Margaret Thompson, Syracuse University); and political scientists (e.g., Mary Segers, Rutgers University; Joann Formicola, Seton Hall University).

14. From this early stage in which feminist theologians came to be recognized and widely read (1970s and 1980s), I include only a sampling of the theological writings or the regular reviews in such publications as the *National Catholic Reporter* (which in one of the September and February issues regularly reviews writings on women and theology). More complete writings are easily traced through such bibliographical sources as the *Catholic Religion and Periodical Index*. See, for instance, Daly (1973, 1975, 1984); Ruether (1974, 1975, 1983 and 1988); Ruether and McLaughlin (1979); Schussler Fiorenza (1983, 1984); Carr (1988); and Swidler and Swidler (1977). For an analysis of some of these writings from this period, see Weaver (1986). See also Weaver's (1993) own more recent and very interesting theological explorations and also Graff (1993). Note the importance to this process of institutionalization of such presses as Harper and Row, Simon and Schuster, and, of course, Beacon Press, which has long specialized in the writings of feminist theologians and feminists writing about spirituality.

15. Some examples: NARW's bimonthly was *Probe;* WOC's *New Women, New Church* is a quarterly with four thousand readers. WATER publishes *WATER-wheel;* the sisters of Loretto network puts out *courRAGE;* Las Hermanas produces *Informes*. The National Coalition of American Nuns has a regular newsletter; Chicago Catholic Women regularly produces information, calen-

dars, and announcement sheets; CFFC produces numerous working papers, brochures, and the newsletter/journal *Conscience*. For further information, see Vidulich (1993, p. 2).

16. See "The Post-Vatican II Church in Latin America," in Ebaugh (1991, pp. 233–45).

17. See the very moving story of friendship and love between two Loretto sisters depicted in Crawley (1995). Ann Manganaro taught barefoot doctor techniques in El Salvador in the late 1980s until her death in 1993.

18. Ferraro and Hussey (1990, p. 196). See the National Assembly of Religious Women's newsletter, *Probe*, of which Tuite was the first editor, for a sense of the deep involvement of some women religious in working on Latin American social justice issues, combatting U.S. imperialism, and assisting with the sanctuary movement.

19. A Brazilian educator, Freire (1970) laid out methods of consciousness raising that could be incorporated within literary classes.

20. I am grateful to David Meyer for suggesting this framing years back when I first undertook this comparison.

10

Transnational Advocacy Networks in the Movement Society

Margaret E. Keck and Kathryn Sikkink

Advocacy networks are one of the main vehicles for transnational activity around rights and social justice issues. Like activists in social movement organizations, activists in transnational advocacy networks seek to make the demands, claims, or rights of the less powerful win out over the purported interests of the more powerful. They do this by presenting issues in new ways (framing), seeking the most favorable arenas in which to fight their battles (paying attention to political opportunity structure), confounding expectations (disruption), and broadening the network's scope and density to maximize its access to necessary information (mobilizing social networks). Although they often include activists who are part of social movements, transnational advocacy networks are not themselves transnational "movements." If we define social movements as sustained, organized, contentious collective action around grievances or claims, these networks depart from the definition in various ways.[1] The clearest of these is in the mobilizational dimension: although advocacy networks may at times stimulate mobilized collective action, more commonly they are alternatives to mass action. This is especially true when the groups on whose behalf advocates organize are blocked from making demands at home—either because the rights violator is the state itself or because their voices are too weak to be heard domestically.

Transnational advocacy networks include those relevant actors working internationally on an issue, who are bound together by shared values, a common discourse, and dense exchanges of information and services.[2] They are *communicative structures* for political exchange. Network nodes (individuals and organizations) vary enormously in nature, density of organization, resources, and domestic standing; their main collective currency is information. Besides nongovernmental actors, networks may include individual officeholders in states or multilateral organizations or even whole agencies.

The conceptual apparatus developed to study domestic social movements remains extremely valuable for understanding transnational advocacy networks. In this essay we first discuss the relevance of concepts of mobilizing structures, political opportunity structure, and framing for our discussion of transnational advocacy networks, and we consider why they travel so well. We then illustrate our points with examples drawn from transnational activity around women's human rights and environment. Finally, we will explain why we believe that much greater attention to the mechanisms of transnational diffusion and persuasion should precede attempts to characterize its results.

In distinguishing between social movements and advocacy networks, we are trying to separate an analysis of what activists in advocacy networks do from an account of the biographies of network members. We recognize that this is a purely heuristic exercise—in real life they are inseparable. As in social movements, activism in advocacy networks occurs "at the intersection of biography and history" in a special way—"as biographies and identities are modified in accordance with the newly perceived historical imperatives" (McAdam 1988, p. 11). Advocacy network activists often have a history of involvement with social movements; some social movement organizations are part of networks, and networks can provide crucial resources for movements. Or, conversely, movements and advocacy networks may compete for legitimacy in the same terrain. Some members of advocacy networks conceive of themselves as part of a transnational social movement; others most decidedly do not.

Core activists in advocacy networks most often work for nongovernmental organizations (NGOs), in the United States, frequently called public interest groups or nonprofits. They are, in other words, career activists. These NGOs may be wholly devoted to international activities (e.g., human rights groups) or barely at all (most environmental organizations). Activists involved in an advocacy network may therefore be speaking for their organizations or may be using the organization as a platform on which to stand. In either case organizational affiliation matters, but the solidity of organizational linkages may affect the resources on which a network can draw.

A brief note on the subject of NGOs is in order. We use the term to refer to professionalized nonprofit organizations (with paid staff, fund-raising capabilities, and, except in highly repressive situations, juridical recognition). In developing countries, NGOs may be involved in service provision or in advocacy and social promotion; many do both. Some are highly politicized, ranging from quasi-governmental fronts to vehicles for radical opposition; others are less so. The origin of the NGO sector varies widely from country to country. In advocacy networks NGOs involved tend most often to be run either by people with histories of activism in other areas (social movements, political parties) or by professionals (e.g., lawyers, ecologists, agronomists) seeking more engaged alternatives to traditional employment. Although NGOs can be involved in a wide range of activities, the ones we discuss in our work are devoted to social change issues.

Social Networks

Social movement theorists have repeatedly stressed the importance of social networks—concrete linkages that derive from locality, shared experience, kinship, and the like—as foundations on which movements are built. In recent explorations, Tarrow (1996a) questions whether or how the functional equivalent of these could be mobilized transnationally. But in fact, many social networks that nourish the creation of transnational advocacy networks and support their work reveal histories of personal relationships and shared experiences that parallel those found in domestic movements.

Just as domestic public interest groups often grow out of social movement struggles, many professional advocacy NGOs involved in transnational activity derive sustenance from earlier movements. Funding from private foundations and religious organizations has similarly played an important role. The Ford Foundation program in public interest law aided in the establishment of U.S. consumer and environmental groups (Berry 1993, pp. 30–33; Ingram and Mann 1989, p. 137); Ford, with NOVIB and other European funders also played a key role in financing human rights groups and Third World environmental advocacy. In developing countries, advocacy NGOs have appeared in response to the push of a particular movement or the pull of funding opportunities that coalesced with strongly held beliefs. During the recent democratic transitions in Latin America, activists involved in popular education or grassroots organizing established new institutes as "private organizations fulfilling public functions" in campaigns against violence and promoting rights of women, racial minorities, indigenous peoples, workers and the landless, the environment, human rights, and so forth (Fernandes 1994; Landim 1993). These professionalized groups, in turn, are linked through social networks forged in past struggles to other activists (Doimo 1995). In countries lacking a history of freedom of association, mobilizing networks of trusted activists for particular campaigns is a more familiar mode of organization than establishing institutions.

Repressive regimes in Latin America (and elsewhere) have spurred the transnationalization of advocacy networks in two ways. Repression forces the externalization of domestic rights struggles. Unable to address issues like human rights, disappearances, and labor rights in situations in which the chief violators of rights were state institutions, activists formed alliances with their counterparts abroad. Together, they sought recourse either by approaching international institutions or by mobilizing foreign pressure to change the behavior of their governments.

Repression also generated diasporas. The thousands of Latin American political exiles who spent part of the 1970s in Europe and the United States inspired a generation of young people, already socialized into movement politics by the events of the late 1960s, with their stories. The exiles developed lasting friendships, political ties, and relations of trust. They also developed relationships with organizations in their host countries—universities, churches, foundations, and research institutes—that became key resources for them when they returned home. Some individuals gained international reputations. Thus, at the onset of democratization, former exiles played an important role in creating new NGOs in Latin America, securing funding, and acting as go-betweens for other initiatives. Some became active in new international NGOs (e.g., Amnesty International, Americas Watch) or other international organizations. Other kinds of international experience became more common as well. In the United States, networks appealed to a public socialized into more cosmopolitan worldviews through participation in student exchange programs, government programs like the Peace Corps, and lay missionary programs that sent thousands of young people to live and work in the developing world.

Social networks forged in earlier social or political struggles are not the only ones relevant to the formation of advocacy networks. Professional networks are also important, and increasingly so. Human rights and environmental lawyers, anthropologists, forensic and environmental scientists, health specialists, agronomists, all may become involved through professional activities in advocacy work. Besides NGO activists, crucial parts of advocacy networks are individuals in governmental agencies or intergovernmental organizations who share the activists' values and try to further their goals within organizations.

International conferences proliferated beginning in the 1970s, bringing activists from around the world together to discuss common concerns. Such meetings led to visits and exchanges. The precipitous fall in airfares that made international travel accessible for more and more people was followed in the 1980s by a revolution in telecommunications. Fax and computer technology made almost instantaneous flows of information that could have taken weeks or never arrived at all. These transnational contacts built the social networks on which advocacy networks were founded; information was the currency by which they gained influence.

Although frequently undertaken by people with strong principled motivations, running effective organizations involves learned techniques and transferrable expertise. NGO or nonprofit management has increasingly become a profession. Transnational networking also involves skills taught by more experienced networkers to newer ones, just as more experienced movement organizers pass on the tools of campaigning to the next generation of campaigners.

Finally, networks have spawned networks (McAdam and Rucht 1993; Meyer and Whittier 1994). Connections forged in the mid-1970s among activists committed to working for a more equitable international economic order, campaigning around food and increasing corporate monopolies of plant germplasm in the International Coalition for Development Action, fed the organization of the International Baby Food Action Network, the Pesticides Action Network, and Health Action International. These in turn were important models for the creation of subsequent generations of health, environmental, and development action networks.

Political Opportunity Structure

Advocacy networks have been the most visible in situations in which domestic access of claimants is blocked or those making claims are too weak politically for their voices to be heard. In such instances, network activists have sought international or foreign venues in which to present claims, effectively transforming the power relationships involved by shifting the political context. Human rights activists brought the "dirty war" in Argentina to the U.S. Congress, producing significant reverberations in Buenos Aires; environmental activists took the problems of rubber tappers in the western Amazon to the multilateral development banks, producing (among other things) the creation of extractive reserves as a legal category.

We call the feedback that comes from this kind of venue shifting "the boomerang effect," and producing it is one of the most common strategic activities of advocacy networks. When the links between state and domestic actors are severed, it initiates the "boomerang": domestic NGOs bypass their state and directly search out international allies to try to bring pressure on their states from outside. Linkages are important for both sides: for the less powerful Third World actors, networks provide access, leverage, information, and material resources they could not expect to have on their own; for northern groups, they make credible the assertion that they are struggling with, and not only "for" their southern partners. Not surprisingly, such relationships can produce considerable tensions. Nonetheless, the practical activity they occasion helps to build the kinds of shared understandings that can form the basis for future work (Calhoun 1995a, pp. 173–76).

Transnational advocacy networks strategize by mapping relationships among a variety of domestic and international institutions. Their ability to get things done frequently depends on their ability to exert leverage over more powerful actors, mainly officials of states (their own or others) or international organizations. Environmentalists and indigenous rights activists lobby members of the U.S. Congress and Treasury Department to influence officials of the World Bank to put pressure on Brazil regarding indigenous land policy. NGO activists in Brasília provide information to mid-level European diplomats tasked with updating their governments on environmental issues, so that their governments, in turn, raise questions in international fora or with the Brazilian government. Mexican pro-democracy and human rights advocates brought Mexican electoral abuses before the Inter-American Commission on Human Rights. These moves involve strategic choices of activity predicated on an assessment of relations among governments and among national and international institutions. These "opportunities" are dynamic; the political opportunity structure relevant for this kind of activity has to do as much with political relations as with political institutions (Tarrow 1996b).[3]

Network members actively seek ways to bring issues to the public agenda, both by framing them in innovative ways and by seeking hospitable venues. Transnational networks normally involve a small number of activists from the organizations and institutions involved in a given campaign or advocacy role. The kinds of pressure and agenda politics in which advocacy networks engage rarely involve mass activism. Boycott strategies are a partial exception. Instead, network activists engage in what Baumgartner and Jones (1991), borrowing from law, call *venue shopping.* "This strategy relies less on mass mobilization and more on the dual strategy of the presentation of image and the search for a more receptive political venue" (p. 1050). Very occasionally, groups become such integral parts of policy networks that they spend very little effort trying to influence public opinion; this kind of purely insider strategy is comparatively rare in transnational advocacy network politics (Walker 1991, p. 12).

In recent work in international relations theory, Thomas Risse-Kappen (1995) stresses the importance of domestic structures in his account of transnational relations. Although crucial, domestic structures do not tell enough of the story. They may account for the more institutionalized and thus more durable aspects of opportunity—the existence of parliaments and Congressional committees, the formal relationship between the executive director of the World Bank and officials at the U.S. Treasury Department, the set of rules governing Mexican elections, the division of labor within diplomatic hierarchies, the policy networks within which information circulates about particular issues or areas. Knowledge of how these "structures" or "institutions" function is clearly an essential aspect of strategy. However, this misses the more dynamic, purely conjunctural, and sometimes even accidental aspects of political opportunity for which transnational networkers—like social movement activists—watch ceaselessly. Such elements might include the replacement of an agency head with another more sympathetic to a particular cause or having preexisting links with an advocacy network, the ability to make global warming and tropical deforestation seem more pressing because of drought and hot weather, recognition that plans for the celebration of the five hundredth anniversary of Columbus's voyages to the Americas opened space for indigenous rights agitation, and so forth.

Thus, beyond recognizing durable patterns of relationships and rules, activists in advocacy networks seek out agitational niches that may provide unexpected access for new ideas and arguments. But to gain access to these niches, they must frame the issue in question in a way that will capture the attention of decision makers.

Framing

Building cognitive frames is an essential component of networks' political strategies. David Snow and his colleagues have called this strategic activity *frame alignment*—"by rendering events or occurrences meaningful, frames function to organize experience and guide action, whether individual or collective" (Snow et al. 1986, pp. 464–465; Snow and Benford 1988, 1992). *Frame resonance* concerns the relationship between a movement organization's interpretive work and its ability to influence broader public understandings. Although initially new frames must be laboriously put into place, over time, "a given collective action frame becomes part of the political culture—which is to say, part of the reservoir of symbols from which future movement entrepreneurs can choose" (Tarrow 1992, p. 197).

The ability of transnational advocacy networks to frame issues successfully is especially problematic, because unlike domestic social movements, different parts of advocacy networks need to appeal to belief systems, life worlds, and stories, myths, and folk tales in many different countries and cultures. This is even more problematic when networks link activists from highly industrialized and less developed countries. We argue that one of the kinds of issues most characteristic of issue networks—involving bodily harm to vulnerable individuals—speaks to aspects of belief systems or life worlds that transcend a specific cultural or political context.

Why do these issues appear so prominently in international campaigns? Although the issue of bodily harm resonates with the liberal ideological traditions in the United States and Western Europe, it is also a component of basic ideas of human dignity. Not all cultures have beliefs about human rights (as individualistic, universal, and indivisible), but most do contain ideas of human dignity (Donnelly 1989, pp. 49–50). Of course, defining bodily harm, and claims about who is vulnerable or innocent, may be highly contested. Nevertheless, we argue that campaigns against practices involving bodily harm to populations perceived as vulnerable or innocent are most likely to be effective transnationally, especially where there is a short and clear causal chain or story assigning responsibility. Issues involving bodily harm also lend themselves to dramatic portrayal and personal testimony that are such an important part of network tactics. Finally, the stark immediacy of the power relationship implied by physical violence against vulnerable individuals relegates the kinds of power asymmetries that frequently divide networks to the background, making possible the development of shared practice that can contribute to a common frame.[4]

The adoption of new frames frequently involves the imagination of political entrepreneurs. The recent coupling of indigenous rights and environmental struggles is a good example of strategic reframing by *indigenista* activists, who found the environmental arena more receptive to their claims than human rights venues were. Although initially the argument that preserving forest peoples' livelihoods and conserving forests were inseparable provoked resistance from some conservationists, this frame very rapidly entered the accepted repertoire of environmentalist discourse (Keck 1995; Conklin and Graham 1995).

Information flows in advocacy networks provide not only hard data but also *testimony*—stories told by people whose lives have been affected. Moreover, they interpret facts and testimony: activist groups frame issues simply, as right and wrong, because their purpose is to stimulate people to take action. An effective frame must show that a given state of affairs is neither natural nor accidental, identify the responsible party or parties, and propose credible solutions. This requires clear, powerful messages that appeal to shared principles and often have more impact on state policy than advice from technical experts. An important part of the political struggle over environmental issues, for example, is precisely the degree to which they are defined primarily as technical questions, subject to consideration by "qualified" experts, or as questions that are properly the concern of a much broader global constituency.

Networks call attention to issues or even "create issues" by using language that dramatizes and draws attention to their concerns. A good example is the recent campaign against the practice of female genital mutilation. Before 1976, the widespread practice of female circumcision in many African and a few Asian and Middle Eastern countries was known outside these regions mainly among medical experts and anthropologists (World Bank 1993, p. 50). A controversial campaign, initiated in 1974 by a network of women's and human rights organizations, began to draw attention to these issues.

One of the main ways the campaign drew attention to the issue was to "reframe" it by *renaming the problem*. Previously the practice was referred to by more technical and "neutral" terms like female circumcision, clitoridectomy, or infibulation. The campaign around female genital mutilation raised its salience, literally creating the issue as a matter of public international concern. By renaming the practice, the network broke the linkage with male circumcision (seen as a personal medical or cultural decision), implied a linkage with the more feared procedure—castration—and reframed the issue as one of violence against women. It thus resituated the problem as a human rights violation. The campaign generated action against female genital mutilation in many countries, including France and the United Kingdom; the United Nations studied the problem and made a series of recommendations for eradicating certain traditional practices (Kouba and Muasher 1985; Slack 1988; Sochart 1988; United Nations 1986).

The tropical forest issue is fraught with scientific uncertainty about forests' role in climate regulation, their regenerative capacity, and the value of undiscovered or untapped biological resources. By reframing the issue, calling attention to the impact of tropical forest destruction on particular populations, environmentalists have made a call for action independent of the scientific status of the issue. Human rights activists, baby food campaigners, and women's groups play a similar role. By dramatizing the situations of the victims, they turn the cold facts into human stories, intended to motivate people to action. For example, the baby food campaign that began in the early 1970s relied heavily on public health studies that proved that improper bottle feeding contributed to infant malnutrition and mortality and that corporate sales promotion was leading to a decline in breast-feeding (Jellife and Jellife 1978; Ambulatory Pediatrics Association 1981). Network activists repackaged and interpreted this information in dramatic ways designed to promote action. The British development organization War on Want published a pamphlet entitled *The Baby Killers*, which the Swiss Third World Action Group translated into German and retitled *Nestlé Kills Babies.* Nestlé inadvertently gave activists a prominent public forum when it sued the Third World Action Group for defamation and libel. In 1977, U.S. campaigners initiated the boycott of Nestlé that made the corporation increasingly a focus of controversy and brought more attention and resources to the issue.

Information Politics

Information binds network members together and is essential for network effectiveness. The main activity of advocacy networks is collecting credible information and deploying it strategically at carefully selected sites. Many information exchanges are informal: telephone calls, E-mail and fax communications, and the circulation of small newsletters, pamphlets, and bulletins. They provide information that would not otherwise be available, from sources that might not otherwise be heard, and they must make this information comprehensible and useful to activists and publics who may be geographically and/or socially distant.

Networks strive to uncover and investigate problems and alert the press and policy makers. One activist described this as the "human rights methodology—promoting change by reporting facts" (Thomas 1993, p. 83; also Lumsdaine 1993, pp. 187–88, 211–13). To be credible, the information of networks must be reliable and well documented. To gain attention it must be timely and dramatic. Sometimes these multiple goals of information politics conflict. The notion of reporting facts does not fully capture the way networks strategically use information and testimony to frame issues.

Testimony by people affected by the abuse being protested serves two informational functions: besides making a problem real to distant publics, it attests to the credibility and reach of the network. Thus, when indigenous rights advocates sponsor international tours for indigenous leaders and environmentalists do so for forest people's leaders, it shows their connection to the people on whose behalf they make claims. The indigenous and forest people's leaders in turn show their compatriots that their claims are recognized abroad.

Even as we highlight the importance of testimony, however, we have to recognize the mediations involved. The process by which testimony is discovered and presented normally involves several layers of prior translation. Transnational actors may identify what kinds of testimony would be valuable, then ask an NGO in the area to seek out people who could tell those stories. They may filter through expatriates, through traveling scholars like ourselves, and through the media. A huge gap often exists between the story's telling and its retelling—in sociocultural context, in instrumental meaning, and even in language. Successful frames become stylized; conflicts told as morality tales may lose the specificity of their local construction as local actors are cast in roles written for them elsewhere. Local people, in other words, normally lose control over their stories in a transnational campaign. How this process of mediation/translation occurs is a particularly interesting facet of network politics.

Nongovernmental networks link testimonial information with technical and statistical information. Without the individual cases, activists cannot motivate people to seek change policies. Increasingly, international campaigns by networks take this two-level approach to information. In the 1980s even Greenpeace, which initially had eschewed rigorous research in favor of splashy media events, began to pay more attention to getting the facts right. While testimony does not avoid the need to manage technical information, it helps to make the need for action more real for ordinary citizens.

A dense web of north-south exchange, aided by comptuter and fax communication, means that governments can no longer monopolize information flows as they could a mere half-decade ago. These technologies have had an enormous impact on moving information to and from Third World countries, where mail service has often been both slow and precarious. We should note, however, that this gives special advantages to organizations that have access to such technologies. A good example of the new informational role of networks occurred when U.S. environmentalists pressured President George Bush to raise gold miners' ongoing invasions of the Yanomami indigenous reserve when Brazilian president Fernando Collor de Mello was in Washington in 1991. Collor believed that he had squelched protest over the Yanomami question by creating major media events out of the dynamiting of airstrips used by gold miners, and a decade ago he would have succeeded. However, since network members had current information faxed from Brazil, they could counter his claims with evidence that miners had rebuilt the airstrips and were still invading the Yanomami area.

The central role of information in all these issues helps to explain the drive to create networks. Information in these issue areas is both essential and dispersed. Nongovernmental actors depend on their access to information to help make them legitimate players. Contact with like-minded groups at home and abroad provides access to information necessary to their work, broadens their legitimacy, and helps to mobilize information around particular policy targets. Most nongovernmental organizations cannot afford to maintain staff people in a variety of countries. In exceptional cases, they send staff members on investigation missions, but this is not practical for keeping informed on routine developments. Forging links with local organizations allows groups to receive and monitor information from many countries at a low cost. Local groups, in turn, depend on international contacts to get their information out and help to protect them in their work.

Finally, the media plays an essential role in network information politics. To reach a broader audience, networks strive to attract press attention. Sympathetic journalists may become part of the network, but more often network activists cultivate a reputation for credibility with the press and package their information in a timely and dramatic way to draw press attention.

Campaigns

Advocacy networks organize around campaigns. For our purposes, campaigns are sets of strategically linked activities in which members of a diffuse principled network develop explicit, visible ties and mutually recognized roles toward a common goal (and generally against a common target). In a campaign, core (usually experienced) network actors mobilize others, initiating the tasks of structural integration and cultural negotiation among the groups in the network. Just as in domestic campaigns, they connect groups to each other, seek out resources, propose and prepare activities, and do public relations. They must also consciously seek to develop a "common frame of meaning," a task complicated by cultural diversity within transnational networks (Gerhards and Rucht 1992, pp. 558–59). Activist groups have long used the language of campaigning to talk about focused, strategically planned efforts. International campaigns by environmental and conservation organizations, for example, traditionally had a topical focus (saving furry animals, whales, tropical forests), while human rights campaigns had either a country (the Argentina campaign) or issue focus (the campaign against torture) (Schiotz 1983, pp. 120-22).

Focusing on campaigns provides a window on transnational relations as an arena of struggles in ways that a focus on networks themselves or on the institutions they try to affect does not. This focus highlights *relationships*—connections among network actors and between activists and their allies and opponents. We can identify the kinds of *resources* that make a campaign possible—information, leadership, symbolic or material capital (McCarthy and Zald 1977). And we must consider the kinds of *institutional structures*—both domestic and international—that encourage or impede particular kinds of transnational activism. Finally, a focus on campaigning lets us explore negotiation of meaning while we look at the evolution of tactics; we can recognize that cultural differences, different conceptions of the stakes in a campaign, and resource inequalities among network actors exist, while we identify critical roles that different actors fill. Campaigns are processes of issue construction constrained by the action context in which they are to be carried out: activists identify a problem, specify a cause, and propose a solution, all with an eye toward producing procedural, substantive, and normative change in their area of concern. In networked campaigns, this process of "strategic portrayal" (Stone 1988, p. 6) must work for the different actors in the network and for target audiences.

The process we describe is interactive: nongovernmental organizations pressure for international events, such as declarations, treaties, theme years, theme decades, and conferences, which in turn serve as arenas for network formation. In the baby food campaign, network pressures motivated U.S. Senator Edward Kennedy to hold hearings on the issue in 1978. Kennedy in turn called on WHO/UNICEF to hold consultative meetings on the issue of the marketing of infant formula, a move favored by industry representatives, who believed that moving to an international venue would help to depoliticize the issue. Industry's expectations were frustrated when these meetings included not only representatives from governments, international organizations, industry, and academia but also NGO and consumer activists. This was the first time NGO activists were full participants alongside industry and government representatives in a United Nations consultation. At the conclusion of the 1979 consultative meeting, NGO activists present formed the International Baby Food Action Network (IBFAN), which eventually brought together a hundred groups working in sixty-five countries on issues of infant nutrition. Network members played a crucial role in helping draft and lobbying government to vote for the WHO/UNICEF Code of Marketing for Breast-milk Substitutes, an innovative effort to regulate transnational business activities in the interest of infant health (Sikkink 1986).

The Global Campaign on Violence against Women

The role of transnational networks of women's groups organizing on violence against women shows how a network can draw attention to issues, set agendas, and influence the discursive positions of states and international organizations. Violence against women is an issue that arrived late and dramatically for the international women's movement, departing from the classic issues of suffrage, equality, and discrimination around which women have long mobilized (Fraser 1994). The 1979 Convention for the Elimination of All Forms of Discrimination against Women does not even mention rape, domestic or sexual abuse, female genital mutilation, dowry death, or any other instance of violence against women. Nonetheless, by the mid-1990s violence against women had become the most important women's issue on the international agenda and the most dynamic new international human rights concern. At the UN Conference on Women in Beijing in 1995, violence against women became a "centerpiece of the platform" (Mufson 1995). The story of its emergence as an international issue shows how two previously separate transnational networks around human rights and women's rights began to converge and transform each other. The network built around violence against women drew on preexisting communications networks that were receptive to the "new ideas of the incipient movement" (Freeman 1973, p. 32). But not all new ideas "resonate" with the submerged networks that must adopt them. This one was especially striking in that it resonated across significant cultural and experiential barriers.

The idea of "violence against women" as a global issue did not initially exist. Instead, activists campaigned independently around different practices: against rape and domestic battery in the United States and Europe, female genital mutilation in Africa, female sexual slavery in Europe and Asia, dowry death in India, and torture and rape of political prisoners in Latin America. It was neither obvious nor natural that one should think of female genital mutilation and domestic abuse as part of the same category. The category "violence against women" had to be constructed and popularized before people could think of these practices as the "same" in some basic way. Once created, the category allowed activists trying to build a transnational campaign to attract allies and bridge cultural differences. It focused on a most basic common denominator—the belief in the importance of the protection of the bodily integrity of women and girls—at the core of understandings of human dignity in many cultures.

The seeds of an international network on violence against women grew out of a series of meetings at the 1980 UN Women's Conference in Copenhagen. Activist-scholar Charlotte Bunch (1996) had organized a set of panels on international feminist networking at the nongovernmental forum held alongside the official conference. Later she recalled:

> We observed in that two weeks of the forum that the workshops on issues related to violence against women were the most successful. . . . They were the workshops where women did not divide along north-south lines, that women felt a sense of commonality and energy in the room, that there was a sense that we could do something to help each other. . . . And they felt there were common issues. I personally had never worked on the issue of violence against women before that. . . . It was so visible to me that this issue had the potential to bring women together in a different way and that it had the potential to do that without erasing difference—because the specifics of what forms violence took really were different. . . . So you get a chance to deal with difference and see culture, and race, and class, but in a framework where there was a sense that women were subordinated and subjected to this violence everywhere, and that nobody has the answers. So northern women couldn't dominate and say we know how to do this, because the northern women were saying, "Our country is a mess; we have a very violent society." So it created a completely different ground for conversation. . . . It wasn't that we built the network in that moment. It was just the sense of that possibility.

Bunch's comment captures the potential of networking. Networks are usually not one-way streets by which activists in one country "help" victims in another. More often they are part of an interactive process by which people in faraway places communicate and exchange beliefs, information, testimony, strategy, and sometimes services. In the process of exchange, they may change each other.

One of the earliest attempts to realize that possibility came in 1981 at the first feminist *Encuentro* for Latin America and the Caribbean in 1981. Participants proposed to call November 25 the International Day to End Violence against Women, in honor of three sisters from the Dominican Republic who were murdered by security forces of the Trujillo dictatorship on that day in 1960 (Anonymous 1988). Many Latin American women's organizations began to stage annual events to commemorate this day. Likewise, women's groups in Asia, Europe, and the United States began to mobilize around issues of violence against women in their regions.

As global consciousness and mobilization around women's human rights grew, four phenomena came together to heighten attention and stimulate action around the issue in the early 1990s: (1) preparations for the World Conference on Human Rights to be held in Vienna in 1993; (2) international news stories that appeared just before the conference, describing the use of rape as an instrument of the ethnic cleansing campaign in the former Yugoslavia (Fraser 1993; Thomas 1995); (3) proactive funding of the issue by the Ford Foundation and other progressive European and U.S. foundations; and (4) the crucial "catalyst" role played by the Global Campaign on Women's Human Rights organized by the Center for Women's Global Leadership.

The absence of any discussion of women's rights in the preparatory documents for the 1993 World Conference on Human Rights stimulated and focused women's organizing efforts. Conference preparations in the early 1990s solidifed relations between the international human rights and women's networks. Women's networks increasingly applied the "human rights methodology" of careful factual documentation to abuses of women's rights, and mainstream human rights organizations gained greater appreciation of women's rights (Fraser 1993; p. 33; Thomas 1993, p. 83).

The issue coalesced in the early 1990s around the Global Campaign for Women's Human Rights coordinated by the Center for Women's Global Leadership (CWGL) at Rutgers University. When the CWGL took up the issue, the groundwork had already been laid by the activities of existing international networks around the issue. Nevertheless, the CWGL played a crucial catalytic role, pulling diverse strands into a single symbolic and visible campaign.

Under its new director, Charlotte Bunch, the center chose to organize around the theme of "women, violence, and human rights," hoping to realize the issue's potential to bridge cultures that Bunch had sensed in Copenhagen in 1980. The preparation for the campaign offers a remarkably clear example of global moral entrepreneurs consciously strategizing on how to frame issues in a way likely to attract the broadest possible global coalition. Participants in an international planning meeting in 1990 and in Women's Global Leadership Institutes helped to develop strategies for linking women's rights to human rights. The two central tactics included the "Sixteen Days of Activism against Gender Violence" campaign to call attention to violence against women through local actions from November 25 (International Day to End Violence against Women) to December 10 (Human Rights Day). By 1993 the Sixteen Days Campaign was being carried out by groups in 120 countries (Bunch 1990, pp. 146–47; Red Feminista 1994, p. 12). It symbolically linked two formerly separate themes—violence against women and human rights—into a single unified theme. In a second tactic, the Center for Women's Global Leadership joined the International Women's Tribunal Center (IWTC) and the International YWCA to initiate a highly successful worldwide petition drive "calling on the 1993 Conference to comprehensively address women's human rights at every level of the proceedings and demanding that gender violence be recognized as a violation of human rights requiring immediate action" (Friedman 1994; Bunch 1993, p. 146; CWGL 1992).

During this period, foundations played a key role in funding groups to do work on women's human rights. Major U.S. foundation grants on projects on women's rights and violence against women increased from less than $250,000 in 1988 to more than $3,000,000 in 1993. Ford Foundation grants account for almost one-half of the total dollar value of grants during this period. Exact amounts are not available for European foundations, but interviews suggest that many increased their funding on women's rights in the same period. The important increase in funding came in 1990, after the explosion of NGO activity in the late 1980s. It suggests that foundations did not lead but did greatly help the growth of work on women's human rights in the period 1989–1993 *(Foundation Grants Index)*.

The developmental path of the issue of violence against women resembles the pattern we see in other global networks. An emerging, dispersed network of groups begins to create global awareness about the issue. These dispersed efforts intensify and unite with the emergence of a "target" (here the World Conference on Human Rights, and later the Beijing Conference) and a condensation symbol. "Condensation symbols evoke the emotions associated with the situation" (Edelman 1995, p. 6). They provoke mass responses because they condense threats or reassurances into one symbolic moment. The routine use of rape in the former Yugoslavia as a tool of ethnic cleansing spotlighted the problem of violence against women. It condensed into a single set of events the fears and threats many women feel in their daily lives: that they will be the targets of special violence by virtue of their gender. In the wake of these symbolic events, the "catalyst campaign" of the CWGL pulled the awareness thus created together into a visible political campaign with concrete outcomes. This pattern—dispersed network→target→condensation symbol→catalyst campaign→strong network and heightened global awareness—is one that appears often in the stories of successful networks.

Network pressures helped to integrate women's concerns into the human rights field, drew global attention to the issue of violence against women, and contributed to institutional innovations, like the naming of a new UN Special Rapporteur on Violence against Women. Also, many governments have adopted new procedures that give women more arenas in which to seek recourse. It remains to be seen what impact the campaign can have on changing practices and ensuring accountability for the abuse of women's rights.

Advocacy Networks and Social Movements

Campaigns undertaken by transnational advocacy networks may include a variety of social movement activity along with the politics of information and pressure more typical of network activity. There is an evident synergy between the locally specific social movements around violence against women and the work of transnational network activists that helped to place female sexual slavery, wife battery, dowry death, and female genital mutilation in the same cognitive frame. There are also cases of frame conflict between social movement groups and particular advocacy networks with which they may be temporarily associated. We can see this quite clearly if we reexamine one of the cases used in Gerhards and Rucht's fine 1992 article on mesomobilization in two West German protest campaigns in the light of an analysis of transnational advocacy networks.

The 1988 Berlin demonstrations during the annual meeting of the Bretton Woods institutions (the World Bank and the International Monetary Fund [IMF]) were the objects of a deliberate process of bringing together various available networks (*mesomobilization*) around a unifying frame (which the authors identify as anti-imperialism). The mobilization was highly successful: a week of events, including a march where eighty thousand demonstrators gathered, garnering extensive media coverage. However, this highly successful local organizing effort must also be seen in the light of two international campaigns in which the Berlin events were embedded and to which they contributed. One was a campaign around Third World debt, in which the IMF's structural adjustment programs were a prime target of the critique. The other was the environmentalists' campaign around the impact of multilateral bank lending on the environment and indigenous peoples.

Spearheaded in the United Kingdom by Oxfam and War on Want, the U.K. debt crisis network formed in the mid-1980s, as did a U.S. Debt Crisis Network made up of New York– and Washington-based NGOs. Over the next few years countless European development and environmental organizations became involved; in 1987–88, several Dutch NGOs (including NOVIB) sponsored an effort to form an international coordinating body, FONDAD (Forum on Debt and Development), and also a network of Latin American groups (Donnelly, forthcoming; Potter 1988). This network has foundered and been revived many times, and it has suffered more than many from long-term divisions between reformist and radical members; nonetheless, the time of the Berlin events in 1988 was arguably a high point in its early development.

The Berlin events were in fact the third annual set of parallel events to the meetings of the Bretton Woods institutions, though they involved much more public mobilization than did the first two. The World Bank and IMF meet annually, but only every third year do they meet outside Washington, D.C., where they are headquartered. (The first parallel meeting and demonstration were held in Washington in 1986). The tone of the Washington meetings tends to be different from those held abroad, with more attention to information sharing and relations among the NGOs present than to public protest. This is due in part to the less radical profile of the Washington NGOs active in the multilateral bank campaign network, most of which are actively involved in lobbying government and multilateral organization officials.

The different campaigning contexts within which social movement activists and advocacy network members situated the 1988 Berlin events thus influenced their interpretations of events. While anti-imperialism may effectively have provided a mobilizational frame for the demonstrations in Berlin, for many foreign participants the international linkages expressed in the various meetings and events, as well as the demonstrations, were the main lesson. The Brazilian *Tempo e Presença*, the magazine of the Ecumenical Center for Documentation and Information (CEDI), headlined its extensive coverage of Berlin "New Internationalism" (Ramalho 1989). Although these approaches were certainly not contradictory, they nonetheless implied different goals and different standards by which to measure success or failure.

Conclusion

What we have described is a process of connection involving exchanges of information, shared ideas, conflict over and negotiation of meanings, and coordinating strategies to motivate action. As advocacy networks multiply, they become an increasingly routinized part of activists' strategic repertoire. Although few networks could be called institutions, the practice of networking has quickly begun to be institutionalized, in the sense that Meyer and Tarrow use the term in the introduction to this volume.

Networks demarcate a nonterritorial space of regularized interaction. As a nonterritorial space, however, the extension of these interactions is unbounded. Core network participants are activists, whose identities are bound up in shared practices of contention and resistance that resonate across borders; the resources to which they have access, however, continue to depend largely on their location. Still, within the loosely defined identities and roles of network participants, there is room for ambiguity, contingency, and even opportunism. Strange bedfellows abound.

We do not believe that the transnational advocacy networks we have studied are accurately understood as transnational social movements. Why not call them transnational social movements? After all, we began this essay by demonstrating the utility of social movement theorists' insights about social networks, political opportunity structure, and framing for the discussion of advocacy networks. Furthermore, our stress on activists and campaigns is consistent with the editors' suggestion that the model of social movement organization is no longer the mass organization of European social democracy but a more fluid and contingent one in which professionalized activists mobilize occasional publics around specific campaigns.

In some situations involving transnational advocacy networks, this might be a reasonable characterization. Clearly, participants in transnational advocacy networks include social movements; it seems equally clear, however, that the networks are not, themselves, social movements. They are not social movement organizations; they are too ephemeral and mobile for that and represent ideas, not constituencies. Where there is significant overlap between principled beliefs and particular bounded constituencies, as with Islamic brotherhoods or militia movements, for example, it may be more appropriate to talk about transnational social movements. However, these groups differ from advocacy networks almost by definition; they require clandestinity, whereas the fundamental currency of the latter is information.

The strategic deployment of information may involve mobilization; more often it involves lobbying, targeting key elites and feeding useful material to well-placed insiders. For activists who cut their teeth in a tradition of intransigent resistance, this kind of activity is hard to take; the *choice* not to mobilize makes little sense if one imagines that the key resource of movements is their capacity for disruption. Because the key resource of networks is information, the choice not to mobilize may be perfectly consistent with the desire to present information and ideas in the most compelling fashion and get it into the hands of politically influential actors.

Not mobilization, perhaps, but "events" serve as points of reference for networks. This has been especially true for women's networks, where international conferences punctuate the standard chronologies of their development. The relationship between such "events," the directionality of information flows in networks, the kinds of strategies imagined, and the types of shared understandings (or misunderstandings) generated by network practices are all areas in which we need further research if we are to grasp the sources and impact of these new linking processes.

We also believe that looking at the constitution and functioning of transnational advocacy networks without seeing links to state actors as central, rather than incidental components, would frequently miss the point. Networks often include actors within states and frequently target the bulk of their activities at states or intergovernmental organizations. Power and money are not the media for all network interactions, but they have not vanished from the story; efforts to leverage more poweful actors are central to network strategies, and network dynamics and effectiveness are at least partly dependent on resource flows.

Nonetheless, whatever we call it, something is happening here. We believe that the current stage of theorizing is better served by examining linkage processes than by trying to draw the outlines of the new patterns these linkages may be producing. The processes we describe and explain in this chapter may contribute eventually to the evolution of transnational social movements, or even to a global civil society. But what we have seen so far is much more fragile, contingent, and contested. However much we are seeing the increasing interpenetration of domestic and international politics, transposing sets of categories from one to the other seems unlikely to make sense of the simultaneity of both. As networks and other kinds of communicative practices multiply, difficulty in determining what is significant and what is noise in international society is likely to persist for a very long time. Still, unless we listen to the full cacophony, we are unlikely to make sense of it at all.

Notes

1. This is similar to their definition by Sidney Tarrow (1996a, pp. 13–14) as "sustained sequences of collective action mounted by organized collective actors in interaction with elites, authorities and other actors in the name of their claims or the claims of those they represent."

2. This discussion of transnational advocacy networks draws heavily on our book, *Activists Beyond Borders*, though this chapter takes steps beyond the book in relating our argument more explicitly to debates in social movement theory.

3. By political opportunity structure, Tarrow (1996b, p. 54) means *"consistent—but not necessarily formal, permanent, or national—signals to social or political actors which either encourage or discourage them to use their internal resources to form social movements. . . .* The most salient kinds of signals are four: the open-

ing up of access to power, shifting alignments, the availability of influential allies, and cleavages within and among elites" (italics in original).

4. We concur with Craig Calhoun (1995, p. 173) in his stress on practice as a basis for the development of shared understandings. He writes, "Indeed, both the translation and metadiscourse models [of shared understandings] are too static, too inattentive to the extent to which our mutual understandings are in fact constructed through processes of historical change, and too exclusively individualistic. . . . [We need to grasp] the historial and political processes by which people come to shared understandings without translations or metadiscourses."

References

Aggarwal, Vinod K. 1986. *Liberal Protectionism: The International Politics of the Organized Textile Trade*. Berkeley: University of California Press.

Aldrich, John H., and Forrest D. Nelson. 1984. *Linear Probability, Logit, and Probit Models*. Beverly Hills, CA: Sage.

Almond, Gabriel, and Sidney Verba. 1963. *The Civic Culture: Political Attitudes and Democracy in Five Nations*. Princeton, NJ: Princeton University Press.

Alvarez, Sonia. 1989. "Politicizing Gender and Engendering Democracy." Pp. 205–51 in Alfred Stepan, ed., *Democratizing Brazil*. New York: Oxford University Press.

———. 1993. " 'Deepening' Democracy: Popular Movement Networks, Constitutional Reform, and Radical Urban Regimes in Contemporary Brazil." Pp. 191–222 in Robert Fisher and Joseph Kling, eds., *Mobilizing the Community: Local Politics in the Era of the Global City*. Newbury Park, CA: Sage.

———. 1994a. "The (Trans)formation of Feminism(s) and Gender Politics in Democratizing Brazil." Pp. 13–64 in Jane Jaquette, ed., *The Women's Movement in Latin America*. 2nd ed. Boulder, CO: Westview.

———. 1994b. "La (Trans)formación del (los) Feminismo(s) y la Política de Género en la Democratización del Brasil." Pp. 227–89 in Magdelena Leon, ed., *Mujeres y Participación Política: Avances y Desafíos en América Latina*. Bogotá: Tercer Mundo.

Alves, Maria Helena Moreira. 1985. *State and Opposition in Military Brazil*. Austin: University of Texas Press.

Ambulatory Pediatrics Association. 1981. "Statement by the Board of Directors on the WHO Code of Marketing of Breast-Milk Substitutes." *Pediatrics* 68 (September).

An, Mildred. 1991. "Free Speech, Post Office Sidewalks, and the Public Forum Doctrine." *Harvard Civil Rights–Civil Liberties Review* 26:633–48.

Anonymous. 1988. "Por que el 25 de noviembre? Un dia de la violencia hacia las mujeres." *Mujer/Fempress* (January).

Applegate, Rex. 1969. *Riot Control: Materiel and Techniques*. Harrisburg, PA: Stackpole Books.

Arriagada, Genaro. 1988. *Pinochet: The Politics of Power*. Boston: Unwin Hyman.

Austine, Glen R., III. 1982. "Time, Place, and Manner Regulations of Expressive Activities in the Public Forum." *Nebraska Law Review* 61:167–86.

Badie, Bertrand. 1995. *La fin des territoires: Essai sur le desordre international et sur l'utilité sociale du respect*. Paris: Fayard.

Baldez Carey, Lisa. 1997. "In the Name of the Public and the Private: Conservative and Progressive Women's Movements in Chile: 1970–1996." Unpublished Ph.D. dissertation, University of California, San Diego.

Ballistier, Thomas. 1996. *Straßprotest: Formen oppositioneller Politik in der Bundesrepublik Deutschland*. Münster: Westfälisches Dampfboot.

Barnes, Samuel H., et al. 1979. *Political Action: Mass Participation in Five Western Democracies*. Beverly Hills: Sage.

Baumgaertner, William L., ed. 1989. *Fact Book on Theological Education: 1987–88*. Vandalia, OH: Association of Theological Schools in the United States and Canada.

Baumgartner, Frank R., and Bryan D. Jones. 1991. "Agenda Dynamics and Policy Subsystems." *Journal of Politic* 53: 1044–74.

Beckwith, Karen. 1996. "Lancashire Women against Pit Closures: Women's Standing in a Men's Movement." *Signs* 21(4): 1034–68.

Bermeo, Nancy. n.d. "Myths of Moderation: The Parameters of Civility during Democratization." Unpublished manuscript, Princeton University, Princeton, NJ.

Bernhard, Michael H. 1993. *The Origins of Democratization in Poland*. New York: Columbia University Press.

Berry, Jeffrey. 1993. "Citizen Groups and the Changing Nature of Interest Group Politics in America." *Annals of the American Academy of Political and Social Science* 528: 30–41.

Berryman, Philip. 1984. *The Religious Roots of Rebellion*. Maryknoll, NY: Orbis Books.

Black, Lisa, and James Hill. 1996. "Dellinger Is Arrested, but World Not Watching: Protests Smaller, Tend to Fizzle Out." *Chicago Tribune*, August 29, section 2, p. 5.

Blumer, Herbert. 1939. "Collective Behavior." Pp. 221–80 in Robert E. Park, ed., *An Outline of the Principles of Sociology*. New York: Barnes & Noble.

Bond, Doug, and Joe Bond. 1995. "Protocol for the Assessment of Nonviolent Direct Action (PANDA): Codebook for the P2 Data Set." Cambridge, MA: Program on Nonviolent Sanctions and Cultural Survival, Center for International Affairs, Harvard University.

Boschi, Renato. 1987. "Social Movements and the New Political Order in Brazil." Pp. 179–212 in John D. Wirth, Edson de Oliveira Nunes, and Thomas E. Bogenschild, eds., *State and Society in Brazil*. Boulder, CO: Westview.

Brecher, Jeremy. 1972. *Strike!* Boston: South End Press.

Bresser Pereira, Luiz Carlos, Jose Maria Maravall, and Adam Przeworski. 1993. *Economic Reforms in New Democracies: A Social-Democratic Approach*. Cambridge: Cambridge University Press.

Bright, Charles, and Susan Harding, eds. 1984. *Statemaking and Social Movements: Essays in History and Theory*. Ann Arbor: University of Michigan Press.

Broek, Andries van den, and Felix Heunks. 1994. "Political Culture: Patterns of Political Orientations and Behaviour." Pp. 67–96 in Peter Ester, Loek Halman, and Ruud de Moor, eds., *The Individualizing Society: Value Change in Europe and North America*. Tilburg, The Netherlands: Tilburg University Press.

Brothers, John. 1985 "Communication Is the Key to Small Demonstration Control." *Campus Law Enforcement Journal* (September/October): 13–16.

Brownstein, Ronald. 1983. "Success Story: Environmentalists amid the Ruins." *Amicus Journal* (fall): 32–35.

Bunch, Charlotte. 1990. "Women's Rights as Human Rights: Toward a Revision of Human Rights." *Human Rights Quarterly* 12 (November): 486–98.

———. 1993. "Organizing for Women's Human Rights Globally." Pp. 141–49 in Joanna Kerr, ed., *Ours by Right: Women's Rights as Human Rights*. London: Zed Books.

———. 1996. Personal interview, (February 21), New York, NY.

Bunyan, Tony. 1977. *The History and Practice of the Political Police in Britain*. London: Quartet.

Burden, Ordway P. 1992. "Law Enforcement and the Preservation of Civil Rights: Peacekeeping and the 'Thin Blue Line.' " *Police Chief* 59 (June): 16–26.

Burstein, Paul. 1997. "Political Organizations: Interest Groups, Social Movements, and Political Parties." In Andrew McFarland and Anne Costain, eds., *Social Movements and the American Political Process*. Boulder, CO: Rowman & Littlefield.

Butterwege, Christoph, Jochen Dressel, Volker Tegeler, and Ulla Voigt, eds. 1990. *30 Jahre Ostermarsch: Ein Beitrag zuer politischen Kultur der Bundesrepublik Deutschland und ein Stück Bremer Stadtgeschichte*. Bremen: Steintor.

Calhoun, Craig. 1995a. *Critical Social Theory*. Oxford: Blackwell.

———. 1995b. "New Social Movements of the Early Nineteenth Century." Pp. 173–215 in Mark Traugott, ed., *Repertoires and Cycles of Collective Action*. Durham, NC: Duke University Press.

Canosa, Romano and Pietro Federico. 1974. *La Magistratra in Italia dal 1945 a oggi*. Bologna: Il Mulino.

Canosa, Romano. 1976. *La polizia in Italia dal 1945 a oggi*. Bologna, Il Mulino.

Carlsen, William. 1996. "Janitors Halt Traffic in Financial District." *San Francisco Chronicle*, July 27, p. A14.

Carr, Anne E. 1988. *Transforming Grace: Christian Tradition and Women's Experience*. San Francisco: Harper & Row.

Carucci, Paola. 1976. "L'organizzazione dei servizi di polizia dopo l'approvazione del Testo Unico delle leggi di P.S. del 1926," Pp. 82–114 in *Rassegna degli Archivi di Stato* 26.

Casa Chile. 1984. *A Nation in Protest*. Berkeley, CA: Casa Chile.

Cauce. 1987, July. "FECH debate inscripción o movilización."

CBOS Report. 1992, February. "Opinia publiczna o roznych formach protestow spolecznych i skierowanych przeciw nim represjom."

Cerny, Philip G. 1995. "Globalization and the Changing Logic of Collective Action." *International Organization* 49: 595–625.

Chandler, C. Lee. 1986. "The Role of Law Enforcement in Student Confrontations." *Law and Order*, October, pp. 74–75.

Chatham, Charles, Ron Pagnucco, and Jackie Smith, eds. 1997. *Solidarity beyond the State: Transnational Social Movement Organizations.* Syracuse, NY: Syracuse University Press.

Chuchryk, Patricia. 1994. "From Dictatorship to Democracy: The Women's Movement in Chile." Pp. 65–108 in Jane Jaquette, ed., *The Women's Movement in Latin America. 2nd ed. Boulder, CO: Westview.*

Clemens, Elisabeth S. 1993. "Organizational Repertoires and Institutional Change: Women's Groups and the Transformation of American Politics, 1890–1920." *American Journal of Sociology* 98(4): 755–98.

Cohen, Jean. 1985. "Strategy or Identity: New Theoretical Paradigms and Contemporary Social Movements." *Social Research* 52: 663–716.

Cohen, Jean, and Andrew Arato. 1992. *Civil Society and Political Theory.* Cambridge, MA: MIT Press.

Conklin, Beth, and Laura R. Graham. 1995. "The Shifting Middle Ground: Amazonian Indians and Eco-Politics." *American Anthropologist* 97(4) (December): 695–710.

Conradt, David. 1980. "Changing German Political Culture." Pp. 212–72 in Gabriel Almond and Sidney Verba, eds., *The Civic Culture Revisited.* Boston: Little, Brown.

———. 1996. *The German Polity.* 6th ed. White Plain, NY: Longman.

Constable, Pamela, and Arturo Valenzuela. 1991. *A Nation of Enemies.* New York: Norton.

Conway, M. Margaret. 1991. *Politics and Participation in the United States.* 2nd ed. Washington, D.C.: CQ Press.

Cooper, Alice Holmes. 1996. *Paradoxes of Peace: German Peace Movements since 1945.* Ann Arbor: University of Michigan Press.

Corso, Guido. 1979. *L'ordine pubblico.* Bologna: Il Mulino.

Costain, Anne N. 1992. *Inviting Women's Rebellion: A Political Process Interpretation of the Women's Movement.* Baltimore, MD: Johns Hopkins University Press.

Cotler, Julio. 1986. "Military Interventions and 'Transfer of Power to Civilians' in Peru." Pp. 148–72 in Guillermo O'Donnell, ed., *Transitions from Authoritarian Rule: Latin America.* Baltimore, MD: Johns Hopkins University Press.

Crawford, Sue E. S., and Elinor Ostrom. 1996. "A Grammar of Institutions." *American Political Science Review* 89(3): 582–600.

Crawford v. Cushman. 1976. 531 F. 2d 114 (2d Cir.).

Crawley, Martha. 1995. "Salvador: Land of Love, Land of War." Pp. 115–37 in Ann Patrick Ware, ed., *Naming Our Truths: Stories of Loretto Women.* Inverness, CA: Chardon.

Cress, Daniel M. 1996. "Nonprofit Incorporation among Movements of the Poor: Pathways and Consequences for Homeless Social Movement Organizations." Unpublished manuscript, Department of Sociology, University of Colorado, Boulder.

Curb, Rosemary, and Nancy Manahan. 1985. *Lesbian Nuns: Breaking Silence.* Tallahassee, FL: Naiad.

CWGL (Center for Women's Global Leadership). 1992, May. "1991 Women's Leadership Institute Report: Women, Violence and Human Rights." New Brunswick, NJ: Rutgers University.

Dalton, Russell. 1996. *Citizen Politics: Public Opinion and Political Parties in Advanced Industrial Democracies. 2d ed.* Chatham, NJ: Chatham House.

Daly, Mary. 1973. *Beyond God the Father.* Boston: Beacon.

———. 1975. *The Church and the Second Sex: With a New Feminist Post-Christian Introduction.* New York: Harper Colophon.

———. 1984. *Pure Lust.* Boston: Beacon.

D'Anieri, Paul, Claire Ernst, and Elizabeth Kier. 1990. "New Social Movements in Historical Perspective." *Comparative Politics* 22: 445–58.

de la Maza, Gonzalo, and Mario Garcés. 1985. *La explosión de las mayorías: Protesta nacional, 1983–1984.* Santiago: ECO.

De Nardo, James. 1985. *Power in Numbers: The Political Strategy of Protest and Rebellion.* Princeton, NJ: Princeton University Press.

della Porta, Donatella. 1990. *Il terrorismo di sinistra.* Mulino: Società Editrice Il Mulino.

———. 1995. *Social Movements, Political Violence and the State: A Comparative Analysis of Italy and Germany.* New York: Cambridge University Press.

———. 1996a, October. "Police Knowledge in Western Europe: A Research Agenda." Paper presented at the conference "Un nouveau champ de la sécurité en Europe: À l'entrecroisement entre sécurité intérieure et extérieure," Paris.

———. 1996b. "Social Movements and the State: Thoughts on the Policing of Protest." Pp. 62–92 in Doug McAdam, John D. McCarthy and Mayer N. Zald, eds., *Comparative Perspectives on Social Movements: Political Opportunities, Mobilizing Structures and Cultural Framings.* New York: Cambridge University Press.

———. 1997a. "Police Knowledge and Public Order in Italy." In Donatella della Porta and Herbert Reiter, eds., *Policing Protest: The Control of Mass Demonstrations in Contemporary Democracies.* Minneapolis: University of Minnesota Press.

———. 1997b. "The Political Discourse on Protest Policing." In Marco Giugni, Doug McAdam and Charles Tilly, eds., *How Movements Matter.* Minneapolis: University of Minnesota Press.

della Porta, Donatella, and Herbert Reiter. 1996. "Da 'polizia del governo' a 'polizia dei cittadini'? Le strategie per il controllo dell'ordine pubblico in Italia." *Stato e Mercato* 48: 433–65.

———. eds. 1997a. *Policing Protest: The Control of Mass Demonstrations in Contemporary Democracies.* Minneapolis: University of Minnesota Press, forthcoming.

———. 1997b. "The Policing of Protest in Contemporary Democracies: An Introduction." In Donatella della Porta and Herbert Reiter, eds., *Policing Protest: The Control of Mass Demonstrations in Contemporary Democracies.* Minneapolis: University of Minnesota Press.

della Porta, Donatella, and Dieter Rucht. 1995. "Left-Libertarian Movements in

Context: A Comparison of Italy and West Germany, 1965–1990." Pp. 229–73 in J. Craig Jenkins and Bert Klandermans, eds., *The Politics of Social Protest: Comparative Perspectives on States and Social Movements*. Minneapolis/London: University of Minnesota Press/University College of London Press.

DiMaggio, Paul J., and Walter W. Powell. 1983. "The Iron Cage Revisited: Institutional Isomorphism and Collective Rationality in Organizational Fields." *American Sociological Review* 48: 147–60.

Doimo, Ana Maria. 1995. *A Vez e a Voz do Popular: Movimentos Sociais e Participação política no Brasil pós-70*. Rio de Janeiro: ANPOCS/Relume Dumará.

Donnelly, Elizabeth Ann. Forthcoming "Transnational Issue Networks: The Case of Third World Debt and Structural Adjustment." In Kathryn Sikkink, James Riker, and Sanjeev Khagram, eds., *The Power of Transnational Networks: Norms and Agency in World Politics*.

Donnelly, Jack. 1989. *Human Rights in Theory and Practice*. Ithaca, NY: Cornell University Press.

Dunnager, Jonathan. 1992. "Ordinamenti amministravat e prassi politica. Le force di polizia a Bologna di fronte al fascismo, 1920–1921." *Italia Contemporanea* 186: 61–89.

Durkheim, Emile. 1995. *Die Regeln der Soziologischen Methode*. Frankfurt M.: Suhrkamp.

Ebaugh, Helen and Rose Fuchs, eds. 1991. *Religion and the Social Order!* Vol. II of *Vatican II and U.S. Catholicism*. Greenwich, CT: JAI Press.

Eckstein, Harry, and Ted Robert Gurr. 1975. *Patterns of Authority: A Structural Basis for Political Inquiry*. New York: Wiley.

Edelman, Murray. 1985. *The Symbolic Uses of Politics*. Urbana: University of Illinois Press.

Eisinger, Peter. 1973. "The Conditions of Protest Behavior in American Cities." *American Political Science Review* 81: 11–28.

Ekiert, Grzegorz. 1993. "Prospects and Dilemmas of the Transition to a Market Economy in East Central Europe." *Research on Democracy and Society* 1: 51–82.

———. 1996. *The State against Society: Political Crises and Their Aftermath in East Central Europe*. Princeton, NJ: Princeton University Press.

Evans, Peter R., Dieter Rueschemeyer, and Theda Skocpol, eds. 1985. *Bringing the State Back In*. Cambridge: Cambridge University Press.

Favre, Pierre, ed. 1990. *La manifestation*. Paris: Presses de la Fondation Nationale des Science Politiques.

Fedeli, Franco. 1981. *Da sbirro a tutore della legge*. Roma: Roberto Napoleone.

Fernandes, Rubem César. 1994. *Privado porém Público: O Terceiro Setor na América Latina*. Rio de Janeiro: CIVICUS/Relume Dumará.

Ferraro, Barbara, and Patricia Hussey with Jane O'Reilly. 1990. *No Turning Back: Two Nuns Battle with the Vatican over Women's Rights to Choose*. New York: Poseidon.

Fillieule, Olivier. 1995, June. "Methodological Issues in the Collection of Data on Protest Events: Police Records and National Press in France." Paper presented at the Workshop "Protest Event Analysis: Methodology, Applications, Problems," Wissenschaftszentrum Berlin.

―――. 1997a. "Du pouvoir d'injonction au pouvoir d'influence? Les limites de l'institutionnalisation." *Cahiers de la Sécurité Intérieure*, no. 27.

―――. 1997b. *Strategies de la rue: Les manifestations en France*. Paris: Presses de Science Po.

Fillieule, Olivier, and Fabien Jobard. 1997. "The Policing of Protest in France: Towards a Model of Protest Policing." In Donatella della Porta and Herbert Reiter, eds., *Policing Protest: The Control of Mass Demonstrations in Contemporary Democracies*. Minneapolis: University of Minnesota Press.

Fish, Steven. 1995. *Democracy from Scratch: Opposition and Regime in the New Russian Revolution*. Princeton, NJ: Princeton University Press.

Flores v. Secretary of Defense. 1973. 355 F. Supp. 93 (N.D. Fla.)

Foote, Evenlyn P. 1993, November. "Institutional Change and the U.S. Military; The Changing Role of Women." Discussion during Peace Studies Workshop, Cornell University, Ithaca, NY.

Foundation Grants Index. In Dialogue Database File #27. New York: Foundation Center.

Foweraker, Joe. 1995. *Theorizing Social Movements*. London: Pluto.

Frankfurter, Felix, and Nathan Greene. 1930. *The Labor Injunction*. New York: Macmillan.

Fraser, Arvonne. 1993. "The Feminization of Human Rights." *Foreign Service Journal* 70: 12.

―――. 1994, November. "International Organizing on Violence against Women." Paper presented at the University of Minnesota.

Freeman, Jo. 1973. "The Origins of the Women's Liberation Movement." *American Journal of Sociology* 78: 792–811.

Freire, Paulo. 1970. *Pedagogy of the Oppressed*. New York: Continuum.

Friedman, Elisabeth. 1994. "Women's Human Rights: The Emergence of a Movement." Pp. 18–35 in Julie Peters and Andrew Wolper, eds., *Women and Human Rights: An Agenda for Change*. London: Routledge.

Frontiero v. Richardson. 1973. 411 U.S. 677.

Fuchs, Dieter. 1991. "The Normalization of the Unconventional: New Forms of Political Action and New Social Movements." Pp. 148–69 in Gerd Meyer and Frantisek Ryszka, eds., *Political Participation and Democracy in Poland and West Germany*. Warsow: Wydaeca.

Gamson, William A. 1990. *The Strategy of Social Protest*. 2nd ed. Belmont, CA: Wadsworth.

―――. 1995. "Constructing Social Protest." Pp. 85–106 in Hank Johnston and Bert Klandermans, eds., *Social Movements and Culture*. Minneapolis: University of Minnesota Press.

Garretón, Manuel Antonio. 1989. *The Chilean Political Process*. Boston: Unwin Hyman.

Gay, Robert. 1994. *Popular Organization and Democracy in Rio de Janeiro*. Philadelphia: Temple University Press.

Geary, Roger. 1985. *Policing Industrial Disputes: 1893 to 1985*. Cambridge: Cambridge University Press.

Gerhards, Jürgen, and Dieter Rucht. 1992. "Mesomobilization: Organizing and

Framing in Two Protest Campaigns in West Germany." *American Journal of Sociology* 98(3): 555–95.

Gillespie, Richard. 1986. "Uruguay's Transition from Collegial Military-Technocratic Rule." Pp. 173–95 in Guillermo O'Donnell, ed., *Transitions from Authoritarian Rule: Latin America*. Baltimore, MD: Johns Hopkins University Press.

Ginsberg, Benjamin, and Martin Shefter. 1990. *Politics by Other Means*. New York: Norton.

Ginsburg, David. 1996, February. "Transition Theory and the Labour Movement." Paper presented at the conference on Social Movements in Durban, South Africa.

Gitlin, Todd. 1980. *The Whole World Is Watching: Mass Media in the Making and Unmaking of the New Left*. Berkeley: University of California Press.

Goldman v. Weinberger. 1986. 475 U.S. 503.

Goldstein, Karl. 1992. "The Green Movement in Brazil." Pp. 119–93 in Matthias Finger and Louis Kriesberg, eds., *Research in Social Movements, Conflicts and Change*. Greenwich, CT: JAI.

Goodman, Jill Laurie. 1979. "Women, War, and Equality: An Examination of Sex Discrimination in the Military." *Women's Rights Law Reporter* 5: 4.

Goodwyn, Lawrence C. 1991. *Breaking the Barrier*. Oxford: Oxford University Press.

Gora, Joel M., David Goldberger, Gary M. Stern, and Morton H. Halperin. 1991. *The Right to Protest: The Basic ACLU Guide to Free Expression*. Carbondale: Southern Illinois University Press.

Gordon, Marilyn A., and Mary Jo Ludvigson. 1990. "The Combat Exclusion for Women Aviators: A Constitutional Analysis." *United States Air Force Journal of Legal Studies* 1: 51–85.

Graff, Ann O'Hara. 1993. "Catholic Feminist Theologians on Catholic Women in the Church." *New Theology Review* 6 (May): 2.

Greenhouse, Linda. 1994. "High Court Backs Limits on Protest at Abortion Clinic." *New York Times*, July 1, pp. A1, A16.

Greiffenhagen, Martin. 1984. "Vom Obrigkeitsstaat zur Demokratie: Die politische Kultur in der Bundesrepublik Deutschland." Pp. 52–76 in Peter Reichel, ed., *Politische Kultur in Westeuropa: Bürger und Staaten in der Europäischen Gemeinschaft*. Frankfurt: Campus.

Greskovits, Bela. 1995. "Hungerstrikers, the Unions, the Government, and the Parties: A Case-study of Hungarian Transformation: Conflict, the Social Pacts and Democratic Development." Occasional papers in European Studies 6, Center for European Studies, University of Essex.

Grillo, Andrea. 1994. *Livorno: Una rivolta tra mito e memoria: 14 luglio 1948 lo sciopero generale per l'attentato a Togliatti*. Pisa: Biblioteca Franco Serantini.

Gruber, Charles. 1990. "The Lesson of Cedar Grove." *Police Chief*, September, pp. 12–15.

Gundelach, Peter. 1995. "Grass-Roots Activity." Pp. 412–40 in Jan W. van Deth and Elinor Scarbrough, eds., *Impact of Values*. New York: Oxford University Press.

Gunther, Richard. 1992. "Spain: The Very Model of the Modern Elite Settlement." Pp. 38–80 in Richard Gunther and John Higley, eds., *Elites and Democratic Consolidation in Latin America and Southern Europe.* Cambridge: Cambridge University Press.

Gurr, Ted Robert. 1989. "Political Terrorism: Historical Antecedents and Contemporary Trends." Pp. 201–30 in Ted Robert Gurr, ed., *Violence in America: Vol. 2. Protest, Rebellion, Reform.* Newbury Park, CA: Sage.

Gutierrezz v. Laird. 1972. 346 F. Supp. 289 (D.D.C.).

Hall, Peter. 1986. *Governing the Economy: The Politics of State Intervention in Britain and France.* New York: Oxford University Press.

Hall, Peter, and Rosemary C. R. Taylor. 1994, September. "Political Science and the Four Institutionalisms." Paper presented at the annual meeting of the American Political Science Association, New York.

Heirich, Max. 1971. *The Spiral of Conflict: Berkeley, 1964.* New York: Columbia University Press.

Hipsher, Patricia. 1994. "Political Processes and the Demobilization of the Shantytown Dwellers' Movement in Redemocratizing Chile." Unpublished Ph.D. dissertation, Cornell University, Ithaca, NY.

———. 1996. "Democratization and the Decline of Urban Social Movements in Chile and Spain." *Comparative Politics* 28: 273–98.

Hochstetler, Kathryn. 1993. "Non-Institutional Actors in Institutional Politics: Organizing about the Environment in Brazil and Venezuela." Unpublished Ph.D. dissertation, University of Minnesota, Minneapolis.

Hocke, Peter. 1996. "Determining the Selection Bias in Local and National Newspaper Reports on Protest Events." Discussion Paper FS III 96-103. Wissenschaftszentrum Berlin.

Huntington, Samuel. 1968. *Political Order in Changing Societies.* New Haven, CT: Yale University Press.

Imig, Doug and Sidney Tarrow. 1996. "The Europeanization of Movements? Contentious Politics and the European Union, October 1983–March 1995." Institute for European Studies Working Paper No. 96.3. Ithaca, NY: Cornell University.

Inglehart, Ronald. 1990. *Culture Shift in Advanced Industrial Societies.* Princeton, NJ: Princeton University Press.

Ingram, Helen M., and Dean E. Mann. 1989. "Interest Groups and Environmental Policy." Pp. 135–57 in James P. Lester, ed., *Environmental Politics and Policy: Theories and Evidence.* Durham, NC: Duke University Press.

International Association of Chiefs of Police. 1992. "Civil Disturbances." *Police Chief,* October, pp. 138–45, 149.

Jäger, Thomas. 1993. *Betriebsschließung und Protest: Kollektive Handlungschancen gegen die Stillegung des Hüttenwerkes Duisburg-Rheinhausen.* Marburg: Schüren.

Jasiewicz, K. 1993. "From Protest and Repression to the Free Elections." Pp. 117–40 in W. Adamski, ed., *Societal Conflict and Systemic Change: The Case of Poland 1980–1992.* Warsaw: IFIS PAN.

Jellife, D., and Jellife, E. P. 1978. *Human Milk in the Modern World.* Oxford: Oxford University Press.

Jenkins, J. Craig, and Craig Eckert. 1986. "Elite Patronage and the Channeling of Social Protest." *American Sociological Review* 51 (December): 812–29.

Jenkins, J. Craig, and Bert Klandermans, eds. 1995. *The Politics of Social Protest: Comparative Perspectives on States and Social Movements*. Minneapolis: University of Minnesota Press.

Jennings, M. Kent, et al. 1990. *Continuities in Political Action: A Longitudinal Study of Political Orientations in Three Western Democracies*. New York: Walter de Gruyter.

Jepperson, Ronald L. 1991. "Institutions, Institutional Effects, and Institutionalism." Pp. 143–63 in Walter W. Powell and Paul J. DiMaggio, eds., *The New Institutionalism in Organizational Analysis*. Chicago: University of Chicago Press.

Jessen, Ralph. 1995. "Polizei und Gesellschaft: Zum Paradigmenwechsel in der Polizeigeschichtsforschung." Pp. 19–43 in Gerhard Paul and Klaus-Michael Mallman, eds., *Die Gestapo: Mythos und Realität*. Darmstadt: Wissenschaftliche Buchgesellschaft.

Kaase, Max. 1982. "Partizipatorische Revolution-Ende der Parteien?" Pp. 173–89 in Joachim Raschke, ed., *Bürger und Parteien*. Opladen: Westdeutscher.

———. 1990. "Mass Participation." Pp. 23–64 in M. Kent Jennings et al., eds., *Continuities in Political Action: A Longitudinal Study of Political Orientations in Three Western Democracies*. New York: Walter de Gruyter.

Kaase, Max, and Kenneth Newton. 1995. *Beliefs in Government*. New York: Oxford University Press.

Karklins, Rasma, and Roger Petersen. 1995. "Decision Calculus of Protesters and Regimes: Eastern Europe, 1989." *Journal of Politics* 55: 588–614.

Katscher, L. 1878. "Die blauen Männer von London: Eine Skizze aus dem Polizeiwesen." *Die Gartenlaube*, pp. 285–87.

Katzenstein, Mary Fainsod. 1995. "Discursive Politics and Feminist Activism in the Catholic Church." Pp. 35–52 in Myra Marx Ferree and Patricia Yancey Martin, eds., *Feminist Organizations*. Philadelphia: Temple University Press.

———. 1998. *Protest from Within: Feminism in the U.S. Military and the American Catholic Church*. Forthcoming. Princeton, NJ: Princeton University Press.

Keck, Margaret E. 1992. *The Workers' Party and Democratization in Brazil*. New Haven, CT: Yale University Press.

———. 1995. "Social Equity and Environmental Politics in Brazil: Lessons from the Rubber Tappers of Acre." *Comparative Politics* 27: 409–24.

Keck, Margaret, and Kathryn Sikkink. 1998. *Activists beyond Borders: Advocacy Networks in International Politics*. Ithaca, NY: Cornell University Press.

King, Mike. Forthcoming. "Policing Social Protest: Some Indicators of Change." In D. Waddington and C. Chritcher, eds., *Policing Public Disorder*. Aldershot: Avebury.

Kitschelt, Herbert. 1986. "Political Opportunity Structures and Political Protest: Anti-Nuclear Movements in Four Countries." *British Journal of Political Science* 165: 57–85.

———. 1992. "The Formation of Party Systems in East Central Europe." *Politics and Society* 20(1): 7–50.

Klandermans, Bert, Marlene Roefs, and Johan Olivier. 1997. "New Cleavages, New Grievances, New Protests: Political Change in South Africa." Unpublished manuscript. Free University, Amsterdam.

Kleidman, Robert. 1994. "Volunteer Activism and Professionalism in Social Movement Organizations." *Social Problems* 41: 257–76.

Kleinknecht, G. H., and Gerald Mizell. 1982. "Abortion: A Police Response." *F.B.I. Law Enforcement Bulletin*, March, pp. 20–23.

Koopmans, Ruud. 1993. "The Dynamics of Protest Waves: West Germany, 1965–1989." *American Sociological Review* 58 (October): 637–58.

———. 1995a, April. "A Burning Question: Explaining the Rise of Racist and Extreme Right Violence in Western Europe." Paper presented to the workshop "Racist Parties in Europe," ECPR Joint Sessions, Bordeaux.

———. 1995b. *Democracy from Below: New Social Movements and the Political System in West Germany*. Boulder, CO: Westview.

———. 1996. "New Social Movements and Changes in Political Participation in Western Europe." *West European Politics* 19: 28–50.

Kornai, Janos. 1994, March. "The Second Government." Unpublished lecture, Princeton University, Princeton, NJ.

———. 1996. "Paying the Bill for Goulash-Communism." Discussion Paper Series No. 1749. Cambridge, MA: Harvard Institute for Economic Research.

Kouba, Leonard J., and Judith Mausher. 1985. "Female Circumcision in Africa: An Overview." *African Studies Review* 28 (March): 95–110.

Kraushaar, Wolfgang. 1996. *Die Protestchronik 1949–1959: Eine illustrierte Geschichte von Bewegung, Widerstand und Utopie*. 4 vols. Hamburg: Rogner & Bernard.

Kriesi, Hanspeter. 1984. *Die Zurcher Bewegung*. Frankfurt: Campus.

Kriesi, Hanspeter, Ruud Koopmans, Jan W. Duyvendak, and Marco G. Giugni. 1992. "New Social Movements and Political Opportunities in Western Europe." *European Journal of Political Research* 22 (2): 219–44.

——— . 1995. *The Politics of New Social Movements in Western Europe: A Comparative Analysis*. Minneapolis/London: University of Minnesota Press/University College of London Press.

Kubik, Jan. 1994. *The Power of Symbols against the Symbols of Power. The Rise of Solidarity and the Fall of State Socialism in Poland*. University Park: Pennsylvania State University Press.

Laba, Roman. 1991. *The Roots of Solidarity: A Political Sociology of Poland's Working-Class Democratization*. Princeton, NJ: Princeton University Press.

Landim Assumpção, Leilah. 1993. *A Invenção das ONGs: Do serviço invisível à profissão sem nome*. Unpublished Ph.D. dissertation, Universidade Federal do Rio de Janeiro, Museu Nacional, Programa de Pós-Graduação em Antropologia Social.

Lane, Ruth. 1992. "Political Culture: Residual Category or General Theory?" *Comparative Political Studies* 25(3): 262–387.

Lange, Peter, and Lyle Scuggs. 1996 September. "A Crisis of Unionism? Developments of Trade Union Power in the 1980s in Postwar Perspective." Paper presented at the Annual meeting of the American Political Science Association, San Francisco, CA.

LeGrande, J. L. 1967. "Nonviolent Civil Disobedience and Police Enforcement Policy." *Journal of Criminal Law, Criminology and Police Science* 58: 393–404.

Lemke, Christiane. 1996, May. "From Peaceful Revolution to Contentious Action: Protest in East Germany before and after Unification." Paper presented at the conference on "Democracy, Markets, and Civil Societies in Post-1989 East Central Europe," Minda de Gunzburg Center for European Studies, Harvard University, Cambridge, MA.

Lens, Sidney. 1969. *Radicalism in America*. New York: Crowell.

Lepine, Louis. 1929. *Mes souvenirs*. Paris: Payot.

Levin, Stephanie A. 1990. "The Deference That is Due: Rethinking the Jurisprudence of Judicial Deference to the Military." *Villanova Law Review* 35: 6.

Liao, Tim Futing. 1994. *Interpreting Probability Models*. Beverly Hills, CA: Sage.

Linhares, Leila. 1991. "La lucha por la democracia calificada." Pp. 23–31 in Isis International, ed., *Transiciones: Mujeres en los procesos democráticos*. Santiago, Chile: Isis International.

Linz, Juan J. 1992. "Change and Continuity in the Nature of Contemporary Democracies." Pp. 182–207 in Gary Marks and Larry Diamond, eds., *Reexamining Democracy: Essays in Honor of Seymour Martin Lipset*. Newbury Park, CA: Sage.

Lipsky, Michael. 1968. "Protest as a Political Resource." *American Political Science Review* 62: 1144–58.

———. 1980. *Street Level Bureaucracy*. New York: Russell Sage Foundation.

Lofland, John. 1996. *Social Movement Organizations: Guide to Research on Insurgent Realities*. Hawthorne, NY: Aldine de Gruyter.

Lohmann, Susanne. 1994. "Dynamics of Informational Cascades: The Monday Demonstrations in Leipzig, East Germany, 1989–91." *World Politics* 47 (October): 42–101.

Lumsdaine, David. 1993. *Moral Vision in International Politics: The Foreign Aid Regime, 1949–1989*. Princeton, NJ: Princeton University Press.

MacRae, Edward. 1992. "Homosexual Identities in Transitional Brazilian Politics." Pp. 185–206 in Sonia Alvarez and Arturo Escobar, eds., *The Making of Social Movements*. Boulder, CO: Westview.

Maguire, Diarmuid. 1995. "Opposition Movements and Opposition Parties: Equal Partners or Dependent Relations in the Struggle for Power and Reform?" Pp. 199–229 in J. Craig Jenkins and Bert Klandermans, eds., *The Politics of Social Protest: Comparative Perspectives on States and Social Movements*. Minneapolis/London: University of Minnesota Press/University College of London.

Mainwaring, Scott. 1986. *The Catholic Church and Politics in Brazil, 1916–1985*. Stanford, CA: Stanford University Press.

———. 1989. "Grassroots Popular Movements and the Struggle for Democracy: Nova Iguaçu." Pp. 168–204 in Alfred Stepan, ed., *Democratizing Brazil*. New York: Oxford University Press.

Malova, Darina. 1996, May. "Protest Events in Slovakia (1990–94)." Paper presented at the conference on "Democracy, Markets, and Civil Societies in Post-1989 East Central Europe," Minda de Gunzburg Center for European Studies, Harvard University, Cambridge, MA.

Mann, Patrice. 1990. *L'activité tactique des manifestants et des forces mobiles lors des crises viticoles du midi (1950–1990)*. Paris: Institut des Hautes Études de la Securité Interne.

March, James, and Johan P. Olsen. 1989. *Rediscovering Institutions. The Organizational Basis of Politics*. New York: Free Press.

Marks, Monique. 1996, February. "Onward Marching Comrades: The Career of the Charterist Youth Movement in Diepkloof, Soweto." Paper presented at the Conference of Social Movements, Durban, South Africa.

Marx, Gary. 1974. "Thoughts on a Neglected Category of Social Movement Participant: The Agent Provocateur and the Informant." *American Journal of Sociology* 80: 402–42.

Mattes, Robert. 1994. "The Road to Democracy: From 2 February 1991 to 27 April 1994." Pp. 1–23 in Andrew Reynolds, ed., *Elections '94 South Africa: The Campaigns, Results, and Future Prospects*. New York: St. Martin's.

McAdam, Doug. 1982. *The Political Process and the Development of Black Insurgency, 1930–1970*. Chicago: University of Chicago Press.

———. 1988. *Freedom Summer*. Chicago: University of Chicago Press.

———. 1995. "'Initiator' and 'Spin-off' Movements: Diffusion Processes in Protest Cycles." Pp. 217–39 in Mark Traugott, ed., *Repertoires and Cycles of Collective Action*. Durham, NC: Duke University Press.

McAdam, Doug, and Dieter Rucht. 1993. "Cross-National Diffusion of Social Movement Ideas and Tactics." *Annals of the American Academy of Political and Social Sciences* 528 (July): 56–74.

McAdam, Doug, Sidney Tarrow, and Charles Tilly. 1997. "Towards a Comparative Synthesis of Social Movements and Revolutions." Paper presented at the Annual Meeting of the American Political Science Association, San Francisco, CA.

McCarthy, John D., and Mayer N. Zald. 1973. *The Trend of Social Movements in America: Professionalization and Resource Mobilization*. Morristown, NJ: General Learning Press.

———. 1977. "Resource Mobilization and Social Movements: A Partial Theory." *American Journal of Sociology* 82: 1212–41.

———. 1987a. *Social Movements in an Organizational Society*. New Brunswick, NJ: Transaction.

———. 1987b. "The Trend of Social Movements in America: Professionalization and Resource Mobilization." Pp. 337–92 in Mayer N. Zald and John D. McCarthy, eds., *Social Movements in an Organizational Society*. New Brunswick, NJ: Transaction.

McCarthy, John D., David W. Britt, and Mark Wolfson. 1991. "The Channeling of Social Movements in the Modern American State." *Social Movements, Conflict and Change* 13: 45–76.

McCarthy, John, Clark McPhail, and John Crist. Forthcoming. "The Emergence and Diffusion of Public Order Management Systems: Protest Cycles and Police Response." In Hanspeter Kriesi, Donatella Della Porta, and Dieter Rucht, eds., *Globalization and Social Movements*. Minneapolis: University of Minnesota Press.

McCarthy, John D., Clark McPhail, and David Schweingruber. 1997. "Policing Protest in the United States: From the 1960s to the 1990s." In Donatella della Porta and Herbert Reiter, eds., *Policing Protests: The Control of Mass Demonstrations in Contemporary Democracies*. Minneapolis: University of Minnesota Press.

McCarthy, John D., Clark McPhail, and Jackie Smith. 1994, July. "The Institutional Channeling of Protest: The Emergence and Development of U. S. Protest Management Systems." Paper presented at the XXIII World Congress of the International Sociological Association, Bielefeld, Germany.

———. 1995, June. "Images of Protest: Dimensions of Selection Bias in Media Coverage of Washington Demonstrations, 1982, 1991." Paper presented at the workshop "Protest Event Analysis, Methodology, Applications, Problems," Wissenschftszentrum Berlin.

———. 1996. "Images of Protest: Estimating Selection Bias in Media Coverage of Washington Demonstrations, 1982, 1991." *American Sociological Review* 61 (3) (December): 478–99.

McIver, John P., and Edward G. Carmines. 1981. *Unidimensional Scaling*. Beverly Hills: Sage.

McKinley, James C. 1994. "Gay Rights March Fight Leaves Mayor in Middle." *New York Times*, June 24, p. B3.

McPhail, Clark. 1985. "The Social Organization of Demonstrations." Paper presented at the Annual Meetings of the American Sociological Association. Washington, D.C.

McPhail, Clark, David Schweingruber, and John D. McCarthy. 1997. "Protest Policing in the United States: From the 1960s to the 1990s." In Donatella della Porta and Herbert Reiter, eds., *Policing Protests: The Control of Mass Demonstrations in Contemporary Democracies*. Minneapolis: University of Minnesota Press.

Medici, Sandro. 1979. *Vite di poliziotti*. Torino: Einaudi.

Melucci, Alberto. 1985. "The Symbolic Challenge of Contemporary Movements." *Social Research* 52(4): 789–815.

———. 1997. *Challenging Codes: Collective Action in the Information Age*. Cambridge: Cambridge University Press.

Meyer, David S. 1990. *A Winter of Discontent: The Nuclear Freeze and American Politics*. New York: Praeger.

———. 1993a. "Institutionalizing Dissent: The United States Structure of Political Opportunity and the End of the Nuclear Freeze Movement." *Sociological Forum* 8: 157–79.

———. 1993b. "Protest Cycles and Political Process: American Peace Movements in the Nuclear Age." *Political Research Quarterly* 46(3): 451–79.

———. 1994, April. "Political Opportunity and Nested Institutions." Unpublished manuscript; earlier versions of the paper were presented at the annual meeting of the Midwest Political Science Association, Chicago.

Meyer, David S., and Thomas R. Rochon. 1997. "Toward a Coalitional Theory of Social and Political Movements." Pp. 237–51. In Thomas R. Rochon and David S. Meyer, eds., *Coalitions and Political Movements: The Lessons of the Nuclear Freeze*. Boulder, CO: Lynne Rienner.

Meyer, David S., and Suzanne Staggenborg. 1996. "Movements, Countermovements, and the Structure of Political Opportunity." *American Journal of Sociology* 101: 1628–60.

Meyer, David S., and Nancy Whittier. 1994. "Social Movement Spillover." *Social Problems* 41: 277–98.

Michels, Robert. 1962. *Political Parties: A Sociological Study of the Oligarchical Tendencies of Modern Democracy.* New York: Collier.

Migdal, Joel S., Atul Kohli, and Vivienne Shue, eds. 1994. *State Power and Social Forces: Domination and Transformation in the Third World.* Cambridge: Cambridge University Press.

Minkoff, Debra C. 1994. "From Service Provision to Institutional Advocacy: The Shifting Legitimacy of Organizational Forms." *Social Forces* 72: 943–69.

———. 1997. "The Sequencing of Social Movements." *American Sociological Review* 62 (October): 779–99.

Momboisse, Raymond M. 1967. *Community Relations and Riot Prevention.* Springfield, IL: C.C. Thomas.

Moore, Kelly. 1996. "Organizing Integrity: American Science and the Creation of Public Interest Organizations, 1955–1975." *American Journal of Sociology* 101: 1592–1627.

Morden, Bettie J. 1990. *The Women's Army Corps, 1945–1978.* Washington, D.C.: Center of Military History, U. S. Government Printing Office.

Morgan, Jane. 1987. *Conflict and Order: The Police and Labour Disputes in England and Wales 1900–1939.* Oxford: Clarendon.

Morris, Aldon, and Cedric Herring. 1987. "Theory and Research in Social Movements: A Critical Review." *Annual Review of Political Science* 2: 137–98, Samuel Long, ed. Norwood, NJ: Ablex.

Mufson, Steven. 1995. "U.N. Women's Meeting Settles Key Disputes." *Washington Post*, September 14, p. A15.

National Abortion Federation. 1997. *Incidents of Violence and Disruption against Abortion Providers in 1996.* Washington, D.C.: National Abortion Federation.

Neal, Marie Augusta, SND de Namur. 1990. *From Nuns to Sisters: An Expanding Vocation.* Mystic, CT: Twenty Third Publications.

Neidhardt, Friedhelm, and Dieter Rucht. 1993. "Auf dem Weg in die 'Bewegungsgesellschaft'? Über die Stabilisierbarkeit sozialer Bewegungen." *Soziale Welt* 44 (3): 305–26.

North, Douglas. 1990. *Institutions, Institutional Change and Economic Performance.* Cambridge: Cambridge University Press.

Oberschall, Anthony. 1973. *Social Conflict and Social Movements.* Upper Saddle River, NJ: Prentice Hall.

O'Brien, Phillip, and Jackie Roddick. 1983. *Chile: The Pinochet Decade.* London: Latin American Bureau.

O'Donnell, Guillermo, and Philippe Schmitter, eds. 1986. *Transitions from Authoritarian Rule: Tentative Conclusions.* Baltimore, MD: Johns Hopkins University Press.

Offe, Claus. 1990. "Reflections on the Institutional Self-Transformation of Movement Politics: A Tentative Stage Model." Pp. 232–50 in R. Dalton and

M. Kuechler eds., *Challenging the Political Order*. New York: Oxford University Press.

Opperwall, Stephen G. 1981. "Shopping for a Public Forum: *Pruneyard Shopping Center v. Robins*, Publicly used Private Property, and the Constitutionality of Protected Speech." *Santa Clara Law Review* 21: 801–43.

Ost, David. 1990. *Solidarity and the Politics of Antipolitics: Opposition and Reform in Poland since 1968*. Philadelphia: Temple University Press.

Ottaway, Marina. 1991. "Liberation Movements and Transition to Democracy: The Case of the A.N.C." *Journal of Modern African Studies* 29: 61–82.

Otto, Karl A. 1977. *Vom Ostermarsch zur APO: Geschichte der Außerparlamentarischen Opposition in der Bundesrepublik 1960–1970*. Frankfurt: Campus.

Owens v. Brown. 1978. 455 F. Supp. 291.

Oxhorn, Philip. 1991. "Popular Sector Response to an Authoritarian Regime: Shantytown Organizations since the Military Coup." *Latin American Perspectives* 67: 66–88.

———. 1995. *Organizing Civil Society: The Popular Sectors and the Struggle for Democracy in Chile*. University Park: Pennsylvania State University Press.

Parker v. Levy. 1974. 417 U.S. 733.

Paterson, Nancy H. 1982–83. "Since the Meadowlands Sports Complex Is Not a Public Forum, the Prohibition of all Literature Distribution and Fund Solicitation by Outside Organizations Does Not Violate the First Amendment." *Villanova Law Review* 28: 741–64.

Petras, James, and Fernando Ignacio Leiva. 1988. "Chile: The Authoritarian Transition to Electoral Politics." *Latin American Perspectives* 15: 97–114.

Pigenet, Michel. 1992. "Au coeur de l'activisme communiste des ánnes de guerrefruide, 'la manifestation Ridgeway'." Paris: L'Harmattan.

Piven, Frances Fox, and Richard Cloward. 1971. *Regulating the Poor: The Functions of Public Welfare*. New York: Vintage.

———. 1979. *Poor People's Movements*. New York: Vintage.

Pizzorno, Allessandro. 1978. "Political Exchange and Collective Identity in Industrial Conflict." Pp. 277–98 in Colin Crouch and Allesandro Pizzorno, eds., *The Resurgence of Class Conflict in Western Europe since 1968*, vol. 2. London: Macmillan.

Post, Robert C. 1987. "Between Governance and Management: The History and Theory of the Public Forum." *UCLA Law Review* 34: 1718–1835.

Potter, George Ann. 1988. *Dialogue on Debt: Alternative Analyses and Solutions*. Washington, D.C.: Center of Concern.

Powell, Walter W., and Paul J. DiMaggio. 1991. *The New Institutionalism in Organizational Analysis*. Chicago: University of Chicago Press.

Prevallet, Elaine. 1995. "Testing the Roots: The Story of *Colegio Loreto* in La Paz." Pp. 91–113 in Ann Patrick Ware, ed., *Naming Our Truths: Stories of Loretto Women*. Inverness, CA: Chardon.

Pridham, Geoffrey, ed. 1990. *Securing Democracy: Political Parties and Democratic Consolidation in Southern Europe*. London: Routledge.

Probst, Lothar. 1995. "Globalization and the Paradigm of Antipolitics in Social Movements: Case Studies from Postwar and Postunification Germany."

Working Paper Series, paper no. 6, Advanced Study Center, International Institute, University of Michigan, Ann Arbor.

Pross, Harry. 1992. *Protestgesellschaft: Von der Wirksamkeit des Widerspruchs.* München: Artemis & Winkler.

Przeworski, Adam. 1991. *Democracy and the Market.* Cambridge: Cambridge University Press.

Pulzer, Peter. 1989. "Political Ideology." Pp. 78–98 in Gordon Smith, William E. Paterson, and Peter H. Merkl, eds., *Developments in West German Politics.* London: Macmillan.

Putnam, Robert. 1995. "Bowling Alone: America's Declining Social Capital." *Journal of Democracy* 6: 65–78.

Ramalho, Luiz Augusto. 1989. "Novo Internacionalismo." *Tempo e Presença,* November, pp. 4–7.

Raymond, M. 1967. *Riots, Revolts and Insurrections.* Springfield, IL: Thomas.

Red Feminista Latinoamericana y Del Caribe Contra la Violencia Doméstica y Sexual. 1994. *Boletin* no. 6 (November).

Reiner, Robert. 1997. "Policing, Protest, and Disorder in Britain." In Donatella della Porta and Herbert Reiter, eds., *Policing Protests: The Control of Mass Demonstrations in Contemporary Democracies.* Minneapolis: University of Minnesota Press.

Reiter, Herbert. 1996. "Le forze di polizia e l'ordine pubblico in Italia dal 1944 al 1948." *Polis* 10: 337–60.

———. 1997. "Police and Public Order in Italy, 1944–1948: The Case of Florence." In Donatella della Porta and Herbert Reiter, eds., *Policing Protests: The Control of Mass Demonstrations in Contemporary Democracies.* Minneapolis: University of Minnesota Press.

Reyneri, Emilio, Ida Regalia, and Marino Regini. 1978. "Labor Conflicts and Industrial Relations in Italy." Pp. 101–58 in Colin Crouch and Alessandro Pizzorno, eds., *The Resurgence of Class Conflict in Western Europe since 1968,* vol. 2 London: Macmillan.

Reynolds, Andrew, ed. 1994. *Elections '94, South Africa: The Campaign, Results, & Future Perspectives.* Johannesburg: David Philip.

Rich, Bruce. 1994. *Mortgaging the Earth: The World Bank, Environmental Impoverishment, and the Crisis of Development.* Boston: Beacon.

Risse-Kappen, Thomas. 1995. "Bringing Transnational Relations Back In: Introduction." Pp. 3–33. In Thomas Risse-Kappen, ed., *Bringing Transnational Relations Back In: Non-State Actors, Domestic Structures and International Institutions.* Cambridge: Cambridge University Press.

Robbins, Rick. n.d. Speech on the history and functions of the U.S. Park Service Demonstration Permitting System (estimated 1986).

Robinson v. Rand. 1972. 340 F. Supp. 37 (D. Colo).

Rochford, E. Burke, Jr. 1985. *Hare Krishna in America.* New Brunswick, NJ: Rutgers University Press.

Rochon, Thomas R. 1990. "The West European Peace Movement and the Theory of New Social Movements." Pp. 105–21 in R. Dalton and M. Kuechler, eds., *Challenging the Political Order.* New York: Oxford University Press.

————. 1998. *Culture Moves: Ideas, Activism, and Changing Values.* Princeton, NJ: Princeton University Press.

Roddi, Cesare. 1953. *La polizia de Sicurezza.* Milano: Giuffrè.

Rosenau, James. 1990. *Turbulence in World Politics: A Theory of Change and Continuity.* Princeton, NJ: Princeton University Press.

Rosenstone, Steven J., and John Mark Hansen. 1993. *Mobilization, Participation, and Democracy in America.* New York: Macmillan.

Rostker v. Goldberg. 1981. 101 S. Ct. 2646.

Roth, Roland. 1985. "Neue soziale Bewegungen in der politischen Kultur de Bundesrepublik: Eine vorläufige Skizze." Pp. 20–82 in Karl-Werner Brand, ed., *Neue soziale Bewegungen in Westeuropa und in den USA.* Frankfurt: Campus.

————. 1994. *Demokratie von unten: Neue soziale Bewegungen auf dem Wege zur politischen Institution.* Köln: Bund.

Rucht, Dieter. 1988. "Themes, Logics, and Arenas of Social Movements: A Structural Approach." Pp. 305–29 in Bert Klandermans, Hanspeter Kriesi, and Sidney Tarrow, eds., *From Structure to Action: Comparing Movement Participation Across Cultures, International Social Movement Research,* vol. 1. Greenwich, CT: JAI.

————. 1990. "Campaigns, Skirmishes, and Battles: Antinuclear Movements in the U.S.A., France, and West Germany." *Industrial Crisis Quarterly* 4: 193–222.

————. 1991. "The Study of Social Movements in West Germany: Between Activism and Professionalism." Pp. 355–84 in Dieter Rucht, ed., *Research on Social Movements: The State of the Art in Western Europe and the United States.* Frankfurt/Boulder, CO: Campus/Westview.

————. 1996a, March. "Forms of Protest in Germany 1950–92." Paper presented at the workshop "Europe and the United States: Movement Societies or the Institutionalization of Protest," Cornell University, Ithaca, NY.

————. 1996b. "Massenproteste und politische Entscheidungen in der Bundesrepublik." Pp. 139–66 in Wolfgang van den Daele and Friedhelm Neidhardt eds., *Kommunikation und Entscheidung.* WZB Jahrbuch. Berlin: Sigma.

————. 1996c. "Mobilizing for 'Distant Issues': German Solidarity Groups in Non-Democratic Issue Areas." Unpublished manuscript, Wissenschaftszentrum Berlin.

————. 1997. "Recent Right-Wing Radicalism in Germany: Its Development and Resonance in the Public and Social Sciences." Pp. 255–74 in Frederick Weil, ed., *Extremism, Protest, Social Movements, and Democracy.* Vol. 3 of *Research on Democracy and Society.* Greenwich, CT: JAI.

Rucht, Dieter, and Friedhelm Neidhardt. 1995, June. "Methodological Issues in Collecting Protest Event Data: Units of Analysis, Selection Bias, Coding Problems." Paper presented at the workshop "Protest Event Analysis: Methodology, Applications, Problems," Wissenschaftszentrum Berlin.

Rucht, Dieter, and Thomas Ohlemacher. 1992. "Protest Event Data: Collection, Uses and Perspectives." Pp. 76–106 in Ron Eyerman and Mario Diani, eds., *Issues in Contemporary Social Movement Research.* Beverly Hills: Sage.

Rucht, Dieter, Peter Hocke, and Thomas Ohlemacher. 1992. "Dokumentation und Analyse von Protestereignissen in der Bundesrepublik Deutschland (Prodat): Codebuch." Discussion Paper FS III 92-103, Wissenschaftszentrum Berlin.

Rucht, Dieter, Peter Hocke, and Dieter Oremus. 1995. "Quantitative Inhaltsanalyse: Warum, wo, wann und wie wurde in der Bundesrepublik demonstriert?" Pp. 261–91 in Ulrich von Alemann, ed., *Politikwissenschaftliche Methoden*. Opladen: Westdeutscher.

Ruether, Rosemary Radford. 1974. *Religion and Sexism: Images of Women in the Jewish and Christian Traditions*. New York: Simon & Schuster.

———. 1975. *New Woman, New Earth: Sexist Ideologies and Human Liberation*. New York: Seabury.

———. 1983. *Sexism and God-Talk: Toward a Feminist Theology*. Boston: Beacon.

———. 1988. *Women-Church: Theology and Practice*. San Francisco: Harper & Row.

Ruether, Rosemary Radford, with Eleanor McLaughlin, eds. 1979. *Women of Spirit: Female Leadership in the Jewish and Christian Traditions*. New York: Simon & Schuster.

Ryan, Charlotte. 1991. *Prime Time Activism*. Boston: South End Press.

Rybczynski, Witold. 1993. "The New Downtowns." *Atlantic Monthly*, May, 98–106.

Salazar, Gabriel. 1990. *Violencia política popular en las "grandes alamedas."* Santiago, Chile: SUR.

Sandora, J. A., and R. C. Petersen. 1980. "Crowd Control and the Small Police Department." *FBI Law Enforcement Bulletin*, December, pp. 2–5.

San Francisco Police Department. 1989. *San Francisco Police Department Crowd Control Manual*. San Francisco, CA: San Francisco Police Department.

Sani, Giacomo. 1996. "I verdetti del 21 aprile." *Il Mulino* 45: 451–58.

Sardino, Thomas. 1985. "The Demonstration Experience at Syracuse University." *Campus Law Enforcement Journal*, September/October, pp. 33–34.

Schiotz, Arne. 1983. "A Campaign Is Born." *IUCN Bulletin* 14 (October–December): 120–22.

Schlesinger v. Ballard. 1975. 419 U.S. 498.

Schmitter, Philippe. n.d. "Some Propositions about Civil Society and the Consolidation of Democracy." Unpublished manuscript, Stanford University, Stanford, CA.

Schneider, Cathy Lisa. 1992. "Radical Opposition Parties and Squatters' Movements in Pinochet's Chile." Pp. 260–75 in Sonia Alvarez and Arturo Escobar, eds., *The Making of Social Movements*. Boulder, CO: Westview.

———. 1995. *Shantytown Protest in Pinochet's Chile*. Philadelphia: Temple University Press.

Schussler Fiorenza, Elisabeth. 1983. *In Memory of Her: A Feminist Theological Reconstruction of Christian Origins*. New York: Crossroad.

———. 1984. *Bread Not Stone: The Challenge of Feminist Biblical Interpretation*. Boston: Beacon.

Scott, W. Richard, and John W. Meyer. 1994. *Institutional Environments and Organizations*. Thousand Oaks, CA: Sage.

Seidman, Gay W. 1994. *Manufacturing Militance: Workers' Movements in Brazil and South Africa, 1970–1985.* Berkeley: University of California Press.

Selznick, Philip. 1949. *TVA and the Grassroots.* Berkeley: University of California Press.

Sikkink, Kathryn. 1986. "Codes of Conduct for Transnational Corporations: The Case of the WHO/UNICEF Code." *International Organization* 40: 815–40.

———. 1993. "Human Rights, Principled Issue-Networks, and Sovereignty in Latin America." *International Organization* 47: 411–41.

Simons, Marlise. 1993. "Mutilation of Girls' Genitals: Ethnic Gulf in French Court." *New York Times,* November 23, p. A13.

Skidmore, Thomas. 1988. *The Politics of Military Rule in Brazil, 1964–1985.* New York: Oxford University Press.

Slack, Alison T. 1988. "Female Circumcision: A Critical Appraisal." *Human Rights Quarterly* 10: 437–86.

Smith, Brian. 1982. *The Church and Politics in Chile: Challenges to Modern Catholicism.* Princeton, NJ: Princeton University Press.

Smith, Jackie, Ron Pagnucco, and Charles Chatfield, eds. 1997. *Solidarity beyond the State. The Dynamics of Transnational Social Movements.* Syracuse, NY: Syracuse University Press.

Smolla, Rodney A. 1992. *Free Speech in an Open Society.* New York: Knopf.

Snow, David A., and Robert D. Benford. 1988. "Ideology, Frame Resonance, and Participant Mobilization." Pp. 197–217 in Bert Klandermans, Hanspeter Kriesi, and Sidney Tarrow, eds., *From Structure to Action: Comparing Social Movement Research across Cultures.* Greenwich, CT: JAI.

———. 1992. "Master Frames and Cycles of Protest." Pp. 133–55 in Aldon D. Morris and Carol McClurg Mueller, eds., *Frontiers in Social Movement Theory.* New Haven, CT: Yale University Press.

Snow, David, E. Burke Rochford, Steven K. Worden, and Robert D. Benford. 1986. "Frame Alignment Processes, Micromobilization, and Movement Participation." *American Sociological Review* 51: 464–81.

Snowden, Frank M. 1989. *The Fascist Revolution in Tuscany, 1919–1922.* New York: Cambridge University Press.

Sochart, Elise A. 1988. "Agenda Setting, The Role of Groups and the Legislative Process: The Prohibition of Female Circumcision in Britain." *Parliamentary Affairs* 41(4) (October): 508–26.

Sommier, Isabelle. 1990. *Analyse des services d'ordre CGT et CFDT.* Paris: Memoire de DEA, École des Hautes Etudes en Science Sociales.

Sontheimer, Kurt. 1983. *Zeitenwende? Die Bundesrepublik zwischen alter und alternativer Politik.* Hamburg: Hoffmann & Campe.

Soule, Sarah. 1997. "The Student Divestment Movement in the United States and the Shantytown: The Diffusion of a Protest Tactic." *Social Forces* 75: 855–83.

Staggenborg, Suzanne. 1988. "The Consequences of Professionalization and Formalization in the Pro-Choice Movement." *American Sociological Review* 53: 585–605.

Stark, Rodney. 1972. *Police Riots.* Belmont, CA: Wadsworth.

Stepan, Alfred. 1988. *Rethinking Military Politics: Brazil and the Southern Cone.* Princeton, NJ: Princeton University Press.

Sternstein, Wolfgang, ed. n.d. "Gottesdienst mit der Drahtschere." Pp. 23–28 in Wolfgang Sternstein, ed., *Abrüstung von unten: Die Pflugscharbewegung in den USA und Europa.* Stuttgart: Sternstein.

Stiehm, Judith. 1989. *Arms and the Enlisted Woman.* Philadelphia: Temple University Press.

Stone, Deborah A. 1988. *Policy Paradox and Political Reason.* New York: Harper-Collins.

Struck v. Secretary of Defense. 1971. 460 F.2d 1372 (9th Cir.), cert. granted, 409 U.S. 497 (1971), vacated and remanded, 409 U.S. 1071 (1972).

Swidler, Ann. 1986. "Culture in Action: Symbols and Strategies." *American Sociological Review* 51: 464–81.

Swidler, Leonard, and Arlene Swidler. 1977. *Women Priests: A Commentary on the Vatican Declaration.* New York: Paulist.

Szabo, Mate. 1994, July. "From Outlawed to Marginalized? Political Movements in Hungary (1990–1994)." Paper presented at the XIII World Congress of Sociology, Bielefeld, Germany.

———. 1995, May. "Trends in Collective Protest in Hungary, 1989–1994." Paper presented at the conference "Democracy, Markets, and Civil Societies in Post-1989 East Central Europe," Minda de Gunzburg Center for European Studies, Harvard University, Cambridge, MA.

Szikinger, Isvan. 1996. "The Institutional Framework of Handling Protest and Demonstrations in Hungary." Pp. 43–58 in Peter Timoranszky, ed., *Uj Rendeszeti Tanulmanyok: Mobilization and Policing of Protest in Western Europe and Hungary.* Budapest: Police Research Institute.

Taft, Philip, and Philip Ross. 1969. "American Labor Violence: Its Causes, Character and Outcome." Pp. 270–376 in Hugh Davis Graham and Ted Robert Gurr, eds., *Violence in America: Historical and Comparative Perspectives.* New York: Signet.

Tarrow, Sidney. 1989. *Democracy and Disorder: Protest and Politics in Italy, 1965–1975.* Oxford: Clarendon.

———. 1992. "Mentalities, Political Cultures, and Collective Action Frames: Constructing Meanings through Action." Pp. 174–202 in Aldon D. Morris and Carol McClurg Mueller, eds., *Frontiers in Social Movement Theory.* New Haven, CT: Yale University Press.

———. 1993. "Modular Collective Action and the Rise of the Social Movement: Why the French Revolution Was Not Enough." *Politics and Society* 21 (1): 647–70.

———. 1994. *Power in Movement: Collective Action, Social Movements and Politics.* Cambridge: Cambridge University Press.

———. 1995. "Mass Mobilization in Regime Change: Pacts, Reform, and Popular Power in Italy (1918–1922) and Spain (1975–1978)." Pp. 204–30 in Richard Gunther, P. Nikiforos Diamandouros, and Hans Jurgen Puhle, eds., *The Politics of Democratic Consolidation: Southern Europe in Comparative Perspective,* Baltimore, MD: Johns Hopkins University Press.

————. 1996a. "Fishnets, Internets and Catnets: Globalization and Transnational Collective Action." Working Paper 78 (March). Madrid; Institutio Juan March de Estudios e Investigaciones.

————. 1996b. "States and Opportunities: The Political Structuring of Social Movements." Pp. 41–61 in Doug McAdam, John D. McCarthy, and Mayer Zald, eds., *Comparative Perspectives on Social Movements.* Cambridge: Cambridge University Press.

————. 1997. " 'The Very Excess of Democracy': Social Movements and the Formation of the American State." In Andrew McFarland and Anne Costain, eds., *Social Movements and the American Political Process.* Lanham, MD: Rowman & Littlefield.

Taylor, Charles, and David A. Jodice. 1983. *World Handbook of Political and Social Indicators.* 3d ed. New Haven, CT: Yale University Press.

Thelen, Kathleen, and Sven Steinmo. 1992. "Historical Institutionalism in Comparative Politics." Pp. 1–32 in S. Steinmo, K. Thelen, and Frank Longstreth, eds., *Structuring Politics.* Cambridge: Cambridge University Press.

Thomas, Dorothy Q. 1993. "Holding Governments Accountable by Public Pressure." Pp. 82–88 in Joanna Kerr, ed., *Ours by Right: Women's Rights as Human Rights.* London: Zed.

————. 1995. Personal interview, October 20, New York, NY.

Tilly, Charles. 1978. *From Mobilization to Revolution.* New York: McGraw-Hill.

————. 1983. "Speaking Your Mind without Elections, Surveys, or Social Movements." *Public Opinion Quarterly* 147: 461–478.

————. 1986. *The Contentious French.* Cambridge, MA: Harvard University Press.

————. 1995a. "Contentious Repertoires in Great Britain, 1758–1834." Pp. 12–42 in Mark Traugott, ed., *Repertoires and Cycles of Collective Action.* Durham, NC: Duke University Press.

————. 1995b. *Popular Contention in Great Britain 1758–1834.* Cambridge, MA: Harvard University Press.

Tilly, Charles, Louise Tilly, and Richard Tilly. 1975. *The Rebellious Century, 1830–1930.* Cambridge, MA: Harvard University Press.

Touraine, Alain. 1985. "An Introduction to the Study of Social Movements." *Social Research* 52(4): 749–87.

Traugott, Mark, ed. 1995. *Repertoires and Cycles of Collective Action.* Durham, NC: Duke University Press.

Tribe, Laurence H. 1988. *American Constitutional Law.* 2d ed. Mineola, NY: Foundation Press.

Tsebelis, George. 1990. *Nested Games: Rational Choice in Comparative Politics.* Berkeley: University of California Press.

U.S. Government Printing Office. 1993. *Code of Federal Regulations.* Section 36: "Parks, Forests, and Public Property," pp. 1–135. Washington, D.C.: Office of the Federal Register, National Archives and Records Administration.

U.S. Government Printing Office. 1959. "Department of the Interior: National Park Service." *Federal Register* 24: 9948–69.

United Nations. 1986. "Report of the Working Group on Traditional Practices Affecting the Health of Women and Children." UN Doc. E/CN.4/1986/42.

United States v. Stanley. 1987. 483 U.S. 669, 671.

Verba, Sidney, and Norman H. Nie. 1972. *Participation and Democracy: Political Democracy and Social Equality*. Chicago: University of Chicago Press.

Vidulich, Dorothy. 1993. "Underground, Women's Press Multiplies." *National Catholic Reporter* 29(2), January 15.

Waddington, P. A. J. 1991. *The Strong Arm of the Law: Armed and Public Order Policing*. Oxford: Clarendon.

———. 1994. *Liberty and Order: Policing Public Order in a Capital City*. London: University of London Press.

Wagman, Robert J. 1991. *The First Amendment Book*. New York: World Almanac.

Waldie v. Schlesinger. 1974. 509 F.2d 508 (D. C. Cir.)

Walker, Daniel. 1968. *Rights in Conflict*. Washington, D.C.: U.S. Government Printing Office.

Walker, Jack L. 1969. "The Diffusion of Innovations among the American States." *American Political Science Review* 63: 880–99.

Walker, Jack L., Jr. 1991. *Mobilizing Interest Groups in America: Patrons, Professions, and Social Movements*. Ann Arbor: University of Michigan Press.

Walker, Samuel. 1990. *In Defense of American Liberties: A History of the ACLU*. New York: Oxford University Press.

Wallace, Michael, and J. Craig Jenkins. 1995. "The New Class, Postindustrialism, and Neocorporatism: Three Images of Social Protest in the Western Democracies." Pp. 96–137 in J. Craig Jenkins and Bert Klandermans, eds., *The Politics of Social Protest: Comparative Perspectives on States and Social Movements*. Minneapolis: University of Minnesota Press.

Wallace, Ruth A. 1992. *They Call Her Pastor: A New Role for Catholic Women*. Albany: State University of New York.

Walsh, Edward. 1996. "This Time Around, Police Take Polite Approach to Protests." *Washington Post*, August 30, pp. A30, A40.

Wapner, Paul. 1995. "Politics beyond the State: Environmental Activism and World Civic Politics." *World Politics* 47: 311–40.

Ware, Ann Patrick. 1985. *Midwives of the Future: American Sisters Tell Their Story*. Kansas City, MO: Leavan.

———. 1995a. "Loretto's Hispanic Tradition: Lights and Shadows." in Ann Patrick Ware, ed., *Naming Our Truth: Stories of Loretto Women*. Inverness, CA: Chardon.

———. 1995b. *Naming Our Truth: Stories of Loretto Women*. Inverness, CA: Chardon. (Available from Loretto Motherhouse, Book Dept., Nerinx, KY 40049-9999.)

Warren, Ellen, and James Warren. 1996. "No Lemmings Here." *Chicago Tribune*, August 30, section 2, p. 2.

Weaver, Mary Jo. 1986. *New Catholic Women: A Contemporary Challenge to Traditional Religious Authority*. New York: Harper and Row. (Reprinted 1995.)

———. 1993. *Springs of Water in a Dry Land: Spiritual Survival for Catholic Women Today*. Boston: Beacon.

Whittaker, Charles. 1964. "The Causes and Effect upon Public Order of Planned Mass Violations of Our Laws." *Police Chief* 34(4): 12–22.

————. 1966. "The Effects of Planned, Mass Disobedience of Our Laws." *FBI Law Enforcement Bulletin* 35(9): 9–13, 25.

Wilson, Frank L. 1990. "Neo-Corporatism and the Rise of New Social Movements." Pp. 67–83 in Russell J. Dalton and Manfred Kuechler, eds., *Challenging the Political Order*. New York: Oxford University Press.

————. 1994. "Political Demonstrations in France: Protest Politics or Politics of Ritual?" *French Politics and Society* 12(2&3): 3–40.

Wilson, James Q. 1973. *Political Organizations*. New York: Basic.

Winter, Martin. 1997. "Police Philosophy and Protest Policing in the Federal Republic of Germany, 1960 to 1990." In Donatella della Porta and Herbert Reiter, eds., *Policing Protests: The Control of Mass Demonstrations in Contemporary Democracies*. Minneapolis: University of Minnesota Press.

Wolfsfeld, Gadi. 1988. *The Politics of Provocation: Participation and Protest in Israel*. Albany: State University of New York Press.

Women Environment and Development Organization (WEDO). 1996. "10,000 Brazilian Women Run for Office." *News & Views* 3–4: 4.

World Bank. 1993. *World Bank Development Report 1993: Investing in Health*. Washington, D.C.: World Bank.

Yin, Jordan. 1996. "The Role of Master Frames in the Sprawl-Busters Movement." Unpublished manuscript, Cornell University, Ithaca, NY.

Zimmerman, Jean. 1995. *Tailspin: Women at War in the Wake of Tailhook*. New York: Doubleday.

Zuzowski, Robert. 1992. *Political Dissent and Opposition in Poland*. Westport, CT: Praeger.

Index

About the Contributors

Matthew P. Crozat is a graduate student in government at Cornell University. His primary research focus is on American public policy. He is coauthor, with Ronald King and Douglas Rose, of "The Downfall of David Duke? Duke, Republicans, and the Structure of Elections in Louisiana," in *David Duke and the Politics of Race in the South* (1995).

Donatella della Porta is professor of political science at the University of Florence in Italy. Her main areas of research include social movements, political violence, public order policies, and political corruption. Among her publications are *Social Movements, Political Violence and the State* (Cambridge University Press, 1995) and, with Herbert Reiter, *Policing Protest* (University of Minnesota Press, forthcoming.)

Olivier Fillieule is a researcher at the Fondation Nationale des Science Politiques, in Paris, France. He is author of *Strategies de la Rue: Les Manifestations en France* (1997) and has written extensively on social movements and protest policing.

Patricia Hipsher is assistant professor of political science at Oklahoma State University. Her research on urban social movement organizations in democratizing Chile has been published in *Comparative Politics*. She is currently studying the women's movement in El Salvador.

Mary F. Katzenstein is professor in the department of government at Cornell University. Her most recent book, *Protest from Within: Feminism in the American Catholic Church and the US Military*, will be published in 1998 by Princeton University Press.

Margaret Keck is associate professor of political science at The Johns Hopkins University in Baltimore, Maryland. She is the author of *The

Workers' Party and Democratization in Brazil (Yale University Press, 1992), and coauthor, with Kathryn Sikkink, of *Activists Beyond Borders: Advocacy Networks in International Politics* (Cornell University Press, 1998). She is currently completing a manuscript on environmental politics in Brazil and intends to pursue research investigating the impact of transnational linkages on domestic political strategies and coalitions.

Bert Klandermans is professor of applied social psychology at the Free University in Amsterdam and has published widely on participation in social movements. He is author of *The Social Psychology of Protest* (Blackwell) and editor of the University of Minnesota's series, *Social Movements, Protest, and Contention*.

Jan Kubik teaches in the department of political science at Rutgers University. He is author of *The Power of Symbols against the Symbols of Power: The Rise of Solidarity and the Fall of State Socialism in Poland*. Among his research interests are the postcommunist transformations, the relationship between politics and culture, protest politics, and social movements.

John D. McCarthy is professor of sociology at the Pennsylvania State University in State College, Pennsylvania. He continues his research on protest events, the policing of protest, media coverage of protest events, and the role of social movement organizations in the mobilization of citizen action. He spent the 1995–96 academic year as a Senior Fulbright Research Scholar at the Wissenschaftzentrum, Berlin.

Clark McPhail is professor of sociology at the University of Illinois, Urbanna-Champaign. His primary interests are the sociology and social psychology of collective action and social movements. He is author of *The Myth of the Madding Crowd* (Aldine De Gruyter, 1991) and numerous articles on collective action.

David S. Meyer is associate professor of political science at the City College of New York and the City University Graduate Center. He is author of *A Winter of Discontent: The Nuclear Freeze and American Politics* (1990); coeditor, with Thomas Rochon, of *Coalitions and Political Movements* (1997); and author of many articles on social protest politics. He is currently studying, with Suzanne Staggenborg, movement/countermovement interaction in the American abortion conflict. Most generally, he is interested in the relationships among social protest, institutional politics, and public policy.

Johan Olivier holds a Ph.D. degree from Cornell University. He is chief research specialist at the Human Sciences Research Council in Pretoria, South Africa. His research interests are in the areas of collective action and social movements, ethnic and racial conflict in the United States and South Africa, and political violence and social change.

Herbert Reiter holds a Ph.D. in history from the European University Institute in Florence. Among his fields of research are the history of political asylum, the police, and the judiciary. His publications include *Politisches Asyl im 19. Jahrundert* (Dunker and Humblot, 1992) and, with Donatella della Porta, *Policing Protest* (University of Minnesota Press, forthcoming).

Marlene Roefs is a student in social psychology at the Free University in Amsterdam, currently conducting a longitudinal research project on social movements in South Africa, sponsored by the HSRC in Pretoria. She is affiliated with the Public Opinion Service of Idasa in Cape Town, where she is pursuing her Ph.D. She is coauthor of an article on intergroup perceptions recently published in the *Personality and Social Psychology Bulletin* and has coauthored a number of articles currently in press.

Dieter Rucht is a senior researcher at the Wissenschaftzentrum Berlin fuer Sozialforeschung in Germany and will be professor of sociology at the University of Kent of Canterbury from 1998 onwards. His main areas of interest are social change, social movements, and political protest. He is editor of *Research on Social Movements: The State of the Art in Western Europe and the USA* (1991) and the author or coauthor of several books and many articles on social movements, mostly in German. Currently, he is engaged in a study on the patterns of protest in Germany since 1950, a collaborative study on the public discourse on abortion in Germany and the USA, and a study on the institutionalization of social movement organizations at the local level in Germany.

Kathryn Sikkink is associate professor of political science at the University of Minnesota. Her recent research focuses on the origins and effectiveness of human rights policies, and on transnational advocacy networks. She is author of *Ideas and Institutions: Developmentalism in Brazil and Argentina* (Cornell University Press, 1991) and, with Margaret Keck, *Activists Beyond Borders: Advocacy Networks in International Politics* (Cornell University Press, forthcoming).

Sidney Tarrow is Maxwell M. Upson Professor of Government and Sociology at Cornell University. He is the author of numerous works on social movements, including *Peasant Communism in Southern Italy* (1967), *Democracy and Disorder* (1989), and *Power in Movement* (1994, 1998). Former president of the Conference Group on Italian Politics and Society, he is currently a fellow of the Center for Advanced Study in the Behavioral Sciences in Stanford, California.